Parenting to Make a Difference. . .

Your One- to Four-Year Old Child

by

Brenda Hussey-Gardner, M.A., M.P.H.

VORT Corporation

Palo Alto, CA 94306

Published by:
VORT Corporation
PO Box 60132
Palo Alto, CA 94306

ISBN 0-89718-118-2

Publisher's Note

We are pleased to have the opportunity to publish this important parenting resource. It is concise and comprehensive, yet we cannot anticipate the circumstances under which a reader may apply its contents. Each child is unique and masters skills and develops at a rate and an age often different from other children. We therefore urge that you seek professional advice if you have any concerns about a child's health or development. We expressly decline liability for the results of conclusions you may reach about a child after reading and applying the contents of this book.

Acknowledgments

I would like to thank the professionals who reviewed this book, adding to its credibility. I am deeply grateful to Vera Lynne Stroup, M.Ed., for her help and encouragement throughout the development of this entire book. Her incisive comments on each chapter were important and much appreciated. Special gratitude goes to Janeece Warfield, Psy.D., for her numerous contributions to the book. I am also thankful to the following professionals who gave their time and expertise to review one or more chapters of this book: Cathy Camp, M.A., R.D., L.D.; Roni Emden, M.S.W., L.C.S.W.; Kathy Swenson Miller, M.S., O.T.R., Renee C. Wachtel, M.D., and Sharon Willig, M.A., CCC-SLP.

I would like to thank the parents who reviewed this book, adding to its practicality. I especially want to thank Judy Esposito for her support and enthusiasm from the moment the idea for this book emerged until the final chapter was written and reviewed. Her experiences and feelings contributed much to each chapter. A special thanks goes to her husband, Tom Esposito, for his assistance and feedback. I am also thankful to the following parents for their helpful reviews and encouraging comments: Shernette Atkins, Lana Barringer, Lorrie and David Groll, Joan L. Kennedy, Jan Lee, Cathy Madden, Catherine Parks, Kathy Pierce, Robin Trenner, and Sandy Wolfgang.

I would like to thank Erich Vogel for his photography skills and assistance during the first few photography sessions. It was the knowledge, expertise, and insights that he shared with me that enabled me to go forward and take the pictures myself. My deepest appreciation goes to the many people who allowed me to come into their homes, classrooms, and lives to take their photographs: Brian Albin; Amanda Bruce; Erica, Judy, and Tom Esposito; Austin and Jack Gardner; Allison Glascock; Zachary, Elliott, Lorrie, and David Groll; Alex Kratochwill; Alex and Garland Jackson; Jillian, Melanie, and Joan L. Kennedy; Elaine Little; Megan Madden; Tiffany Manzoline; Brianna McCaffery; Pamela Newman; Valerie Nowak; Kathy and Kaitlin Pierce; Cinthia, Christopher, Christina, and Luis Ruiz; Cliff Sass; Sandra Sehman; David and Robin Trenner; Adrian, Janeece, and Lamar Warfield, Jr.; Kimberly and Sandy Wolfgang; and Jonathan C.L., Christopher C.J., and David C.S. Wu. I would also like to extend my appreciation to Louise Walker of Glen Mar Preschool for her cooperation and assistance with photographing children at her school.

I would like to thank my family and friends for listening to me talk about the book and supporting my efforts. I most especially want to thank my husband Jack for his constant help, support, encouragement, and understanding. He provided me the time and confidence that I needed to write this book. He also provided valuable advise on many chapters and photographs. A very special thank-you also goes to my son Austin for giving me the personal day-to-day parenting experience that has taught me about the love, fun, creativity, consistency, and patience involved in being a parent. My experiences with him have contributed much to this book.

Finally, I would like to thank Tom Holt and all those at VORT who worked so hard to make this book a reality.

Table of Contents

Introduction Letter

Dear Parent,

Parenting is probably the most important and meaningful thing that you will ever do. Through your love and guidance you will help an infant develop into a child and grow into an adult. The first few years of your child's life are very important. During these early years, the times you spend talking, playing, and cuddling with your child, as well as the time you spend guiding his behavior, all contribute to his future development and self-esteem.

Unfortunately, no one teaches us how to be good parents. In school many of us take numerous classes in subjects such as math, science, and English. However, very few of us take classes in child development. As we grow into adults, many of us move miles away from our own parents. When we have children of our own, we often do not have the advice and guidance of extended family members.

Fortunately, the career I chose prepared me well for being a parent. I had taken numerous courses in early childhood development and intervention. I worked with many families on issues such as fostering development, sleeping through the night, toilet training, and guiding behavior. However, when I had my son Austin I realized that parenting a child can be more difficult than offering advice as a professional. For instance, I found how very hard it can be to listen to your child cry at night as you teach him to sleep through the night, and I found how frustrating it can be to clean up an accident right after spending ten minutes in the bathroom while your child tried to go potty. But I also found that things can be more rewarding with your own child. Seeing your own child take his first steps is exciting and something you will never forget. Hearing your child say, "Love you," touches your heart like nothing else ever will. Playing chase with your child makes running more fun than imaginable. Walking in the park or along the seashore with your child opens your eyes to nature and brings your attention to things we usually overlook and take for granted. Parenting is a difficult but extremely rewarding responsibility.

Loving your child and providing him with a sense of safety, security and trust are probably some of the most important things that you can do for your child. With the right information, parenting can become a little easier and less frustrating; it can also become more enjoyable and fun. I wrote this book to help parents learn more about young children—how they think, learn to talk, move, develop social skills such as sharing, cope with separation anxiety and fears, form a positive self-esteem, and become independent children who can dress themselves and brush their own teeth. I also wrote this book to provide parents with additional information on everyday issues, such as feeding and food throwing, time-outs and sticker paths, bedtime routines, toilet training, preparing for a new baby and adjusting to a new sibling, choosing a nursery school and supporting your child through that educational experience.

Accordingly, this book has two sections. The first section presents information on understanding and fostering your child's development in each of the following domains: cognitive/ thinking, language, motor, emotional, social, and self-help. The second section contains tips and insights on: nutrition and mealtime behavior, guiding your child's behavior, sleeping through the night, toilet training, a new baby, and preschool. Each chapter contains an introduction, a description of the parent and child perspective on the issue discussed, informative text, a parent's story that brings the chapter to life, and a list of references and recommended readings. Although this book contains a lot of information, no one book can provide you with all the guidance you may need. Refer to your child's doctor and the list of readings at the end of each chapter for additional information.

In writing this book I had to decide what information and suggestions to include and what to leave out. In an attempt to validate my decisions, each chapter was reviewed by a series of professionals and parents. For example, the chapter on language development was reviewed by a language pathologist, child development specialist, mother, and father; the chapter on nutrition and mealtime behavior was reviewed by a pediatrician, several nutritionists, a child development specialist, and two mothers. Feedback from reviewers was incorporated into the final version of this book. In addition to making content decisions, I also had to address the issue of pronouns. I use "you" to refer to you, the parent. "You" refers to both parents when both are involved and to either parent when one must parent alone. I alternate, by chapter, the use of masculine and feminine pronouns when referring to young children. Alternating within one chapter was confusing and using one gender exclusively seemed unfair. Except for when gender influences the child, the information and suggestions apply to both boys and girls. Where there is an exception, in toilet training for example, a specific gender is specified.

Throughout the book age ranges are often presented for skill development. These age ranges are approximations. Your child may develop at a different rate or in a slightly different order. If you ever have concerns about your child, contact your child's pediatrician or your family practitioner to talk about these issues. If you are concerned that your child may have a developmental delay, you can also contact your local Child Find program. Under Public Law 99-457 (IDEA), Child Find provides free screening and assessment to identify children who may have special needs. You can find the phone number for your local Child Find program by contacting your county Department of Education, Department of Health and Human Services, or Department of Public Welfare. You can also get the phone number for the Child Find program in your area by calling the U.S. Department of Education in Washington, DC.

This book can be helpful to parents of all young children. If your child was born prematurely or with special needs, most of the information and many of the suggestions in this book are appropriate. If your child has a developmental delay, he may take a little longer to develop some skills and may need extra practice to learn various activities. Talk with your child's doctor, teacher, or therapist about how to best adapt the information in this book to meet your child's individual needs. For instance, if your child has a motor delay you can disregard the age ranges presented in the motor chapter, determine what skills your child can do, and foster his development at the point where skills are just emerging.

Parenting to make a difference means loving and caring for your child, talking with and listening to your child, playing with your child to have fun and to foster his development, setting limits and guiding your child's behavior. Parenting to make a difference also means being consistent. Your child needs to know that he can trust you and that you mean what you say. If you tell your child that you will read a story when you get home, you should do so. Likewise, if you tell your child he will get a time-out if he continues to throw his toys, you should give him a time-out if the throwing doesn't stop. Yet, at the same time, flexibility needs to exist. If your child becomes ill, you may want to bend nighttime routines and allow extra cuddling. When doing so explain to your child, in a very simple manner, why you are deviating from the norm. For instance, you could say, "Because your tummy hurts, I will rub it while you go back to sleep as a special treat." If you want to you can add, "Tomorrow night when you feel better, we will do things the way we usually do them." In the beginning it may take more time and energy to parent in this manner, but the rewards you and your child will reap are well worth the effort.

I hope that you enjoy the book and that it helps make your job as a parent a little easier. Even more importantly, enjoy your child—children grow up so fast. Take the time each day to play with your child and to have fun together.

Sincerely,

Brenda Hussey-Gardner, M.A., M.P.H.

Chapter 1
Thinking/Cognitive Skills

A one-year-old plays with blocks by banging them, hammer-style, on the floor or coffee table. Months later, she stacks them to build a teetering tower. Eventually she constructs a house with the same blocks. And by the time a child is four, she pretends one of the blocks is the peanut butter sandwich she offers to an imaginary friend. At play, a child is in the serious business of learning.

Between one and four years of age, children become increasingly sophisticated in the way they think and do things. Thinking skills include developing concepts such as color, size, time, and shape. A child also uses thinking skills when she imitates others, identifies body parts, learns nursery rhymes, and answers questions. Your pediatrician may refer to these thinking skills as cognitive skills. As a parent, you can foster your child's development of thinking skills by:
- Understanding the sequence in which young children learn
- Providing your child with opportunities to learn through play and enhancing activities

Parent Perspective

Parents know that toddlers and preschoolers play a lot. But some parents do not realize that through play with toys and household objects, young children develop many of their thinking skills. Once parents realize how important play is, most of them want to know how their child should play, where, when, and with what. Many parents also want to know what role they should take in their child's play. As you play along with your child, you may become bored and antsy, especially when your child plays with the same toy for an extended period. Maybe you find it hard to keep up with her because she bounces from one toy to another so quickly. Or maybe you wish your child would play independently once in a while instead of always insisting that you play with her. But most parents are willing to do whatever they can to foster their child's thinking skills, and they are eager to learn good activities to accomplish this.

<u>Child Perspective</u>
Most toddlers and preschoolers love exploring, building, imitating, and pretending. They like to go at their own pace and become frustrated when someone asks them to go faster or to do something that is too difficult. Young children want to know everything about their world. They want to know why it happens, where it lives, what it does, who does what, and how it works.

DEVELOPMENT OF THINKING SKILLS

You can establish a base for fostering your child's thinking skills by understanding at what ages children learn which skills. This knowledge can help you set appropriate expectations for your child. If you are not familiar with the progression of thinking skills, you may frustrate both your child and yourself by offering toys or concepts that are too complex. On the other hand, you could

DEVELOPMENT OF THINKING SKILLS[1]

<u>One-Year-Olds</u>
• Play with household objects as often as toys.
• Play to figure out how things work.
• Place a round block into a shape sorter; then learn to place a square block, and then a triangle.
• Pull a string horizontally, then vertically, to get a toy.
• Imitate new gestures they can see themselves do (stir, rub stomach).
• Imitate gestures they cannot see themselves do (wriggle nose, pat head).
• Think things out in their minds.
• Find an object that is hidden, even if they don't see where it goes.
• Point to pictures of some animals and objects.
• Point to clothing items.
• Identify at least six body parts.

<u>Two-Year-Olds</u>
• Are very inquisitive and want to know why.
• Enjoy nursery rhymes, singing songs, and dancing.
• Play with water and sand.
• Understand concept of one, then two, and then three.
• Find details in pictures.
• Engage in pretend play.
• Match shapes, colors, and simple pictures of objects.
• Learn about opposites.
• Know own sex and sex of others.

- Look at books independently.
- Sort shapes and colors.
- Assemble three- to four-piece puzzles.
- Understand the concepts of larger, smaller, and longer.
- Enjoy playing house.

Three-Year-Olds
- Engage in more complex dramatic play involving props and themes.
- Identify square and round.
- Understand up, down, top, bottom, under, over, next to, beside, fast, slow, empty, full, tall, short, more, and less.
- Say two nursery rhymes or sing two songs with an adult.
- Count six objects in a row.
- Add 1 to 1, 2, 3, 4, and 5.
- Identify silly or wrong pictures.
- Understand that different activities occur at different times of the day.
- Answer "Why do" and "What do you do when" questions.
- Understand heavy, light, around, in front of, behind, between, high, low, bigger, biggest, smaller, smallest, larger, and largest.
- Recall two points from a story just read.

[1]Skills are presented in the order that most children learn them.

potentially slow your child's development by providing only toys that are below her level.

One-Year-Olds

Most one-year-olds play to figure out how things work—they play with household objects as often as they play with toys. The one-year-old drops the lid of a pot on the floor to see it wobble and listen to the sound it makes. Then she takes the lid into the living room where she drops it on the carpet to see if it moves differently or makes a different sound. If her discovery fascinates her, she may go from the kitchen to the living room five or six times, dropping the lid and squealing with delight at the results with each trip. To learn more about the lid, she may hit it with her hand, then with a spoon and then again with her hand to determine how to make the loudest noise.

Through play, the one-year-old learns that the round block fits in the round opening and not in the square one—no matter how hard she pushes and pounds in an attempt to get the round block into the square opening. After she masters placing a round block in a shape sorter, she learns to put a square one in, and then a triangle. She also learns that by pulling a string, she can get the toy at the end. While she plays, she imitates actions she has seen you do, such as stirring with a spoon or wrinkling her nose. Through play she develops concentration as well as concepts of color, size, and shape.

The older one-year-old (between eighteen and twenty-four months of age) doesn't always need to manipulate an object or a toy to figure out how it works. Instead, she can now think about things in her mind. For instance, she understands that to reach a glass of milk in the middle of the table, she needs to use a long wooden spoon to scoot the glass over to her. This new ability to think in her mind also enables her to find a ball quickly and easily after it rolls under the couch and into the kitchen. She simply runs around the couch and into the kitchen to spot and retrieve the ball. As a younger one-year-old, she probably would have looked under the couch for the ball. If the ball wasn't under the couch, because it had rolled into the kitchen, she most likely would not look in the kitchen unless you had suggested it.

The older one-year-old gradually understands the names of objects. Between eighteen and twenty-four months of age, she learns to point to clothing items such as her shirt, pants, diaper, socks, and shoes. During this same time span, she also learns to point to pictures of animals and objects. For instance, when you read her a book about a farm and ask, "Where is the horse?", she will point to the horse. In addition, she learns to point to body parts. The six body parts that young children usually identify first are the nose, eyes, ears, mouth, hands, feet, tummy, and hair.

Two-Year-Olds

The two-year-old is very inquisitive. Through her desire to know why, she learns that birds have wings so they can fly in the sky, but that cars can't fly because they don't have wings, but wheels instead. This curiosity helps her learn that she is a girl because she has a vagina and that Daddy is a boy because he has a penis. Water and sand intrigue the two- year-old. While playing with these materials, she experiments with concepts such as full and empty, heavy and light. Other concepts, such as time, emerge at this age. Once she understands "now" versus "later," your two-year-old may ask, "In a little while?" after you say "no" to her request for a cookie.

The two-year-old is eager to learn about numbers, colors, and opposites. She learns to match shapes, colors, and identical pictures of objects. If, while playing with a pegboard, you ask her to find a blue peg like the one you have, she will pick a blue peg.

In the beginning she does this in a random fashion, picking pegs up and turning to you to find out if she chose the right one. But once she has a good understanding of colors, she will pick the matching peg without hesitation. While learning about matching, she learns about the number "one." When she is two and a half years old, she will give you one—and only one—item when you ask her for one. Before that time, you may get one, two, or five items when you ask for one. Once she masters the concept of one, she begins to learn about two, and then three.

The ability to sort items comes after the skill to match items. The two-year-old usually learns to sort first by shape and then by color. Sorting is more complex than matching. It involves separating a mixed group of circles, squares, and triangles into one group of circles, one of squares, and another of triangles. The two-year-old demonstrates her increased understanding of shapes by her ability to sort complex shapes and assemble three- to four-piece puzzles.

The concept of size develops as your child approaches three years of age. You may notice the first signs that your child understands size during play. When she can stack rings in the correct order, she has a basic understanding of size. As she nears three, she will be able to point to the larger or smaller of two objects and will identify the longer item in a group of two items.

In addition to developing concepts, the two-year-old enjoys learning rhymes, songs, and dances. She likes to make rhymes or sing songs along with other people. She even repeats phrases of rhymes or songs while playing with her toys or taking a bath. With her interest in rhymes and songs, a two-year-old also becomes interested in stories. The two-year-old looks at books independently, understands stories and can find details about the story in the pictures. Many two-year-olds develop a preference for one book. If your child has a favorite book, she may insist you read the same book again and again.

With all her new skills and abilities, the two-year-old is delightful to play with. She can engage in simple pretend play; she likes to play house. She may invite you over for coffee in her kitchen, and if you're lucky, will offer you a peanut butter and jelly sandwich (a toy block) to go with it.

Three-Year-Olds

Dramatic play blossoms and becomes more refined at this age. It involves props that may be real, substitute, or make-believe. Real props include old milk cartons, shoes, or hats that Mom or Dad makes available. Real props also include child-size, plastic versions of real items available in many stores. Substitute props are toys or objects that a child uses to represent something else. While playing

with her kitchen, a three-year-old may take a can of clay and put a mound of it into a baking pan. Then she sticks toothpicks vertically into the dough, one at a time. That accomplished, she turns to another child and says, "Here's my cake! Let's sing 'Happy Birthday.'" Make-believe props are invisible to the human eye but are very much visible to the child using them. The dramatic play of a three-year-old usually revolves around a plot. Themes reflect what the child sees and experiences. Playing house, dress-up, doctor, school, and dentist are five popular themes. Children at this age also begin to incorporate stories from books and TV shows into their play.

Three-year-olds also learn to play very simple games with rules. Imaginary monsters, friends and enemies, and singing and chanting are three types of games many three-year-olds play. As children approach four years of age, they begin to play hide-and-seek and easy board games. The rules for these games require and foster skills such as understanding and following rules, and using strategy, negotiation, and sportsmanship to play.

Throughout her day and especially as she plays, the three-year-old is very busy learning about concepts. Concepts of shape continue to emerge; she learns to identify square and round. Number, spatial, and time concepts become well formed in the three-year-old. She learns to count to 10 from memory, to count 6 objects in a row, and to add 1 to 1, 2, 3, 4, and 5. The three-year-old's awareness of where things are in space becomes keen. She develops an understanding of up, down, top, bottom, under, over, next to, beside, around, in front of, behind, between, high, and low. She also discovers how objects and people move in space (fast/slow) and how things occupy space (full/empty). In addition, she learns to differentiate night from day. She understands that different activities occur at different times of the day, for instance, that she eats breakfast in the morning and takes her nap in the afternoon.

The three-year-old continues to enjoy nursery rhymes and learns to say at least two nursery rhymes with an adult. She also learns to sing simple songs by herself. She may feel very proud of her new ability to remember and sing songs independently. Once in a while she may ham it up with an original song and dance, along with a request that you not sing with her.

Your three-year-old's book skills are also improving. She begins to "read" a book by looking at the pictures and identifying silly or wrong pictures. If she sees a picture of a boy walking in the rain holding a closed umbrella upright, she will laugh and tell you, "The umbrella's closed. It suppose to be open so you don't get wet. He needs to open it." As she approaches four, she will be able to recall two points about a story without hints. She will answer "why do" and "what do you do when" questions. If you ask her, "Why do we use soap?", she will answer, "To get clean." If you ask, "What do you do when you are hungry?", she will answer, "Eat something."

TALK TO YOUR DOCTOR IF YOUR CHILD IS UNABLE TO[2]

By The Age Of Two...
- Place a round block in a pegboard.
- Pull a string to get a toy.
- Find an object hidden under one of two cups.
- Imitate invisible gestures.
- Identify one body part.
- Enjoy messy play.

By The Age Of Three...
- Identify six body parts.
- Point to pictures of animals or objects.
- Understand the concept of one.
- Engage in simple pretend play.
- Match colors or shapes.
- Listen as you read for ten minutes.

By The Age Of Four...
- Assemble a four-piece puzzle.
- Participate in dramatic play.
- Identify square and round.
- Understand concepts like up, down, fast, slow, tall, and short.
- Say a nursery rhyme or sing a song with an adult.
- Count six objects in a row.

[2]Most children are able to do these items by the age listed. If your child is unable to do them, it may or may not mean there is a problem with her development. It only means that you should mention it to your doctor so that together, you can determine whether your child's development needs to be assessed. You can also consult with your local Child Find program. Under Public Law 99-457 (IDEA), Child Find provides free screening and assessment to identify children who may have special needs. You can find the phone number for your local Child Find program by contacting your county Department of Education, Department of Health and Human Services, or Department of Public Welfare.

PLAY

Play is extremely important to the development of young children. Young children attain many of their thinking skills through play. You can facilitate your child's play in four ways. The first is to allow your child to lead play; in other words, let her set the tone and pace. The next is to provide your child with opportunities to engage in experimental, pretend, and constructive play. A third way is to balance your child's play by providing both indoor and outdoor play, active and quiet play, play with you and independent play. The fourth is to choose appropriate toys for play. When your child uses a toy or engages in an activity, the main issue is that it must be _safe._ *Read all labels and instructions carefully. Remove all wrappings, pins, and staples.* Check for small parts. If a toy has small parts, remove the parts that are small, and use the toy only when supervised by an adult, or put the toy away until the child is older. Supervise *carefully.*

Allow Your Child to Lead Play

As your child plays, take cues from her and her interests. You should play with your child, but allow her to set the tone and pace of play. In this way, she can show you what she can do—and she will probably surprise you. Facilitate the development of current skills and encourage the attainment of new skills according to your child's signals. Many young children don't respond well to direct teaching; often, they refuse to perform. Instead of teaching her, use a natural approach by providing your child with play activities that will encourage cognitive development. If your child is into filling and dumping, give her different items to fill and dump. For example, save your junk mail and let her fill an oatmeal container with the mail and dump it out. If your child likes tea parties, watch her play to determine how to encourage her pretend play. If she is good at pouring tea from a child-size teapot and at passing out plastic cookies, introduce substitute props. Say something like, "I want some ice cream," then grab a block and say, "Now I have some ice cream."

During play, your child may ask you to show her how to use a toy or an object. While you try to teach her, you may become tense or insistent. If you find yourself feeling this way, stop trying to teach. Instead, ask her to show you what to do with the toy or redirect her attention to another toy. Do the same if your child becomes tense, irritable, or too frustrated. Remind yourself that play should be fun, and that while your child plays, she is learning.

Provide Experimental, Pretend and Constructive Play

Experimental Play

Experimental play includes play with messy substances, sand and water, and toys that invite exploration. Most children love **messy play**. Among the favorite substances for messy play are Jello, pudding, applesauce, yogurt, and whipped cream. Not only can children smear and squeeze these substances, but also they can taste them. For messy play, you may want to put a large towel or plastic tablecloth under the high-chair or table where your child is playing. You may also want to put a big bib or smock on your child. On a warm day, you might consider allowing her to play in her diaper or underwear. Each of these suggestions will make cleaning up a little bit easier. And often the easiest way to clean your child after messy play is to give her a bath.

Play with **sand and water** is excellent for developing concepts such as full/empty, light/heavy, pour/dump, dry/wet, and sink/float. You can do sand play at a park, in a sandbox, or even in a roasting pan with a couple pounds of sand. Provide your child with items like a pail, shovel, cup, spoon, funnel, and colander to play with in the sand. Give her the opportunity to experiment with the sand. Show her how to scoop the sand and put it in containers, how to make sand molds, and how to pour sand through a funnel or colander. If the idea of having sand in your house does not appeal to you, try play with rice or dried beans during the winter months when it is too cold to go outside to play in the sand. Provide for water play in a sink, tub, large bowl, or sprinkler.

Provide your child with cups, containers with and without spouts, squeeze and spray bottles (*empty and clean* dishwashing detergent or Windex-type bottles are excellent), sponges or wash-cloths, spoons and ladles. Show her how to fill the containers, then how to pour and squirt. Give her a small rock, twig, leaf, and feather to play with in the water. Talk about what happens when she drops these items into the water, using words like sink and float. Spread a couple of towels over the floor where your child plays. Water play is fun, but it's not very neat, especially in the beginning.

Toys that lend themselves to **exploration** include musical instruments, pull toys, and pop-up toys. Through play with these types of toys, children learn that actions they do make certain responses occur. Through musical instruments, a young child learns to tap a xylophone with a stick to make pretty sounds and to blow into a harmonica to make music. She also learns to tap or blow softly to make soft sounds, and to tap or blow hard to make loud sounds. As she plays with a pull toy, a child learns to pull a string to make the toy move, and she also learns that the speed of her pull determines how fast or slow the toy moves. Similarly, playing with a pop-up toy may teach her to turn a knob clockwise to make a clown pop out of a box.

Pretend Play

Through pretend play a young child can fulfill her desire to be grown up. She fixes the car and puts out a fire. She cleans the house and hosts a tea party. Pretend play can also be the channel through which she acts out her fears and problems. She saves her friend from the big bad wolf and scolds her teddy bear for spilling juice. Facilitate your child's pretend play by providing props like hats, shoes, dolls, dishes, a broom, plastic tools, and cars. Props may be real or child-size, plastic versions. Young children often prefer real props; they are thrilled when Mommy or Daddy add an empty cereal box, a hat, or necklace to their toy box.

Constructive Play

Constructive play includes building with blocks and playing with clay. When building with blocks, children learn about size, shape, and balance. Provide your child with blocks of all sizes. For the large blocks, give your child cardboard blocks instead of wooden blocks. Young children are just beginning to learn about balance, and their creations often topple over. Be careful—the wooden blocks *can hurt small fingers and toes* when they come crashing down. You can buy cardboard blocks the size of a shoe box in most toy stores. Some of these blocks hold up to 120 pounds of weight, so children can walk and climb on them. Or offer your child old shoe boxes to play with. Many shoe stores even give boxes away. Simply tape the box shut before giving it to your child. To make the boxes more attractive, let your child decorate them with markers or cover them with contact paper. Providing your child with toy figures and cars encourages her to combine constructive play with pretend play.

While they play with clay, children learn about color, actions (pound, smash, squeeze, poke), size (long/short, big/small, skinny/fat), and shape (round, oval, square). You may purchase clay in a variety of colors at your local toy store. To make your own clay, mix the following ingredients in a large bowl: 2 cups flour, 2 cups salt, and 3 tablespoons cream of tartar. Then add 3 tablespoons oil and enough water to get the clay to the consistency you want. To color the clay, mix in a few drops of food coloring.

Balance Play

Indoor and Outdoor Play

Although it may not be possible to allow your child to play outside every day, it is important for her to play outside at least two times each week. Children learn things while playing outside that they cannot learn while playing indoors. During outdoor play, children learn about the wind, bugs, birds, shadows, leaves, sticks, and clouds. Your child may become familiar with these items through books and television, but she can only experience them outdoors.

Active and Quiet Play

Each day your child needs to spend some time playing actively and playing quietly. Active play allows your child to expend energy and develop physical skills—while it fosters her thinking skills.

Active play can occur outdoors or indoors. Outdoors, your child climbs **up** the steps and comes **down** the slide. She climbs to the top of a hill slowly and runs to the **bottom** of the hill **fast.** Indoors, you play airplane with her, holding her so she flies up. She bounces **fast** or **slow** on your lap while you sing a song about a train: "Charlie the s-l-o-w train is going down the track—choo, choo. Charlie the fast train is going down the track—choo, choo." While you pretend to be a tunnel and she pretends to be a car, she crawls **under, over, behind** and in **front of** you.

Quiet play provides your child with opportunities to calm down and to work with small objects while enhancing thinking skills. Like active play, quiet play can occur outdoors or indoors. Outdoors, you and your child lay on a blanket or sit on a bench as you read and turn the pages of a book or look for shapes in the clouds. Indoors, she puts a puzzle together, builds with blocks, or scribbles with crayons.

Playing with You and Independent Play

Your child also needs to spend time each day both playing with you and playing independently. During parent-child play, your child learns with you, teaches you, and has fun with you. It is important to spend between 30 and 60 minutes each day actively playing with your child. This play may be indoors or outdoors, quiet or active, messy or pretend. During play, give your child the opportunity to learn by trial and error. As a parent, resist the strong temptation to jump in the moment it appears that your child can't do something. In the same situation during independent play, your child would possibly succeed after a few attempts. However, you should help your child when she becomes frustrated or requests help. If your child routinely requests more help then she needs, encourage her confidence by gently guiding her to try things herself. Guide her by showing her the activity, by talking her through the activity, or by doing half the activity and letting her do the other half.

You may also use play to increase your child's attention span. If she goes from toy to toy without spending much time on any one toy, try to keep her with a toy a minute or two longer. Do this by showing her different things to do with the toy. For instance, if your one-year-old is banging with a toy car, show her how to spin the wheels fast and slow with her finger.

During independent play, your child learns to do things by herself, learns to entertain herself, and develops independence. If your child insists on constant parental entertainment, you need to encourage her to play independently. To facilitate independent play, get your child involved in an activity, and then move to the side. Explain to her that you must read a magazine or fold clothes. Tell her you will help her if she needs help. Watch her play out of the corner of your eye. If she looks as if she is becoming frustrated, verbally suggest a way that she can play. In the beginning, try to get her to play alone for five minutes. Increase the time by a minute or two every few days. Like many parents, you may feel uncomfortable or guilty about "making" your child play alone. To lessen these feelings, spend 15 to 20 minutes playing with your child before the independent play, or follow independent play by offering a special snack that you eat together.

Choose Appropriate Toys

When you choose a toy for your child, the main issue is that it must be _safe_. *Read all labels and instructions carefully. Remove all wrappings, pins, and staples. Check for small parts.* Young children cannot anticipate consequences and may swallow a piece if it is too small. If a toy has small parts, remove the parts that are small, and use the toy only when supervised by an adult, or put the toy away until the child is older.

Besides being safe, toys must be appropriate for your child's developmental level. Toys that are above her level will frustrate her and cause her to feel inadequate. Providing only toys below her level will slow her development. Most toys should be at her level, with a couple slightly above and a few below. Look for toys that are motivating, that lend themselves to exploration and that have sensory appeal. Your child's toys should vary in color, shape, size, texture, sound, and weight. In addition, choose toys that allow her to play next to other children and that encourage pretend play.

Also consider the durability and longevity of a toy. Select a toy that will withstand banging, dropping, and pulling. You want a toy that will grow with your child and encourage the development of new skills. You can increase the longevity of all of your child's toys by rotating them. Make two or three different sets of toys available. Keep one set in her bedroom, another set in the family room or living room, and the third set in another room. Put all other toys away in a box or a closet. Rotate the toys once a month, taking some out of the box and putting others into it. By rotating toys, you can offer your child different toys every month. Your child might never notice many of her toys if they are all stored in one large toy box. After not seeing a toy for a month or two, your child will be excited when it reappears. Because of the new skills she gained while the toy was in the box or the closet, she is likely to play with it in a different way then she did before.

Enhancing Activities

You can foster the development of thinking skills through "enhancing" activities that incorporate books, nursery rhymes, rhythm experiences, colors, shapes, the alphabet, and counting. Young children can experience these activities at home, in play groups, and at preschool.

Books

Reading is beneficial for children of all ages. You should read to your child every day. Read your child short stories in the beginning and progressively build up to the longer ones. At first, books with many pictures are best. Remember—five minutes of attentive story time is better than twenty minutes of squirming and daydreaming. If you find that the text in the books you have is too long, "read" the book from the pictures. Ask your child questions as you read the story. As you read to a one-year-old, ask her to point to details in the pictures. If you are reading to a two-year-old, ask her simple questions about the story that she can answer by looking at the pictures. And when your child is three years old, continue to ask questions she can answer from the pictures, but also ask her to tell you about the story after you finish reading it. If she is unable to recall the story, prompt her with a verbal hint or show her a picture from the book. Give your child the opportunity to tell you the story from the pictures.

Nursery Rhymes

Most three-year-olds can say or sing at least two nursery rhymes with minimal help from an adult. By four years of age, many children say or sing a couple of nursery rhymes independently. To get your child to that point, read stories and sing songs about nursery rhymes. As you sing nursery rhymes in the car together, occasion-

ally leave out a word or two to see whether your child can fill it in. When possible, add finger gestures to go with the words. For instance, when you sing, "Twinkle, Twinkle, Little Star," open and close your fingers in a twinkling manner for the first verse, point up for the second verse, use your fingers to make a diamond shape for the third verse, and so on.

In addition, act out nursery rhymes with your child. For "Humpty Dumpty," have your child sit on the couch. Together say, "Humpty Dumpty sat on a wall." As you say, "Humpty Dumpty had a great fall," have her lay on the floor. Then say, "All the kings horses and all the king's men couldn't put Humpty Dumpty together again," as you try to "fix" your child by moving her arms and legs. Feel free to add a phrase like, "So they decided to tickle Humpty Dumpty instead," and tickle her.

Rhythm Experiences

Listen to music with your child—children's songs, soft rock, country, or whatever you like to listen to. Sing with your child while you listen to music. Whenever you have the chance, dance with her. Hold her in your arms and dance around the room, dipping her every now and then, or dance standing side by side. Provide her with opportunities to play instruments. Children love playing drums and cymbals, and they like pots as much as toy drums. Start an impromptu parade now and then, marching together through the house while you both play instruments.

Colors, Shapes, the Alphabet, and Numbers

These are concepts that toddlers and preschoolers need to learn. By the time that your child is four, she should know primary colors, some of the alphabet, and the numbers 1-10. Teach your child these concepts during everyday experiences. While you fold clothes, talk to your child about the colors of her shirts and count the number of washcloths.

While grocery shopping, talk to her about the colors and shapes of the fruits, and point out large letters on cans or boxes. While you unload the dish-washer, talk about the number of spoons you are putting away, the shape of the plates, the color of the glasses. As you put toys away, count how many there are and discuss their different colors and shapes. Several good books on these concepts are available; read some of them with your child. You can also do simple art projects to reinforce these concepts with your child. For instance, cut out pictures of blue objects from a magazine, and glue them on a piece of paper. Another fun project is to make a triangle or a block letter out of a piece of paper and allow your child to finger-paint it with *non-toxic*, washable paint.

A PARENT'S STORY

I'll never forget the week that I was "quarantined" to the house with my two girls. It all started on a Sunday morning in February when I noticed a flat red rash on Erin's back and chest. At first I didn't give the rash much thought, but by afternoon the rash had spread to her stomach and consisted of watery blisters that were red at the base. At that point I pulled out my *Childhood Medical Guide* and looked up the chart on skin rashes. According to the chart, it appeared as though Erin had the chickenpox. The section in the book on chickenpox stated that it was important to call the doctor to have the condition confirmed. So the next morning I called the doctor and spoke with the receptionist. By the time our pediatrician called me back, my other daughter had the same flat red rash that Erin had the morning before. Our pediatrician confirmed the diagnosis—Erin and Megan both had chickenpox. She told me that I would need to keep the children home from day care for the next week.

I remember not having a clue as to what I should do to entertain my two girls. Erin was three and a half at the time and Megan was a little over a year old. I had always worked full time, which meant that I picked the girls up from day care at 5:30, went home, and made dinner while my husband played with the girls. We ate dinner, and I cleaned the kitchen while my husband bathed the girls and read them bedtime stories until we kissed them good-night. On the weekends we always did these wonderful family outings, like duck-pin bowling with bumperguards or visiting a children's museum.

After three days of coloring and watching every possible children's video, I decided that we needed a change or we would all go crazy. I was at my wit's end and had no creative ideas. Then suddenly I had a brilliant thought—to call Carol. Carol, my roommate in college, had majored in early childhood education and was a preschool teacher. That evening I called Carol. She was full of ideas, and as we talked on the phone I became excited about the next day.

Wearing a green sweatshirt, a pair of green and white stirrup pants, and green socks, I greeted the girls the next morning and made the declaration, "Today is green day, and we're going to have a lot of fun!" We went to the kitchen to eat green pancakes and drink green milk. Before my conversation with Carol, I had never thought of using food coloring to jazz up food or drinks. Erin and Megan thought it was the neatest thing! After breakfast I gave them a long bath (adding the traditional 1/2 cup of baking soda to the water to help relieve their itching). Instead of having them get in the tub, wash, and get out, I filled the tub with odds and ends from the kitchen. We had a blast! After the bath I suggested they each wear something green. Erin eagerly ran to her room in search of her favorite green shirt, while Megan and I went to her room to pick out some clothes.

Once the girls were dressed, we did the greatest color experiment. I gave each of the girls two glasses. I filled Megan's glasses halfway with water and had Erin do the same for herself. Then I put a drop of blue food coloring into one of Megan's glasses, and a drop of yellow into the other glass. I had Megan stir the water, and when she did, she got so excited about the water becoming blue and yellow. While Megan was stirring, I had Erin repeat what I had just done for her sister. Next, I had them each (Megan with some help, of course) pour their blue water into their yellow water. When the water turned green the two girls got so excited. Megan waved her arms in the air, chanting, "Green! Green! Green!" Erin screamed, "It turned green Mommy, it turned green!" and asked to do it again. We repeated our little experiment four more times before they were willing to stop.

After lunch we made what we call a "beep story tape"— an audio tape of a story read with a beep to indicate when to turn the page. The story was about Kermit (who else would we read about on green day?!) I read the story, Erin turned the pages when I made the beep sound, and Megan held the tape recorder. After we made the beep story tape, we listened to it as our nap time story.

Exhausted from their busy morning and from having the chickenpox, the girls took a long afternoon nap. While they slept, I thought about how great our morning had been. I had really enjoyed myself ,and knew that the girls had a lot of fun, too. Later that afternoon, we baked sugar cookies together and topped them with green sprinkles (of course!). When my husband got home from work, he was amazed by our adventurous day.

The rest of the week was just as much fun. We made sock puppets and had a puppet show one day. Another day, we went on a scavenger hunt looking for different shapes. On that same day, we cut our cheese sandwiches in the shape of triangles and our apples into rectangles. Spending the week at home with my two girls was a wonderful experience. I not only learned a lot about Erin and Megan, but I had fun. Now when I come home from work, the girls and I spend 30 minutes of "girl time" together. Then they have the choice of playing with Dad or helping me make dinner.

SUMMARY

Thinking skills include the development of concepts like color, size, time, and shape. They also include imitating, identifying body parts, learning nursery rhymes, and answering questions. To foster your child's thinking skills, you need to understand at what ages children develop which skills. As a parent, you can facilitate your child's thinking skills through play by: (1) allowing your child to lead the play; (2) providing opportunities for experimental, pretend, and constructive play; (3) balancing play; and (4) choosing appropriate toys. You also can facilitate thinking skills through activities that incorporate books, nursery rhymes, rhythm experiences, colors, shapes, the alphabet, and counting.

REFERENCES AND RECOMMENDED READINGS

For Children:

Glazer, T. (1973). *Eye Winker Tom Tinker Chin Chopper...Fifty Musical Fingerplays.* Garden City, NY: Doubleday & Company, Inc.

Hall, N. (1987). *Snoopy's ABC's.* New York, NY: Western Publishing Company, Inc.

Hall, N. (1987). *Snoopy's Book of Colors.* New York, NY: Western Publishing Company, Inc.

Hall, N. (1987). *Snoopy's Book of Opposites.* New York, NY: Western Publishing Company, Inc.

Ingoglia, G. (1987). *Look Inside Your Body.* New York, NY: Grosset & Dunlap, Inc.

Nez, J. (1985). *Mother Goose Rhymes.* New York, NY: Western Publishing Company, Inc.

Tallarico, T. (1982). *Numbers.* New York, NY: Tuffy Books.

Tallarico, T. (1982). *Alphabet.* New York, NY: Tuffy Books.

Wilburn, K. (1987). *Nursery Rhymes.* New York, NY: Western Publishing Company, Inc.

For Parents:

Burtt, K. & Kalkstein, D. (1981). *Smart Toys.* New York, NY: Harper and Row.

Dworetzky, J. (1981). *Introduction to Child Development.* St. Paul, MN: West Publishing Co. Chapters 12 & 13.

Furuno, S., O'Reilly, K., Hosaka, C., Inatsuka, T., Zeisloft, B., & Allman, T. (1988). *HELP Checklist.* Palo Alto, CA: VORT Corporation.

Fisher, J. (1986). *Toys To Grow With.* New York, NY: Perigee Books.

Johnson-Martin, N., Attermeier, S., & Hacker, B. (1990). *The Carolina Curriculum for Preschoolers with Special Needs.* Baltimore, MD: Paul H. Brookes Publishing Co.

Parks, S. (1988). *HELP...at Home.* Palo Alto, CA: VORT Corporation.

Rothenberg, B., Hitchcock, S., Harrison, M., & Graham, M. (1983). *Parentmaking.* Menlo Park, CA: The Banster Press.

Schneider, B. (1986). *Let's Sing and Play.* New York, NY: Western Publishing Corporation, Inc.

Time-Life Books (1987). *Childhood Medical Guide.* Author.

Chapter 2
Language Development

The first time that your child looks up at you and says "Mama" or "Dada" is very exciting. Hearing your child say "I love you" touches your heart like nothing else. The development of language is one of the most amazing changes that occurs between the ages of one and four years. To understand what it's like for your child to learn to speak, imagine yourself in a foreign country surrounded by a foreign language. At first you would try to understand the meaning of all the strange sounds you hear. You would understand best if the person speaking to you used as few words as possible and many gestures. If he pronounced his words slowly and clearly, it would be easier for you to learn to repeat them.

You would probably need to hear the same words over and over before you would feel comfortable enough to try saying them yourself. The same goes for your child. You can foster your child's language development by understanding the order in which language skills emerge, talking with your child, encouraging speech, helping your child learn to listen, and reading to your child.

Parent Perspective
Your child's speech development probably amazes you. One day he is babbling and the next thing you know, he says four or five words. As your child begins to speak, you may feel that he is no longer a baby and that he is becoming a toddler. The first time your child says "Juice." while pointing to the refrigerator may make you feel that for the first time, you truly know what he wants. As your child uses more words, you may feel that you are no longer talking to him, but are now talking with him. It may, however, frustrate you when he says something that you can't understand. You may feel badly when you see how your inability to understand him makes him frustrated. You may wonder when his articulation will get better. If you have trouble understanding your child's speech, you may wonder if you should be concerned. Once your child is two and a half or three years old, has a large vocabulary, and fairly clear articulation, you may find yourself wishing that he didn't talk quite as much and that he wouldn't ask "Why?" quite as often.

Child Perspective
With speech, your child learns that he can tell you what he wants. Sometimes he knows what he wants to say and thinks he is saying it, but has trouble making himself understood. At times this frustrates him; at other times it makes him upset. As your child develops more words and as his articulation improves, it becomes easier for him to communicate. He really enjoys talking and may try to begin a conversation but not know what to say. He likes it when you include him in conversations, and needs you to be patient as he tries to express himself. If you say something like, "Hurry up, we don't have all day," he may become anxious. If you tell him to take his time and to think about what he wants to say, he will feel confident enough to continue trying to express himself.

LANGUAGE DEVELOPMENT

To foster your child's language development, you need to know what language skills are appropriate at what ages. This will allow you to encourage skills that are at your child's developmental level. You also need to understand there are two important parts to language: receptive and expressive skills. Receptive skills refer to your child's ability to understand language. When your child hands you a ball after you say, "Give me the ball," he is demonstrating a receptive skill. Expressive skills refer to your child's ability to produce language. "Mama," "More juice," and "Tomorrow I going to see big trains" are all examples of expressive skills.

DEVELOPMENT OF LANGUAGE SKILLS[1]

One-Year-Olds
Receptive:
• Understand more than express.
• Follow simple one-step directions.
• Begin to follow two-step directions when accompanied by gestures.

Expressive:
• Point to desired objects.
• Say "Mama" for Mommy and "Dada" for Daddy.
• Say first word between ten and fourteen months of age.
• Use words and/or gestures to communicate needs.
• Use their own name to refer to themselves.
• Imitate sounds of animals, cars, etc.
• Attempt to sing the words to songs.
• Use 10-15 words by eighteen months.
• Begin to use two-word sentences around eighteen months.
• Use 50 words at twenty-four months.

Two-Year-Olds
Receptive:
• Want to learn new words.
• Point to objects, then pictures of objects, then objects described by
   their use, then pictures of objects described by function.
• Follow two-part directions with gestures.
• Respond to "where" questions.
• Understand action verbs.
• Understand simple stories.
• Follow one-part directions involving prepositional phrases.

Expressive:
• Use 50 words at twenty-four months and 300 or more words by
   three years.
• Develop clear sentence structure.
• Use three-word sentences.
• Start to use word endings (s, ing, ed).
• Use speech for many purposes.
• Name objects and simple pictures.
• Tend to say the same thing over and over again.
• Pronounce p, b, m, k, g, w, h, n, d, and t correctly at two and a half
   years of age.
• Use words more than gestures to communicate.
• Ask many questions.
• Request help.
• Want to know more about colors and numbers.
• Begin to use time-related words.
• State first and last name.
• Recite a few nursery rhymes.
• Answer simple questions.

Three-Year-Olds
Receptive:
• Understand and respond to a wide variety of questions.
• Follow two-step directions involving sequence.
• Respond to verbal guidance.

Expressive:
- Like to sing and love to talk.
- Use four or more words in sentences.
- Participate in conversations.
- Change speech according to listener.
- Speak clearly but may still have difficulty pronouncing r, l, s, and th.
- Talk about the future.
- Use words to describe shape, size, color, texture, spatial relationships, and functions of objects.
- Describe parts of pictures.
- Tell a simple story from a picture.
- Use words to get what they need.
- Ask questions frequently to which they already know the answer.
- Use action verbs, adjectives, pronouns, and prepositional phrases correctly.
- Add s to end of words to indicate possession.
- Use most irregular past tense verbs correctly.
- Use different voices for different people while playing.

[1]Skills are presented in the order that most children learn them.

One-Year-Olds

Receptive
At twelve months of age, a toddler understands a lot more than he can express. For instance, he gets excited and looks at his highchair when you say, "It's time to eat," but he may not yet say "eat." Between twelve and twenty-four months of age, the one-year-old becomes increasingly sophisticated in his ability to follow directions. At first he can follow one-part directions that are accompanied by a gesture. For example, he will give you a ball if you point to it and say, "Give me the ball," while you hold out your hand. He then learns to follow similar directions without needing a gesture. This is a big help because now you can say, "Get your shoes," and he will go get his shoes, even if they are in another room—assuming he knows where his shoes are and that they are not hiding under a mound of toys. As he approaches two years of age, he will start to follow two-step directions with gestures. If you say, "Put the bucket and the shovel in the basket," while you point to the bucket and then the shovel, he will put the bucket and the shovel in the basket. In the beginning, he may only put the bucket in the basket, and will need you to say, "Remember to put the shovel in too."

Expressive
Most twelve-month-olds babble very well and say "Dada" for Daddy and "Mama" for Mommy. By fourteen months of age, most toddlers say their first word. Many children say 10-15 words by

eighteen months and 50 words by two years. Girls generally talk sooner than boys, and first-born children talk sooner than other children. Until one-year-olds have a good grasp of speech, they use gestures with their words to communicate their needs. To get you to read him a book, your child may say, "Book," and bring you a book. To get you to look at a picture in his book, he may say, "Book," and point to a picture.

The one-year-old's first words are associated with the experiences, things, and people important to him. To some extent his first words reflect his parents' verbal style. If his parents spend a lot of time pointing to and labeling objects, he may use early words to name objects, for example, "ball" or "kitty." If they use language to describe or guide his behavior, he may use words to make requests and socialize such as "more" or "bye-bye."

One-year-olds sometime identify the meaning of a word by only one or two attributes. The first time a one-year-old goes to the zoo he may call a tiger, a zebra, and a lion "dog," because all three have a similar shape and way of moving. When he sees an elephant, a sophisticated one-year-old may call it a big dog. This child knows that the animals are different; he simply doesn't know the right word. From his small vocabulary, he chooses the word that best fits the situation. If your child calls apples, balls, oranges, circles, and the moon "ball," he could probably pick out the apple in the group if you said, "Get the apple."

To learn the names of objects, animals, and people, the one-year-old carefully listens to the words you use and he imitates what you say. He can't differentiate between "good" and "bad" words; he imitates everything. Remember that you are a role model for your child. If there are certain words you don't want your child to use, try to avoid using them yourself. The one-year-old also learns names by asking, "Uh?" while pointing to a car, or "Dada?" while pointing to the mailman.

The one-year-old needs a lot of repetition to learn, so he asks for the same name over and over. While learning language, he talks to himself as much as to others. He even practices talking in bed. Most parents feel a great sense of joy from listening to these early words. Some stand near the bedroom door; others turn on the old baby monitor to eavesdrop proudly for a moment or two. Bedtime and one-on-one times are ideal for marveling over your child's developing speech. Many one-year-olds are shy as they learn to talk, and they talk much less in a group setting.

While first learning to talk, the one-year-old says the one most important word to make his point. If he is drinking apple juice and wants more apple juice, he will say, "More." He doesn't consciously think, "What do I need? What does Mom already know? What word should I use?"; he just says, "More." He may say "Up" to get you to make something go up or to let you know where something is. To decipher what he means, you must read his gestures in addition to listening to his one word. If he says "Up" while he lifts both arms in the air, he wants you to pick him up. But if he says "Up" while he points to his book on a shelf, he wants you to get his book.

The one-year-old talks about the present, not the past or future. He often uses words like "uh-oh" and "no-no." He names familiar objects, and he uses his own name to refer to himself. When speaking, he usually omits consonants, saying "tee" for tree or "ba" for bath. He enjoys imitating the sounds of animals and cars, and he tries to sing the words to songs. However, his speech may reach a plateau while he learns to walk. Walking and talking each require much concentration and effort. In the beginning, one-year-olds can't do both at the same time. Once he is comfortable with his ability to walk, the one-year-old will focus on developing speech once again.

The older toddler (between eighteen and twenty-four months) often mimics what others say. When mimicking, he doesn't always understand what he says. He may mimic to practice a word or a phrase. He may also mimic what you say to get you to rephrase the information to help him understand it. Most toddlers begin to use two words together at around eighteen months. Some toddlers don't combine words until closer to twenty-four months of age. As he makes the transition from using one to two words, the older one-year-old lists: "More milk," "Dada bye-bye," "No cookie." Next, he uses "this" and "that" in sentences—"More this" or "That ball." By two years of age, his speech is understandable at least 50 percent of the time.

Two-Year-Olds

Receptive
The two-year-old is word-hungry and wants to learn all the words he can. He listens carefully to new words. He may ask, "What you say?" or request, "Say that one again," if he doesn't hear you clearly or doesn't quite understand. Between two and three years of age,

he becomes increasingly sophisticated in his ability to point to objects upon request. At first he points to objects that you name; he then points to pictures of objects; by the age of three, he points to objects described by their use. For instance, at your request he will point to a cup, then to a picture of a cup, and finally, when you say, "Show me which one is for drinking," he will point to a cup among other dishes.

Between twenty-four and thirty months of age, the young two-year-old learns to follow two-part directions without gestures. If he is told, "Give Grandpa the paper and his glasses," he will do so without any additional prompts. The young two-year-old also begins to understand complex sentences. When you tell him, "You may play in the tub when we get home," he will say, "Home now. Play in tub," the moment you walk into the house. The older two-year-old (between two and a half and three years) responds appropriately to "where" questions by pointing to or stating the location. When he is asked, "Where is Daddy?", he may point outside or say, "My Daddy outside fixin' the car." The older two-year-old also understands action verbs, such as sleeping, walking, and eating. Many children at this age can point to pictures of people or animals involved in these actions. In addition, the older two-year-old understands simple stories and can follow more complex one-part directions involving prepositional phrases. For example, he is able to put a book on, under, or beside the shelf.

Expressive

Speech continues to develop at an amazing rate for the two- year-old. Many children have 50 words by the time they are twenty-four months of age. Most children have 300 or more words by the time they are three years old.

The young two-year-old (between twenty-four and thirty months) uses speech in a variety of ways: to express his needs—"Give me juice."; to indicate posses-  sion—"My doll!"; to describe action—"I eating cheese."; and to request recurrence—"More milk." He also uses speech to show nonexistence— "Daddy bye-bye."; to spec- ify objects—"This hat."; to describe—"Big boy!"; to greet familiar people—"Hi Grammy!"; and to ask simple questions—"What doin'?". He has the vocabulary and knowledge to name objects he sees, hears, or touches. He can also label simple pictures of familiar objects in books. The young two-year-old tends to say the same things over and over: "This pretty hat. See my hat. My hat pretty. This pretty hat." His articulation is imperfect, but as he matures physically and as he practices saying more words, his articulation improves. At two and a half years of age, most children pronounce p, b, m, k, g, w, h, n, d, and t correctly.

The older two-year-old (between thirty and thirty-six months) uses words more than gestures to communicate his needs, and he likes to engage in conversations. He asks many questions; "Why?" and "how come?" are his favorites. He even asks questions when he knows the answer. Frequently, he does this to test his own knowledge and memory. Other times, he asks the question because he wants to tell you something, but he wants you to ask him the question. In addition to asking questions, he uses speech to request help—"Help me"—and to request permission—"I do it?". The older two-year-old uses size words and opposites, but he frequently mixes them up. He wants to know more about colors and numbers, and he begins to use time-related words, such as night, day, now, and later. He can tell you his first and last name, recite a few nursery rhymes, and sing parts of songs. He answers simple questions, such as, "Where are your shoes?" Although his articulation continues to improve, he may still have difficulty pronouncing several sounds. Unlike the younger two-year-old, the older two- year-old becomes frustrated when you don't understand his speech.

Between two and three years of age, children develop clear sentence structure. They begin to incorporate rules of grammar into their speech; they use three-word sentences with nouns, verbs, and adjectives, for example, "Big dog runned." or "Give me juice." When children start to use word endings, they use "s" to form plurals, "ing" on verbs, and "ed" to show past tense. Young children over-general- ize many grammatical rules as they learn them. Over-generalization continues until school age, when most children have mastered adult language. A two-year-old who goes from saying "ate" to "eated" is not regressing, but making progress. He is learning an important rule, to add "ed." Once he learns there are exceptions to the rule, he will go back to saying "ate." When learning pronouns, the two-year-old uses me, you, my, and mine before he uses I. He uses these pronouns incorrectly before he learns to use them correctly. When using prepositions, he uses prepositional phrases as sentences—"In your box." or "On big rock." Later, at around three and a half years of age, he will use prepositional phrases within sentences—"Put it in your box" or "The bird is on the big rock."

Three-Year-Olds

Receptive

The three-year-old understands and responds to a wide variety of questions. He understands "what do you do?" and "why do we do" questions. If you ask him, "What do you do when you are hungry?", he is likely to respond, "Eat." If you ask, "Why do we wear raincoats?", he may say, "To keep the water off." or "To stay dry." Between three and four years of age, he begins to respond correctly to yes and no questions. Before this time, he frequently responded with a firm "no" though he sometimes meant "yes." When asked, "Did you have fun at the park?", he may have answered, "No," and then asked, "When we goin' back? I wanna feed the ducks again." He probably said no more than yes because he learned no first, heard no a lot, or used no to exert control. Now when you ask, "Did you like the puppet show?", he may say, "Yes, I liked the turtle the bestest. You know why I liked the turtle the bestest? I liked the turtle the bestest he nice to the girl." The three-year-old also correctly responds to who and whose questions. For example, if you ask "Whose shoes are these?", he will appropriately answer, "Mine" or "Daddy's." As he approaches four, he begins to understand that questions involving "how many" require him to answer with a number and "which" questions require him to point to or to name a person or an object. At this age he will respond with the  right type of answer, but his answers won't always be correct. For instance, he will answer "three" when there are really five cars.

The older three-year-old (between three and a half and four years) learns to follow two-step directions involving sequence. If you say, "Put the drum in the toy box, and then bring me the book," he will put the drum away and bring you the book. In the beginning he may need you to emphasize the words, "and then." He may also need you to point to the drum and then to the book while you give the direction. As he gets better at following two-step directions, he may only need an occasional reminder if he starts to come back after completing only one of the two steps: "Remember to get the book." As the three-year-old gets better at following directions involving sequence, he becomes more responsive to verbal guidance. Verbal guidance works well for a young child who wants to do something for himself but doesn't know how and doesn't want you to help. Take, for instance, the following example: Your child's hands are full of toys, and he is ready to go outside to play, but he wants to be the one to open the front door. You watch him as he struggles to grasp the door handle while holding onto all four toys. You try to help him open the door, but he tells you, "Don't do it. I wanna open the door myself." You can help him by saying, "Put the toys down, and then open the door."

Expressive

The three-year-old likes to sing and loves to talk. He talks to almost anyone who will listen, and he enjoys talking on the telephone. He speaks in fluent sentences containing four or more words and participates in conversations for several turns. When talking with others, he changes his speech depending on the listener. For instance, he uses a simple, more high-pitched voice with babies. The three-year-old speaks clearly; he is understandable to more than just family, relatives, and close friends. About 80 percent of what he says is easily understood by all listeners. He may, however, still have difficulty pronouncing r, l, s and th. Between three and four years of age, his language becomes more complex as he learns to use well-formed sentences that follow grammar rules.

Between three and three and a half years of age, the younger three-year-old begins to talk about the future and uses words to describe shape, size, color, texture, spatial relationships, and the functions of objects. He may say, "Tomorrow I going to see the big, black trains" or "Put the blue one next to the green one that moves." He also uses words to describe what he sees or what is happening, for example, "The big jet is flying high." In addition, he describes parts of pictures, and he can tell a simple story by looking at a picture: "The big bad wolf is blowing. But this house is a strong house. He can't blow it down."

Between three and a half and four years of age, the older three-year-old begins to use words to get others to get him what he needs. He often makes statements such as, "Give me the crayon" and "You get my shoes." If he's polite, he may even add "please" to his request, for example, "Mom, get me more milk, please." During this time he discovers the power of questions; he continues to ask questions to which he already knows the answer. Often he asks the question to test his own knowledge and memory of the answer. The older three-year-old uses action verbs, adjectives, pronouns,

**TALK TO YOUR DOCTOR OR A LANGUAGE PATHOLOGIST
IF YOUR CHILD DOES NOT[2]**

By the Age of Eighteen Months...
• Follow a one-step direction with gesture.
• Point to desired objects.
• Say "Mama" for Mommy or "Dada" for Daddy.
• Say three words.

By the Age of Two Years...
• Point to a few pictures of familiar objects.
• Point to one body part.
• Say ten words.
• Use two-word sentences.

By the Age of Three Years...
• Point to six body parts.
• Name a few pictures of familiar objects.
• Speak clearly 80 percent of the time.
• Pronounce b, p, m, t, w, d.

By the Age of Four Years...
• Follow a two-step direction involving sequence.
• Use three- or four-word sentences
• Use action words.
• Use adjectives.
• Speak clearly 90 percent of the time.

[2]Most children are able to do these items by the age listed. If your child is unable to do them, it may or may not mean there is a problem with his development. It only means that you should mention it to your doctor or consult with a language pathologist, so you can determine whether your child's development needs to be assessed. You may contact language pathologists privately or through your local Child Find program. Under Public Law 99-457 (IDEA), Child Find provides free screening and assessment to identify children who may have special needs. You can find the phone number for your local Child Find program by contacting your county Department of Education, Department of Health and Human Services, or Department of Public Welfare. You can also get the phone number for the Child Find program in your area by calling the U.S. Department of Education in Washington, D.C. For additional information, contact The American Speech-Language-Hearing Association in Rockville, MD.

and prepositional phrases correctly. He correctly adds s to the ends of words to show possession. He also uses many irregular past tense verb forms correctly. He says, "Mommy went to the store" instead of "Mommy goed to the store." In play, the older three-year-old uses different voices for different people.

TALKING WITH YOUR CHILD

Talk with your child throughout the day. As you dress your child in the morning, talk about the picture on his shirt or the color of his pants. Use breakfast time to talk about what his day will be like. While you clean the house, describe what you are doing. In the car with him, sing a song about where you are going, imitate car horns and sirens as you hear them, or look for a big

truck and then a small car. At the grocery store, discuss the colors, shapes, and names of various foods. While you cook, talk about the textures and smells of different foods, allowing your child to touch or taste the food when appropriate. At bath time, name body parts and talk about opposites, such as dirty/clean, wet/dry, and out/in. Before your child goes to bed each night, spend a few minutes talking about how his day went and what his day will be like tomorrow.

Use simple and clear speech as you talk with your child. If you are making oatmeal cookies, say to him, "I'm putting the butter and sugar in the bowl. Now I'm putting in the vanilla and eggs." instead of, "I'm putting two tablespoons of butter and three-quarters cup of sugar in the mixing bowl. Now I'm adding an eighth teaspoon of vanilla and two eggs to the ingredients."

Talk about things that interest your child. If your child is watching a ladybug crawl across the sidewalk, talk about the ladybug instead of the birthday party he is attending the following week. If a helicopter flies overhead while he is looking at the ladybug, mention the helicopter, but if he is not interested in the helicopter, continue talking about the ladybug. In addition to talking about things that interest your child, describe the things he does; say, for example, "Wow! You're sliding down!" or "You're hopping on one foot!"

ENCOURAGING SPEECH

Encourage your toddler to make sounds or use words in addition to pointing. If you meet your child's needs immediately, he doesn't need to speak. If he points to his highchair and you say, "Oh, you want to eat," he doesn't need to use his words to communicate. Anticipating your child's needs too quickly and too often can slow his speech development. However, it is important to find a balance between responding too quickly and not quickly enough. Your goal is to encourage him to speak, but not to frustrate him. When your child runs into the kitchen and points to the refrigerator, ask, "What do you want?". If he says, "ja," then say, "Oh, you want juice. Mommy will get you some juice."

When your child starts using words, pronounce words correctly, as opposed to using baby talk. Your child learns which words to use and how to pronounce these words by listening to you speak. If he says, "Me want bankie." and you respond, "Here's your bankie," you make it hard for him to learn to say "blanket." Do not, on the other hand, require him to say "blanket" before you give him his blanket. Penalties and threats take the fun out of talking and do very little to foster speech development. Instead, simply respond to his request in a manner that incorporates the correct word—"Here is your blanket."

Show enthusiasm for your child's efforts, and make him feel proud of his successes and attempts. Statements such as "Thank you for telling me you want more juice!" and "Way to go! You said 'Up!'" foster positive feelings about talking. Help your toddler use gestures with his words when you don't understand him. If he comes to you, pulls on your hand, and says, "Deek! Deek!", you may not know what he wants. In such situations, say, "Show me what you want." If he walks to the kitchen and points to the refrigerator, you will know that he wants a drink. On the other hand, if he goes to the table and points to a toy duck that is out of his reach, you will know that he wants the duck. Occasionally, you may help your  child by casually talking for him when he cannot make himself understood. If he tells a neighbor, "My Daddy gone workin' puter," you might say, "That's right; Daddy has gone to work, and he's working on a computer." As your child grows older, he may have trouble expressing his thoughts because his mind is racing. If this happens, help him slow down by saying, "Stop a moment, and think about what you want to say with your brain. Then tell me with your words."

HELPING YOUR CHILD LEARN TO LISTEN

You can foster your child's listening skills in three ways. The first way is to **bring everyday sounds to your child's attention.** If you are outside playing and an airplane flies by, say something like, "I hear an airplane. The airplane makes a loud noise." or ask, "Do

you hear that noise? What's making that noise?" The second way is to **use words as a form of play**. You might do finger plays while singing songs. For instance, use your hands to act out "The Wheels on the Bus." You can also do tickling games while you say nursery rhymes. For example, you can say, "The itsy bitsy spider went up the water spout," as you creep your fingers up your child's stomach. The third way is to **play listening games**. You might play "Bring me a ____," changing the name of the object each time and praising his successes. Or you can also play hide-and-seek, describing verbally where your are— "Daddy is hiding in the kitchen. Daddy is under the table."

READING TO YOUR CHILD

Reading to your child fosters both receptive and expressive language skills. Many children first see a picture of a cow and learn that a cow says "Moo" during story time. It is also during story time when many children hear their first nursery rhyme. **Read to your child every day.** Hard-paged books, with a couple objects on each page, are best in the beginning. Then choose books that

capture your child's imagination and interest. When reading to your child, don't feel as if you have to read exactly what the book says. Instead, you should adapt it to meet your child's level of interest. With a one-year-old, you might initially only name the pictures on each page, as you point to them. Later, you might tell an abbreviated version of the story. While reading, occasionally **ask your child questions**, such as, "Where is the dog?" or "What color is the girl's dress?" or "What do you think will happen next?". As your child gets older, encourage him to "read" the book to you by talking about the pictures. Keep story time enjoyable. If your child gets tired of listening to a story, don't force him to stay for the rest of the book. Five minutes of enjoyable reading with your child's full attention is better than 20 minutes of squirming.

A PARENT'S STORY

When I brought Russell to the pediatrician for his two-year checkup, our pediatrician was concerned about his speech and hearing. Russell was talking in three- and four-word sentences, but Dr. Young was worried about his articulation and the fact that he said "huh?" all the time. Even though I clearly understood Russell, not too many other people did. When Dr. Young first mentioned that she was concerned, I told her that I wasn't worried. But on the way home from the doctor's office, I began to wonder if maybe there was something wrong with Russell and that maybe I was trying to deny it.

After Russell was in bed that evening, my husband and I talked about Dr. Young's concerns. At first my husband agreed with me, and then he agreed with Dr. Young. He said that when he stopped to think about it, he realized that I did interpret much of what Russell said and that Russell definitely said "huh?" a lot.

The next morning I called our pediatrician to tell her that I wanted to pursue a speech and hearing assessment for Russell. Unfortunately, I reached Dr. Young's answering service and was told it was the first day of her two-week vacation. I told the service it wasn't an emergency and said I would call Dr. Young in two weeks when she returned.

A few days later I was telling a neighbor about Russell. She recommended that I call our local elementary school. She told me that a friend of hers had a toddler with Down's syndrome who was getting a variety of services from the school. I called the school and told the secretary I had a two-year-old who needed a speech and hearing evaluation because of poor articulation. She explained there was a program called "Child Find" for screening and testing infants, toddlers, and preschoolers for possible delays. She gave me the phone number and encouraged me to call.

I called Child Find right away. They asked me a few questions and said someone would call me back in the next day or two. Ms. Chen, an educator from the infant and toddler program, called that afternoon. We set up an appointment for her to come to my house to explain the program and to do a brief screen of Russell's development.

Ms. Chen came to our house the next week and explained that Russell was entitled to evaluations and, if needed, services under a law called PL 99-457. She told me that in our state the evaluations and services were free. She asked me a number of questions about Russell and spent some time playing little games with him. She had Russell do things, such as play with blocks, kick a ball, point to body parts, and name pictures. At the end of our meeting, she told me that Russell should get a full audiological assessment and a speech evaluation. She said the rest of his development looked great. She explained that according to the law, Russell would be tested within 45 days. Before she left, we called the necessary departments and set up an audiological assessment for the following day and a speech evaluation in three weeks.

Russell's audiological assessment took more than an hour. The audiologist, Mr. Hood, began by asking questions about Russell's health and development. He played some sound games with Russell. Mr. Hood rang bells, shook rattles, and spoke to see whether Russell would turn and look for the sounds. Russell did a great job and turned every time except once. Next, Mr. Hood brought Russell and me to a soundproof booth where different sounds were presented through speakers to Russell's left and right. Again, Russell turned to almost all the sounds. For the last test, Mr. Hood put a plug in Russell's ear canal and presented a sound to see how the sound bounced off Russell's eardrum at different pressures. This was to make sure Russell's middle ear was functioning properly. Mr. Hood said that, as with all the other tests, Russell performed within the normal range. Mr. Hood told me that as far as he could tell, Russell's hearing was perfectly normal. He said he would bring a copy of his report to the meeting we would have following the speech evaluation. The purpose of the meeting was to review all the assessment information to determine if Russell needed any services and if so, what type. He asked me if I wanted him to send a copy of the report to my pediatrician. I said yes and asked him to send me a copy of the report as well.

Russell's speech evaluation took a little longer than the audiological assessment, about an hour and a half. Before beginning the speech test, Mrs. Cammel, the language pathologist, spent some time playing with Russell and me. She said she would learn a lot about his speech just by watching him play. After he played for about 15 minutes, she began her testing. The test involved a lot of different little games in which she would ask Russell to do things, such as pointing to a picture and telling her the name of an object. Throughout the evaluation session, Mrs. Cammel asked me a number of questions about Russell's ability to understand and to use speech. After the session, Mrs. Cammel said she thought Russell did nicely. She said she needed to score the tests before she could tell me exactly how he did. She told me we would review both the audiological and speech results at our meeting the next week. I asked her to forward a copy of her report to my pediatrician and requested that she bring an extra copy of the report to the meeting for me.

That week was one of the longest weeks of my life. I thought Russell had done fine, but I wasn't sure. I hoped he was okay, but if he weren't, I would be glad we found out about it early. The day of the meeting finally came, and my stomach was in knots. What if Russell really did have a speech problem, and what if it were something that couldn't be fixed? My husband was pretty concerned, but he kept telling me that I shouldn't worry until we knew we had something to worry about. Ms. Chen, Mr. Hood, Mrs. Cammel, my husband, and I attended the meeting. I was prepared to hear that Russell had a speech impairment, but we were told that his speech was within normal limits. Mrs. Cammel explained there is a wide range as to when children develop various speech skills. She told us Russell was on the low end of normal. She gave us a few suggestions on how to facilitate his speech and asked us to make an appointment to see her again in three months so she could check Russell's progress. I was relieved.

It's been six months since that meeting. Russell has been to two follow-up appointments with Mrs. Cammel so she could check his speech. Yesterday she told us that Russell had caught up and that we didn't need to come back to see her anymore. She told us to feel free to call her anytime we had any concerns. The infant and toddler program is a wonderful program, and although Russell never needed actual speech therapy services, it is nice to know they are available.

SUMMARY

The development of language is one of the most amazing changes that occur between the ages of one and four years. Receptively, children go from pointing to a ball when you ask, "Where is the ball?" to answering, "I got one blue car and two red cars" when you ask, "How many cars do you have?". Expressively, children go from saying "Mama" to "Mommy, more juice, please. I so thirsty."

There are five ways to foster your child's language development. First, become familiar with the developmental progression of language skills so you can encourage skills that are at your child's level. Second, talk with your child throughout the day. Use simple speech, and talk about the things that interest your child. Third, encourage your child's speech. When he points, also encourage him to make sounds or to use words. When he starts using words, give him a good role model by saying words correctly, as opposed to using baby talk. When he talks, show enthusiasm for his efforts and make him feel proud of his successes and attempts. Fourth, help your child learn to listen by bringing everyday sounds to his attention, using words as a form of word play and playing listening games. Finally, foster receptive and expressive language skills by reading to your child every day.

REFERENCES & RECOMMENDED READINGS

Coplan, J. (1983). *The Early Language Milestone Scale.* Tulsa, OK: Modern Education Corporation.

Dworetzky, J. (1981). *Introduction to Child Development.* St. Paul, MN: West Publishing Co. Chapter 11.

Furuno, A., O'Reilly, K., Hosaka, C., Inatsuka, T., Zeisloft- Falbey, B., & Allman, T. (1988). *HELP Checklist.* Palo Alto, CA: VORT Corporation.

Frankenburg, W. and Dodds, J. (1990). *Denver II.* Denver, CO: Denver Developmental Materials, Inc.

Johnson-Martin, N. Attermeier, S., & Hacker, B. (1990). *The Carolina Curriculum for Preschoolers with Special Needs.* Baltimore, MD: Paul H. Brookes Publishing Co.

Ohanian, B. and Vollmer, G. (1989, October). Now we're talking. *Parenting,* pp 64-69.

Parks, S. (1988). *HELP...at home.* Palo Alto, CA: VORT Corporation.

Rothenberg, B., Hitchcock, S., Harrison, M., and Graham, M. (1983). *Parentmaking.* Menlo Park, CA: The Banster Press.

Chapter 3
Motor Development

Watching your child take his first step from the sofa to your outstretched arms is something that you will probably always remember. As is watching him draw his first picture of you—the almost perfect circle for your head, the two dots for your eyes, and the crooked line for your mouth. From that first step at around twelve months of age to the portrait at three and a half years, many other motor skills emerge. Your child will learn to run, climb stairs, go down a slide, and ride a tricycle. He also will learn to put a circle into a shape sorter, build a tower out of blocks, put a puzzle together, and snip with scissors. You can foster your child's motor development in three ways. First, understand your child's temperament and the progression of motor development so you can pick activities that encourage rather than frustrate your child. Second, arrange your child's outdoor and indoor environment to encourage motor skills. Third, provide your child with a variety of motor experiences.

<u>Parent Perspective</u>
Most parents feel an overwhelming sense of pride the first time their child takes a step. As your child's walking and running skills improve, you may feel concerned if your child is afraid to climb a jungle gym or go down a slide. You may wonder if you should push him a little. Later, when he is an "expert" at the playground, you may feel anxious if he climbs too high or tries to go down a slide head first while lying on his back. At those times you may wonder if you should limit what your child does.

Most parents also feel proud when their child draws or paints his first picture. As your child gets involved with art projects, there may be days when the clean-up process frustrates you. At those times you may wonder how long it will take before he can paint without getting the paint all over his clothes, the table, and the floor. If he mixes the black paint with the yellow paint or paints the grass pink, you may wonder if you should encourage him to keep the colors separate or tell him that grass is green. When your child can't get his paints to mix a certain way, can't stack his blocks the way he wants to, or can't figure out how to put a puzzle together, you probably want to do all you can to help him without helping too much.

Child Perspective

Young children are very pleased with their new abilities to walk, run, climb, and jump. Your child may want to practice doing these things over and over. When a skill is emerging, he may be afraid. Climbing up a ladder to go down a slide may frighten him just as much as climbing a ladder to get on a roof might frighten you. Sometimes he simply wants to watch others do these things. By watching he learns how others do things. As his skills improve, he may have trouble determining his limits. He may not realize, for instance, that he cannot climb as high as his older sister. He may also not understand the importance of having you "spot" him. He may insist on doing it himself, and think that if you are standing near him then you are helping him. He may accept "spotting" better if you tell him that you are standing near him to make sure he doesn't get hurt and will only help if he needs it.

Young children are equally proud of their artwork, block structures, and puzzles. Your child will need you to show him how to do these things, but he will probably want to do them by himself. Mixing the colors and experimenting with various strokes and smudges may be more important to him than the end art project. Your child will need you to be patient and will do best if you allow creativity and experimentation. Your child may become upset when his paints smear the wrong way, his blocks fall down before he knocks them down, or his puzzle piece won't fit where he thinks it should. To him, these are devastating events. At these times he needs your empathy and he needs you to show him how to make things okay again.

UNDERSTAND MOTOR DEVELOPMENT

As a parent, you can better foster your child's motor development when you key into his individual temperament and when you know what skills are appropriate for your child's age. Temperament plays a big role in a child's motivation and interest to learn and practice motor skills. Some children are "motor driven" and want to try everything. Other children are "motor cautious" and need time to watch others before trying things themselves. An understanding of your child's temperament will help you offer activities in a manner that is appropriate for your child.

TABLE 1 DEVELOPMENT OF MOTOR SKILLS[1]

One-Year-Olds
Gross Motor:
• Creep on hands and knees.
• Walk with both hands held.
• Stand alone.
• Walk forward.
• Walk backwards.
• Throw a ball underhand in sitting.
• Creep or hitch upstairs.
• Walk sideways.
• Run.
• Throw a ball forward.
• Pull toy behind while walking.
• Throw a ball overhand landing near target.
• Creep downstairs.
• Walk upstairs with one hand held.
• Carry large toy while walking, and push and pull large toys or boxes around the floor.
• Kick ball.
• Throw a ball into box.
• Use "ride on" toys.
• Walk downstairs with one hand held.
• Walk upstairs holding rail, two feet on step.

Fine Motor:
• Remove pegs from pegboard.
• Put objects into container.
• Mark paper with crayon.
• Build tower using two cubes.
• Place one round peg in pegboard.
• Build tower using three cubes.
• Place one round peg in pegboard.
• Build tower using four cubes.
• Pull pop beads apart.
• Imitate vertical stroke.
• Imitate circular scribble.
• Imitate horizontal stroke.
• Build tower using six cubes.

Two-Year-Olds
Gross Motor:
• Jump in place with both feet.
• Go up and down slide.
• Walk upstairs alone with both feet on step.
• Walk downstairs holding rail with both feet on step.
• Jump from 8 inches high (bottom step) with one foot leading.
• Walks downstairs alone with both feet on step.
• Walk on tiptoes.
• Jump backwards.
• Jump sideways.
• Stand on one foot.
• Hop on one foot.
• Climb jungle gyms and ladders.

• Make sharp turns around corners when running.
• Walk a few steps on balance beam.
• Catch a ball with arms straight in front of body.
• Kick a ball a few feet.

Fine Motor:
• Place ring on ring stack toy.
• Hold crayon with thumb and fingers.
• Imitate simple train made of three blocks.
• String one-inch beads.
• Snip with scissors.
• Build tower using eight cubes.
• Hold pencil with thumb and fingers.
• Place square pegs in pegboard.
• Imitate bridge made of three cubes.
• Copy circles.

Three-Year-Olds
Gross Motor:
• Walk upstairs using alternate feet without holding rail.
• Walk down few stairs alternating feet holding rail.
• Jump from 16-18 inches with one foot leading.
• Broad jump about 4-23 inches.
• Jump off ground or hurdles 2-8 inches.
• Jump from 18-24 inches with feet together at takeoff and landing.
• Gallop.
• Ride tricycles.
• Hop.
• Jump rope for two cycles.
• Throw balls underhanded 9 feet.
• Catch a ball with elbows bent.
• Kicks ball 4-12 feet.
• Balance on one foot 3-5 seconds.

Fine Motor:
• Make continuous cut across paper with scissors.
• Build tower using 10 blocks.
• String one-half inch beads.
• Show hand preference by picking up most items with the same
    hand.
• Cut on line using scissors.
• Copy a cross.
• Copy a square.
• Draw a person with head and one to three features.
[1]Skills are presented in the order that most children learn them.

An understanding of motor development will enable you to pick activities that enhance your child's current skills and foster the development of emerging skills. When looking at your child's motor development, remember to look at both gross and fine motor skills. Gross motor skills involve your child's large muscle movements. Walking, throwing a ball, and riding a tricycle are examples of gross motor skills. Between one and four years of age, gross motor skills fall into three areas: movement, using stairs, and play. Fine motor skills involve the small muscle movements of your child's hands and fingers in coordination with his eyes. Vision plays a critical role in most fine motor skills. Talk with your child's doctor or a pediatric ophthalmologist if you are concerned about your child's vision. Putting a block into a shape sorter, drawing a line on a piece of paper, and cutting with a pair of scissors are examples of fine motor skills. Between one and two years of age fine motor skills fall into four areas: putting in, building up, putting together, and writing. In addition to these areas the two- and three-year- old can engage in craft fine motor skills.

One-Year-Olds

Gross Motor
Movement.
At twelve months of age, most toddlers can creep on their hands and knees. At this age most children also can walk when you hold both their hands. About the same time a child learns to walk with one hand held, he learns to stand alone. At first he stands for only a split second before toppling over. Soon he can stand alone for

minutes at a time. After learning to stand alone, he learns to take a few steps by himself. By the time he is eighteen months old, he will probably walk forwards very well. He also will take a few steps sideways and backwards. As his walking skills improve, he will start to pull a toy on a string behind him while walking. Before you know it, he will carry large toys while walking and push and pull large toys or boxes around on the floor. By twenty-four months of age he runs well.

Using stairs.
Almost as soon as the toddler can creep or walk to a set of stairs, he tries to climb them. He starts by creeping or hitching up stairs. He then learns to creep down stairs. Some children learn to go down stairs by sliding on their bottoms at very fast speeds. Once he is skilled at creeping up and down stairs and as his walking skills improve, he tries to walk up stairs while you hold one of his hands. To go up the steps, he puts his right foot on the first step and then his left foot on the first step; next, he puts his right foot on the second step and then his left foot on the second step. After he

learns to walk up stairs holding one of your hands, he learns to go down stairs in a similar fashion. As he approaches two years of age, he will walk up stairs holding onto a rail instead of your hand. At this age most children continue to place both feet on each step as they walk up stairs.

Play.

One-year-olds like to climb on everything, but they need to learn what is and what is not acceptable to climb. Children at this age also enjoy playing with balls. The toddler can throw a ball under-hand when he is sitting before he can throw overhand in standing. When a child first learns to throw, his aim is generally not very good. You may be standing directly in front of him only two feet away, and the ball may end up three feet behind your toddler. With practice, the one-year-old can get the ball within three feet of his target. Soon after that, he can throw a ball into a box. In addition to throwing balls, the toddler enjoys trying to kick a ball. At first he tries to kick the ball by walking into it, sometimes tripping over the ball as he does so. Through practice, he learns to kick the ball forward. As he nears two years of age, he begins to move on "ride on" toys without pedals.

Fine Motor
Putting in, building up, and putting together.
Toddlers learn to take out before putting in, to knock down before building up, and to take apart before putting together. At twelve months of age, most children love to take pegs out of pegboards and objects out of containers. They like to knock down block towers as fast as you can build them. They also enjoy pulling a string of pop beads apart and taking rings off ring stack toys.

When learning to put in, the one-year-old will put one item in and take it out, put one in again and take it out. Once he is good at putting one peg in a pegboard or one block in a container, he learns to put many pegs and blocks in without removing them. The toddler usually learns to put a round shape into a shape sorter before he can put a square one in. While learning to use a shape sorter, he may try three or four times to fit the square shape into the round opening. When he doesn't succeed, he may take the lid off the bucket and simply toss the square in. If you try to encour-age a toddler to build a tower out of the blocks, he will first build only with two blocks. He then learns to build a three- and then a four-block tower. Around two years of age, he can build a teetering tower of six blocks. As he learns to build up with blocks, he contin-ues to enjoy knocking the blocks down. He may get upset if some-one else knocks down one of his towers because he wants to be the one to knock it down. By two years of age, many toddlers can put simple puzzles together by placing big non-interlocking pieces in the correct spot.

Writing.
Most one-year-olds can mark and scribble on paper with a crayon. Most children can imitate vertical strokes before circular scribbles. Imitating horizontal strokes generally comes next. *When using a crayon, the toddler needs close supervision.* He may occasionally try to put the crayon in his mouth, or he may decide that the wall or a chair cushion would make a good writing surface.

TWO-YEAR-OLDS

Gross Motor

Movement.
Between two and three years of age, young children become very skilled jumpers. They begin by jumping in place on both feet. Next they jump forwards, then backwards, and then sideways. In addition, they learn to jump two inches high, jump over a two-inch hurdle, broad jump, and jump down from eight inches high with one foot leading. Two-year-olds love to jump. Your heart may almost stop the first time you see your child in mid-air jumping off the living room sofa. *He needs to learn what he may and may not jump off.* The two-year-old's balance is improving. Between two and two and a half years of age, he learns to walk on tiptoes, stand on one foot for a second, and take two or three steps on a balance beam. As he approaches three, he may even try to hop on one foot. As his balance improves, so does his running. By three years of age, he runs very well and can make sharp turns around corners when running.

Using stairs.
The two-year-old no longer needs to hold onto your hand or a rail; he walks up the stairs by himself. He does, however, continue to place both feet on each step as he goes up the stairs. He is getting better at going down the stairs, but going down is a little scarier than going up; although he doesn't need to hold your hand, he still needs to hold onto the rail. Between two and a half and three years of age, he walks upstairs alternating his feet placing only one foot on each step. Since alternating feet is new to him, he usually holds onto the rail.

Play.
The two-year-old is an excellent climber. He goes up and down slides and climbs on jungle gyms. If he comes down a slide a little too fast and falls off the end or climbs too high on a jungle gym and can't figure out how to get down, he may become scared and

cry. He may need some extra support and encouragement to try these things again. Between two and three years of age, his ball skills continue to improve. He learns to throw a ball five to seven feet underhand, to catch a ball with straight arms in front of his body, and to kick a ball a few feet.

Fine Motor

Putting in, building up, and putting together.

In addition to putting circles and squares into a shape sorter, the two-year-old can put a triangle into it. He continues to develop more advanced block-building skills, and by two and a half years of age, he can imitate a simple train made out of blocks and build a tower using eight blocks. By three years of age, he can imitate a simple bridge made out of three blocks. As he did when he was a one-year-old, he continues to get upset when his block structures accidentally fall or are purposely knocked down. Between two and three years of age, he learns to put a number of different types of

toys together. He learns to place rings on a ring stacker, string a few one-inch beads, and put three-piece puzzles together.

Writing.

The two-year-old has a much better understanding of what he should and should not write on. He may, however, need an occasional reminder. With practice he learns to hold a crayon or pencil with his thumb and fingers, and by three years of age, he can copy a circle. He may or may not have shown a hand preference by this age.

Crafts.

As his fine motor skills become more refined, the two-year-old can do very simple craft activities. He enjoys projects that involve paint, scissors, and glue. At first he does best with finger paints, but soon he learns to paint with a brush. When he is first given a pair of scissors, he can barely hold them with both hands. By the time he is two and a half years old, he will hold a pair of scissors in one hand and snip a piece of paper. As he nears three, he will snip on a line using scissors. Most two-year-olds love squeezing glue out of the bottle. Many, however, can't judge when to stop. As a result, the two-year-old often needs you to tell him when he has enough glue. Between two and three years of age, *all craft activities require constant adult supervision.*

THREE-YEAR-OLDS

Gross Motor

Movement.
The three-year-old progresses from being a skilled jumper to an expert jumper. Between three and four years of age, he learns to jump eight inches off the ground and to jump over an eight-inch hurdle. He goes from broad jumping four inches at three years to broad jumping almost two feet at four years. At three, he can jump from a sturdy object 16-18 inches high with one foot leading, and at three and a half, he can jump from a height of two feet with both feet together on takeoff and landing. At three and a half, he can also jump rope for two cycles, hop on one foot, stand on one foot for two to five seconds, and gallop.

Using steps.
Between three and three and a half, he learns to walk up stairs using alternating feet without holding onto a rail. During this time he also learns to walk down stairs, placing both feet on the same step, without holding onto a rail. At around four years of age, he will begin to walk down stairs using alternating feet while holding onto the rail.

Play.
The three-year-old likes playing ball. He kicks and throws a ball well. At three he can kick a ball four feet and by four years of age he can kick a ball twelve feet. The three-year-old can throw a ball underhand nine feet, and he is beginning to learn to throw overhand. Catching a ball is harder for the preschooler. The ball never comes at exactly the same speed, direction, or height. Catching involves eye/hand coordination and the ability to react and move quickly. Coordinated catching skills generally don't develop until close to ten years of age and requires a lot of practice to master. At three, a child can catch a large (8 inch) ball with both his arms extended straight in front of his body. He then learns to catch a large ball with his elbows bent. In addition to playing ball, the preschooler enjoys climbing on jungle gym bars

and will drop several inches to the ground. He also likes riding a tricycle and can pedal about ten feet before needing to take a break.

Fine Motor

Putting in, building up, and putting together.
The fine motor skills in this area become increasingly sophisticated between three and four years of age. During this time the preschooler learns to do more complex shape sorters—ones with stars, rectangles, and octagons. He also learns to build a ten-block tower, assemble 7 to 15 piece puzzles, and string one-half inch beads. He enjoys playing with many different types of construction toys such as Legos. The three-year-old likes these quiet activities and enjoys doing them over and over. He may spend 15 or more minutes playing independently with one activity. By three and one half years of age, many children demonstrate hand preference by picking up most items with the same hand.

Writing.
Between three and four years of age, the preschooler develops the writing skills necessary to copy a cross and then a square. He may also attempt to copy a few letters, especially those in his name. By the time that he is four years old, he can draw a person with a head and one to three features. When a preschooler draws a person, he often draws the head larger than the rest of the body, and he may draw the arms and legs extending from the head rather than from a torso.

Crafts.
The three-year-old takes pride in the fact that he is more skilled with crayons and paint. He may say, "I draw good now. I don't scribble-scrabble anymore," as he draws with a crayon. His scissor skills are also improving. At three years of age, he can make a continuous cut across a piece of paper. At around three and a half, he can cut a straight line, staying within a half inch of the guideline. By the time he is four years old, he is pretty good with glue, except he may squeeze too much from the bottle.

ARRANGE THE ENVIRONMENT

Gross Motor
Arrange outdoor and indoor play spaces for gross motor activities. Places for outdoor gross motor play include a backyard, the park, or a playground. The exact location isn't important as long as your child gets experiences with jungle gyms to climb; toys to ride on; slides to go up and down; balls to throw, kick, and catch; and objects to push, pull, jump off, and over.

TALK TO YOUR DOCTOR IF YOUR CHILD IS UNABLE TO[2]

By the Age of eighteen Months...
- Walk.
- Crawl up steps.
- Throw a ball.
- Put nine small blocks in a cup.
- Scribble with a crayon.

By the Age of Two...
- Crawl down steps.
- Run.
- Walk up steps, placing one foot on each step.
- Kick a ball forward.
- Build a tower of four small blocks.
- Place a circle and a square into a shape sorter or puzzle.

By the Age of Three...
- Walk up steps alternating feet.
- Jump up.
- Pedal a tricycle a few feet.
- Build a tower of six small blocks.
- Imitate a vertical and horizontal stroke with a crayon.

By the Age of Four...
- Broad jump over a piece of paper 8 1/2 inches long.
- Balance on one foot for two seconds.
- Build a tower of eight small blocks.
- Copy a circle.

[2]Most children are able to do these items by the age listed. If your child is unable to do them, it may or may not mean there is a problem with his development. It only means that you should mention it to your doctor or consult with a physical or occupational therapist so that you can determine whether your child's development needs to be assessed. You may contact physical or occupational therapists privately or through your local Child Find program. Under Public Law 99-457 (IDEA), Child Find provides free screening and assessment to identify children who may have special needs. You can find the phone number for your local Child Find program by contacting your county Department of Education, Department of Health and Human Services, or Department of Public Welfare. You can also get the phone number for the Child Find program in your area by calling the U.S. Department of Education in Washington, D.C.

Indoors, your child should have several safe toys for gross motor play. Provide him with large boxes to push, pull, crawl through, and sit in. Place a six-foot piece of wood (four to six inches wide and two to four inches thick) on the floor for your child to use as a balance beam. Have him walk around or on the balance beam, and have him jump off or over it. Allow him to use a ride-on toy in the house. Give your child a large pillow to jump on. Give him small, safe objects to practice throwing and catching.

Routinely check all indoor and outdoor equipment and toys to make sure they are in safe condition. *Check for potential dangers, such*

as rough splinters, sharp edges, loose nuts or bolts, and protruding nails. Make sure the ground or floor under jungle gyms, slides, swings and other equipment is soft. Wood chips, sand, and grass are much safer to land on when playing outdoors than cement or gravel. A thick mat or carpeting is safer for indoor play than hardwood floors, linoleum, or tile.

Fine Motor

Arrange outdoor and indoor play spaces for fine motor play. Indoors, provide your child with a small table and chair to play at. On nice days, bring a few fine-motor toys outdoors. Your child can play with these toys at a picnic table or while sitting on a blanket in the grass. Offer your child a variety of fine-motor toys. Encourage putting in by offering him small blocks and a box, junk mail and an oatmeal container, and plastic measuring cups and a nonbreakable mixing bowl. To promote building up, provide small and large lightweight blocks to play with. You can foster putting together by giving him pop beads, shape sorters, ring stackers, and puzzles. To introduce writing, supply him with pencils, crayons, markers, and paper. You also can allow him to write with chalk on a chalkboard or outdoors on a sidewalk. Inspire craft projects by allowing him to use paints, scissors, and glue *with your supervision.*

As your child gets older and his toys have more pieces, the toy box is no longer the best place to store all his toys. Store fine motor toys with many pieces in their own box, dishpan, or basket. To

help your child identify what is in each container, put a picture of the toy on the outside of the container. Place these containers on sturdy shelves. Put safe toys on low shelves and objects that require adult supervision on high shelves. Routinely check containers for broken or lost pieces. *Broken pieces can be dangerous* and lost pieces can frustrate your child because they will prohibit him from successfully completing the activity.

PROVIDE A VARIETY OF EXPERIENCES

Gross Motor

Movement.
Give your child the time and space he needs to crawl, walk, run, and jump. Make movement fun for him by playing little games. When going from one room to another, have your child walk backwards, sideways, or on tiptoes. At another time, have him move like an animal to get to the next room. For instance, your child can hop like a rabbit, crawl slow like a turtle, or flap his arms like a bird. On a nice day, go outside and blow bubbles. Encourage your child to bend, stretch, reach, and jump to pop the bubbles. Another fun outdoor activity is to play follow-the-leader through an obstacle course. Have your child crawl through a tunnel, step over a rock,

go down the slide, run around a tree, and jump in a small pile of leaves. On a rainy day, you can make an indoor obstacle course. Have him crawl under a kitchen chair, step over a book, scoot across the floor on his bottom, run down a hallway, and jump on a big floor pillow. Another good rainy day activity is to have a circus. Your tightrope walker can walk across a long piece of masking tape that you lay on the floor or across a long piece of board (four to six inches wide and two inches thick) that you lay on the floor. Your animal trainer can dance around the room holding onto stuffed animals while listening to music. Your acrobat can tumble and roll across a soft rug or mat. You can join the action
or play the role of ringmaster and announce your child's performance to your imaginary audience. Add music to make the circus more fun. Children's music is available on tapes and records from

your library. Most children love moving to music.

Play.

Encourage your child to play on swings, slides, and jungle gyms. Take him to the park or playground to play on these pieces of equipment. *Slides and jungle gyms should be low, and you should "spot" your child in case he falls.* If your child is afraid of climbing or sliding, don't push or frighten him. Some children need much "warm-up" time at the playground. Foster his self-confidence by making these early experiences positive and fun. Allow him to watch other children climbing and sliding— children learn a lot of motor skills by watching others and imitating them. Describe what they are doing to focus your child's attention on the more important aspects. Say, for instance, "The little girl is holding onto the side of the ladder, and she is going up the steps. She's going up the ladder like you go up the steps at home..." If there are no other children to watch, demonstrate the activity for him so he can see how it is done. After your child spends some time watching, offer to do the activity with him. You can, for example, go down the slide together with your child sitting on your lap. Swings should also be low and should have safety buckles. *Remind your child always to hold onto the swing. Teach your child important playground safety rules,* such as "Sit on the swing, don't stand" and "Use the ladder, don't climb the slide." *Some children require very close supervision at a playground* because they see no danger and may go beyond their capabilities. Encourage your child to use protective equipment, such as helmets and knee pads as needed.

In addition to playing at the playground, spend some time playing ball. If your child is a beginner, try playing catch with a partially inflated beach ball or sponge ball. Both are easy to grab onto. If your child is more advanced, put an old box or laundry basket in the middle of a room and give your child a few small objects to practice throwing into the box. Good objects include lightweight balls, small sponge balls, bean bags, a pair of socks folded into a ball, marshmallows, and cotton balls. You can add variety to the game by putting the box or basket on a chair or by having your child throw from different distances.

Finally, engage in family exercise. This is much better than signing your young child up for a competitive and structured sports program. At this age, your child needs to practice his gross motor skills in a noncompetitive environment. There is plenty of time for organized and competitive sports later. Family exercise allows your child to practice gross motor skills in a noncompetitive environment and enables you to serve as a role model. It also can help promote healthy exercise behaviors for a lifetime. Your exercise program could include five to ten minutes of warm-up exercises and a short walk. Simple exercises work best with young children. Try stretching high and low, twisting back and forth, swinging your arms in circles, and "riding" a bicycle with your legs while lying down. Be sure to give your child water to drink after exercising, especially on hot days. Also remember to offer him plenty of water to drink when he is playing outside during hot weather.

Fine Motor

Putting in.
Give your child a variety of experiences putting smaller objects into larger containers. Everyday fun examples include putting mail into a mailbox, clothespins into a small opening in the lid of a coffee can, and coins into a jar or bank. *Always supervise your child carefully when he is using small objects*, such as coins, to make sure that he doesn't put them in his mouth- -otherwise he may choke on them. Once your child is skilled at putting objects in, move onto pegboards and shape sorters.

Building.
Provide your child with small and large blocks to build a tall tower or to make a long road. To make knocking down tall towers even more fun, have your child toss a bean bag at a tower made of small blocks or let him use his whole body to walk into and knock down a tower made of large blocks. Empty shoe boxes taped together with masking tape make excellent large blocks. To make them more attractive, you can cover the boxes with contact paper or let your child paint them. Unlike the more

sturdy and reinforced commercially available giant blocks, shoe boxes will not support your child's weight. Be sure to tell him not to stand on these boxes.

Putting together.
Offer your child popbeads, a ring stacker, and puzzles so he can practice putting things together. First puzzles should have large non-interconnecting pieces. Puzzle pieces with knobs attached make handling pieces even easier for the toddler. You can make your own simple puzzles by cutting a square, a circle, and a triangle out of a piece of thick cardboard. If you want to, you can add a knob by gluing a small, empty spool of thread to each puzzle piece. When teaching your child how to put puzzles together, have him run his finger around the shape of the piece and inside the opening in the puzzle. Talk about the shape and how it feels, say for example, "The circle is round and smooth. It doesn't have any points." When your child is ready for interlocking puzzles, cut the front of his favorite cereal box into a three-, five- or seven-piece puzzle. When teaching your child to put interlocking puzzles together, help him look for context clues in addition to shape clues. For instance, point out there is half a bowl of cereal in the piece, and ask him to find the puzzle piece with the other half of the bowl. You also can make puzzles out of magazine pictures. To make the puzzle more durable, glue the picture to a piece of cardboard and cover with clear contact paper.

Writing.
As a precursor to writing, provide your child with opportunities to draw with crayons and chalk. Draw with him, and show him how to make horizontal and vertical lines. To make this activity a little more fun say, "Vroooom!" and "Zzzzip!" as you draw. To develop the fine motor control required for writing, provide your preschooler with path activities. To make a path, draw two, four-inch lines about an inch apart. At the front draw a stick person and at the end draw a ball. Tell your child to help the boy get to the ball by drawing a line from the boy to the ball. As your child gets better at this, you can make a curvy path or one that zigzags.

When your preschooler is interested in learning to write letters, describe the shape of the letters in a fun manner, say for example, "To make the letter N, your pencil has to go up the mountain and down the mountain, then up the mountain again." In the beginning, draw a dotted version of the letter for him to trace. Once he is skilled at tracing letters, write letters and let him try to copy them.

Crafts.
Provide your child with opportunities to use paints. You may want to use paints that are washable because children can be rather messy while painting. You may also want to have your child wear a smock or an old shirt of yours as a cover-up when painting.

Let him paint with his fingers, a sponge, or a brush. Talk about the colors he uses and ask him to describe his creations. What may look like a house to you may really be a big dinosaur, and his feelings may be hurt if you misinterpret his work. For a fun outdoor painting activity, give your child a small pan of water and a big brush to "paint" the sidewalk or house. If your child  is too young for crayons and paints because he puts these items in his mouth, let him experiment by using pudding or yogurt as paint and his highchair tray as the paper.

When your two- or three-year-old is ready, *give him supervised experiences with child safety scissors.* At first you will need to show your child how to hold a pair of scissors. Have him place his thumb and middle fingers in the handle holes, with his index finger on the handle next to the hole. Tell him to squeeze the scissors shut to cut the paper. At first you will need to hold the paper for your child while he snips. In the beginning, cutting and holding the paper will be too difficult for him. Once he is successful at making cuts, have him try to hold the paper while he cuts. A placemat is a nice little project for him to make with his new skill. To make a placemat, have your child snip the edges of a rectangular piece of paper. To teach your child to make continual cuts across a piece of paper, give him strips of colored paper to cut across. Once he can make continual cuts, draw straight lines on the paper for him to follow.

Instead of throwing away the pieces of cut paper, let your child glue them onto a piece of construction paper or a paper plate. When your child first uses glue, hold the bottle with him to teach him how much glue to squeeze out. If your child has a difficulty controlling the flow of glue or if he has trouble getting the glue on the paper, pour a small amount of glue on a paper plate and allow your child to brush the glue on with an old paint brush. Young children love gluing almost anything. On a nice day, take your child for a nature hike to collect leaves, twigs, and stones to glue onto a piece of paper.

A PARENT'S STORY

My son, Charlie, was born prematurely. When I was six and a half months pregnant, I woke up in the middle of the night with sharp abdominal pains. At first I wasn't sure what was going on. Twenty minutes later I knew something was wrong. I was terrified as my husband raced me to the hospital—the abdominal pains were almost unbearable, and I was bleeding vaginally. When we got to the hospital, the doctor did a quick examination and told me I had placenta abruptio. He said the placenta was separating from the uterine wall. He told me, as I was being rolled to the surgical suite, he was going to have to perform an emergency Cesarean section. He explained that because of the placenta abruptio, my baby was in danger of not getting enough oxygen. Within 30 minutes of my getting to the hospital, Charlie was born. He weighed only three pounds and five ounces. After spending two months in the Neonatal Intensive Care Unit (NICU) at our hospital, Charlie finally came home.

At our first visit to the NICU follow-up clinic, the doctors explained that Charlie was at risk for developing developmental delays. My husband and I were told that we would need to monitor Charlie's development closely. We were told that we needed to bring Charlie to the NICU follow-up clinic every three months. They explained that specialists would evaluate his cognitive, motor, and language development at each visit.

At our nine-month follow-up appointment, the doctors told us Charlie had hypotonia in his lower extremities. They said this meant the muscles in Charlie's legs were floppier than they would like them to be. The physical therapist gave us exercises to do with Charlie at home and recommended that we stop using the walker. She told us that a walker would not help Charlie learn to walk. She explained that what he really needed was time playing on the floor.

At our twelve-month appointment, Charlie was not yet crawling, and the specialists at the follow-up clinic recommended that Charlie get physical therapy twice a week from a program called Infants and Toddlers. They explained that the physical therapist would come to our home twice a week and that there would be no out-of-pocket cost to us.

Two weeks later Jan, Charlie's physical therapist, came to our house for the first time. Each time Jan came, she worked with Charlie for an hour. During this hour she did various exercises and played little games with Charlie. She showed me how to do these things with Charlie, so I could do them between her visits. Charlie finally started to crawl when he was fourteen months old. Jan said this was very good. Charlie began pulling to stand when he was nineteen months old, and he took his first steps when he was twenty-three months old. We were all very excited, and we will never forget the moment Charlie took his first two steps to go from me to my husband during one of our therapy sessions with Jan. Although Charlie was walking, the quality of his movements were poor so the therapy sessions continued and the visits to the NICU follow-up clinic continued as well.

Charlie is now three and one half years old. Jan no longer comes to our home on a weekly basis—she simply monitors him by evaluating his progress every six months. Charlie is now walking and running well. He loves to climb on jungle gyms and go down slides. His absolute favorite thing is to jump in a mud puddle on a rainy day. When he jumps in one of those mud puddles, I don't ask him to stop, I watch him and thank God that he can jump.

SUMMARY

There are two types of motor skills—gross and fine motor. Gross motor skills involve large muscle movements and fine motor skills involve the small muscle movements of your child's hands and fingers. You can foster your child's motor development in three ways. First, understand the progression of motor development so you can pick activities that encourage rather than frustrate your child. Second, arrange your child's environment to enhance motor skills. This involves arranging safe and stimulating outdoor and indoor play spaces for motor activities. Examples include providing a place outdoors for your child to run and climb, and offering your child a place indoors to draw and paint. The third way to foster your child's motor development is to provide your child with a variety of motor experiences. Appropriate activities range from playing follow the leader through an obstacle course, to having your child make a placemat by snipping the edges of a rectangular piece of paper with a pair of scissors.

REFERENCES AND RECOMMENDED READINGS

Cryer, D., Harms, T., & Bourland, B. (1988). *Active Learning for Threes.* Menlo Park, CA: Addison-Wesley Publishing Co.

Furuno, S., O'Reilly, K., Hosaka, C., Inatsuka, T., Zeisloft- Falbey, B. & Allman, T. (1988). *HELP Checklist.* Palo Alto, CA: VORT Corporation.

Folio, M. & Fewell, R. (1982). *The Peabody Motor Development Scale.* Allen, TX: DLM.

Frankenburg, W. & Dodds, J. (1990). *Denver II.* Denver, CO:Denver Developmental Materials, Inc.

Johnson-Martin, N., Attermeier, S. & Hacker, B. (1990). *The Carolina Curriculum for Preschoolers with Special Needs.* Baltimore, MD: Paul H. Brookes Publishing Company.

Parks, S. (1988). *HELP...at Home.* Palo Alto, CA: VORT Corporation.

Rothenberg, B., Hitchcock, S., Harrison, M., & Graham, M. (1983). *Parentmaking.* Menlo Park. CA: The Banster Press.

Chapter 4
Emotional Development

When a toddler moves freely about the house on his own two legs, his parents know for sure that he has conquered the developmental milestone of walking. When a young child says, "I do it; you don't do it for me," there is no doubt in his parents' mind that he has mastered pronouns. But emotional development in a child is not as obvious as the development of motor or language skills. When a child clings to Mommy or throws a tantrum for Daddy, parents easily forget that these are signs of emotional development. As a parent, you can facilitate your child's emotional development in five ways:
- Understanding the emotional development of your child
- Supporting your child through separation anxiety
- Handling tantrums consistently
- Helping your child gain control over his fears
- Fostering the development of a positive self-esteem

Parent Perspective
Leaving your child with another caregiver may cause you to feel anxious, especially the first few times. However, you probably feel more distressed during the actual separation than your child does—Maybe you even call a few times to see how things are going.

Your child's temper tantrums may irritate or even anger you, especially at the end of this or a similar scenario: You gave him apple juice because he asked for it, and now he wants milk.

If the sound of the vacuum cleaner running frightens your child, you may try to help him deal with his fear by showing him that the sound of the vacuum cleaner can't hurt him. You feel frustrated that you can't finish vacuuming because your son cries every time you turn the vacuum cleaner on. But once you decide to vacuum anyway and let him cry for five minutes, you feel guilty.

Parents want their child to feel good about himself. They want to do everything they can to foster the development of a positive self-esteem.

Child Perspective

Your child cries when you move out of his sight because he is afraid you won't come back. Usually he stops crying soon after you leave and plays happily while you are gone. When you return, he may cry again because your returning reminds him that you left and he is afraid you will leave again.

Your child probably becomes frustrated and upset easily. Since he doesn't know how to express these feelings with words, he expresses them by screaming, hitting, kicking, or throwing. Since your child is unaware of the major problems of the world, he may feel truly devastated that you cut his sandwich in two pieces, even though he himself asked you to do it just a minute ago.

Your child has not had much experience with big animals or loud noises. He does not realize that the neighbor's bull dog is on a leash and can't get him or that the loud thunder can't hurt him. Things like these really frighten your child and hearing you say, "He won't hurt you," or "Of course, you're not afraid!" doesn't help him.

Your child is likely to see himself as you see him. If he hears you say, "You're a bad boy," he feels bad about himself and may even walk around saying, "I bad boy."

UNDERSTANDING EMOTIONAL DEVELOPMENT

As a parent, it is very important and helpful to fully understand the order in which young children develop emotionally. This knowledge will help you understand why your child behaves the way he does. If you are not familiar with the progression of emotional milestones, you may feel confused and frustrated that your child clings to your leg when you try to leave him with another person. On the other hand, if you are familiar with the emotional development of young children, you will recognize this "clinging" as separation anxiety and will handle this phase of your child's development appropriately.

One-Year-Olds

Most one-year-olds continue to experience anxiety when they are separated from a parent. Separation anxiety usually emerges around nine months of age and generally peaks between twelve and twenty-four months. Separation anxiety is usually expressed in two ways. The first is when a parent leaves a child with another person.

A one-year-old cries when Mommy leaves because he fears that Mommy will be gone forever. He may burst into tears when Mommy returns. He cries because her return reminds him of how he felt when she left, and now that she's back, he fears she will leave again. After a while, a toddler learns that Mommy always returns. Separation anxiety is also expressed when Mom is home but is not right beside her child. Even though Mommy may be in the same room, young  toddlers may become anxious and cry because she isn't close enough to them. This may occur even though the child was the one who crawled or walked to a different part of the room. As their motor skills improve, young toddlers have the option of physically moving away from their parents. The prospect of being on their own scares them, even though internally they are driven to explore. As a result, a one-year-old frequently needs to touch base with his parents. In the beginning, a young child cries to get Mom or Dad to come to him to reassure him. Later he learns to touch base by going to Dad for a hug or by getting Mom's attention to see her wave at him.

Between one and two years of age, children begin to develop and exert independence. At this age, most children like to make decisions for themselves; they are eager to make their own choices and often express very strong opinions about what they like and do not like. However, most one-year-olds grow frustrated when they are presented with too many choices. The younger one-year-old (twelve to eighteen months) may say "no" when he means "yes" simply because he learns to say no before yes. Later, the older one-year-old (eighteen to twenty-four months) may say "no," when he means "yes," out of habit or because it's his only way of exerting independence. The one-year-old also begins to direct his own behavior by saying no to himself in dangerous situations. For instance, he may say "no-no" as he starts to touch an electrical outlet. The one-year-old also uses no to stop others from doing something and to resist you. He does this in an attempt to gain some control and to exert independence. The one-year-old wants to do things for himself, but he becomes frustrated easily when he can't.

Temper tantrums frequently result when a one-year-old gets

frustrated. He becomes frustrated when he doesn't get his way. The one-year-old can be demanding, and he wants things right away. He has no concept of "later," and he is often concerned only about himself. Therefore, he has great difficulty understanding that he needs to wait until afternoon to go outside to play because Mommy must do some work in the morning. A one-year-old also loses patience when he can't make something work the way he thinks it should work. Young children are more likely to become frustrated when they are hungry or tired. As a result, the one-year-old is more likely to throw a temper tantrum when he misses a snack, doesn't take a nap, or goes to bed late. Temper tantrums may consist of screaming, kicking, punching, and crying. Although these tantrums may be frightening to see and difficult to cope with, they **are** normal.

The one-year-old enjoys being the center of attention and is very affectionate. He is developing his own self-esteem, and he is learning to identify and express emotions such as jealousy, fear, anger, sympathy, joy, and empathy. For example, a one-year-old can empathize with another child who falls and cries by summoning his mommy to help the child.

Rituals become important at this age. A toddler likes rituals and needs them, because he is changing and growing rapidly. The rituals keep certain aspects of a child's life reliable and routine. A one-year-old who normally brushes his teeth before his bath may flop on the floor or run away if you try to put him into the tub first. Another one-year-old may want to eat the same lunch every day or wear the same pajamas every night.

Two-Year-Olds

Separation anxiety usually decreases between two and three years of age. At this stage, children generally separate easily from their

parents when they are left with a familiar person. However, two-year-olds still tend to be shy with strangers. Even though the two-year-old is more willing to separate from his parents, sometimes he has difficulty with it. One day he doesn't want to hold his mom's hand while they go for a walk, and he may even run ahead. But the next day he clings to Mom and insists she carry him. Carrying a 26- to 32-pound toddler is hard for some parents to do. When Mommy tells him he has to walk and refuses to carry him, the two-year-old may sadly burst into tears or may angrily throw a temper tantrum. On the other hand, the two-year-old is likely to cooperate if Mom gives him a hug, explains that he is getting too heavy to carry, and promises to hold him while they sit in the rocking chair after they get home. Mom can further ease the situation by offering him the choice of holding either her left or her right hand while they walk. When they are provided with such an option, many two-year-olds make a choice gladly, with a feeling they have some control over the situation.

Most two-year-olds go through a period when they relate better to one parent at a time. During this phase, they want only Mommy or only Daddy to help them. This may be difficult for parents. If the child wants Mommy only, Mommy grows exhausted from trying to meet all her child's needs while Daddy feels left out and unloved. At the same time, a two- year-old is often very possessive of his mommy, daddy, and siblings. For example, a two-year-old may tell another child, "You can't talk to him; he is my daddy."

The two-year-old wants to be independent, but he is still somewhat dependent. He tries to do a lot for himself, but he still needs help. Often, he resists help just so he can try something until he finally gets it or gives up and asks for help. The two-year-old experiences extreme emotional shifts while he tries to do things for himself. He is very proud of his accomplishments, and he resists help so he can try to do it himself. For instance, after putting on his coat by himself, he claps excitedly and says proudly, "Hip hip hooray for me! I did it!" A minute later, he collapses onto the floor, sobbing because he can't zip it. But as his dad starts to help him, he kicks his feet and screams, "I wanna do it! Let me do it! You don't help me!" Two minutes later, he goes to his dad and says, "Help me. I need help with this zipper."

Most two-year-olds have difficulty with transitions, such as getting dressed, ending play, and going to bed. A two-year-old may be dictatorial and demanding, sometimes talking with a loud, rough voice. He may be physically aggressive; pushing, hitting, and kicking to get his way. Frustration tantrums peak between two and three years of age, and many two-year-olds develop fears. The most common fears of young children are large animals, loud noises, and the dark. The two-year-old doesn't really know why he is afraid. All he knows is that he wants to avoid these things. He strives to control his fears, sometimes acting them out as he plays. As he approaches three years of age, he may be afraid of getting lost, of sleeping alone, and of monsters.

Three-Year-Olds

The three-year-old continues to separate easily from his parents. As long as he is familiar with the person and the place, he may not even remember to wave or kiss his parents good-bye unless someone  reminds him. The three-year-old continues to feel proud of his achievements; he enjoys praise, and at this stage, he calls attention to unnoticed accomplishments. For example, as he stands in front of a mirror, smiling at himself, he says, "See, I combed my hair. I look good now. I like my hair. Do you like my hair?". The three-year-old praises himself and makes positive statements about himself. It is common for parents to hear comments such as, "I'm good at puzzles. The other day I did the bunny all by myself! When I was a little baby, I couldn't do that."

The three-year-old can identify when he or another person feels happy, sad, angry, tired, or hungry. When talking about his own feelings, he may explain why he feels that way and say what ought to be done. For instance, he may say, "That makes me soooo happy! I like it when I drink my apple juice in the living room. We should do this all the time!" or, "That makes me sad. You shouldn't go out of the room when I talk to you. That is not polite. Next time you wait till I stop talking before you leave. Can you listen to me this time?" When the three-year-old sees a hurt, sad, or angry child, he will try to comfort the child in addition to labeling how the child feels. For example, to a child who spills a drink, he says, "Don't cry. It is okay you spilled milk 'cause it was an accident. Your daddy can get you more milk when he cleans up this mess. Don't be sad; you can have more milk."

Between three and four years of age, children try to please their parents. If it will make Mommy or Daddy happy, they will do it, and if it makes Mommy or Daddy unhappy, they will try hard not to do it. During this period, young children try to conform to rules and requests, and the negativism when he was two-years old is gone. Instead of saying "no" and running away every time his mother tries to dress him, he cooperates. Ritualism also decreases, and the three-year-old can handle changes in routine.

SEQUENCE OF EMOTIONAL DEVELOPMENT[1]

One-Year-Olds
- Develop independence.
- Are eager to make choices.
- Have strong opinions about likes and dislikes.
- Say no a lot.
- Begin to direct their own behavior.
- Want to do things for themselves.
- Have frequent temper tantrums.
- Enjoy being the center of attention.
- Hug and kiss parents.
- Learn to identify and express moods.
- Want to control others.
- May be more demanding.
- Become frustrated easily.
- Like and need rituals.
- Develop feelings of self-worth.
- Try to comfort others who are upset.
- Exhibit separation anxiety.

Two-Year-Olds
- Are shy with strangers.
- Feel very possessive of their mom, dad, and siblings.
- Cling and like to be carried.
- May be physically aggressive.
- Have frustration tantrums.
- Relate best to one parent at a time.
- Develop fears.
- Separate easily from parents in familiar surroundings.
- Have extreme emotional shifts.
- Can be dictatorial and demanding.
- Talk with a loud, rough voice.
- Have difficulty with transitions.
- Are proud of what they can do.
- Resist help so they can do it themselves.

Three-Year-Olds
- Continue to separate easily from parents.
- Are proud of their achievements.
- Try to please and conform.
- Enjoy praise.
- Make positive statements about themselves.
- Call attention to what they do.
- Can identify their own feelings.
- Express when another child is hurt, sad, or angry.
- Comfort peers who are upset.
- Exhibit less ritualism.

[1]Skills are presented in the order that most children learn them.

SUPPORTING YOUR CHILD THROUGH SEPARATION ANXIETY

It is very important for your child to feel that his needs for food, drink, warmth, and love will always be met. During the first year of his life, your child learns that you are the one who meets his needs. He then develops a sense of trust in you to meet these needs. The one-year-old thinks that you must be present in order to meet these needs. When you leave, he fears that you will not come back and that his needs will not be met. With time, the two-year-old learns that you always return and that when you go away, you leave him with someone who can meet his needs while you are absent. The three-year-old is so confident of this fact that he experiences little or no distress during normal separations.

You need to provide your child with separate experiences so that he learns to trust other adults and that he begins to establish bonds with other people. Separate experiences expose your child to

new environments and learning situations. These experiences also give you time to work, run errands, or simply relax. Before leaving your child with a new person, try to make arrangements for the three of you to play together for a brief period of time. Use the time to familiarize your child with his new caregiver. By playing together, you can show your child that you like this new person and that it is safe and fun to be with her. Next, leave your child with the caregiver for a short period of time. If possible, before you leave your child with the new caregiver for an entire day, arrange for your child to stay with her for an hour or two while you run a few errands. That way, when you leave, you can tell your child you will be back soon. Returning in an hour or two is coming back soon, and this will build your credibility. The next time you leave and promise to be back after nap time that day, your child will believe you. Whenever you leave your child with a caregiver, leave him with a loving person who will give him the calm and confident care he needs, both as you leave, and right after you leave.

When you leave your child with another person **always say good-bye.** As tempted as you may be, don't sneak off thinking that will make the separation easier. Although your child will probably cry when you say good-bye, he will stop crying soon after you leave. If you don't say good-bye, you risk the chance of making your child always anxious and on guard, a child who is constantly afraid you will leave. When you tell your child good-bye, let him know where you are going and when you expect to return. If you tell him you are going to work, he can picture you at work. This image will be more realistic if he has seen where you work or if you have discussed your work place with him. Although he can't tell time, knowing when you will return gives him an idea of when he should expect you back. If you tell him you will be back from the grocery store after lunch, he won't look for you until after lunch.

Be cheerful and confident when you tell your child good-bye, and **try not to linger**. It is the **act** of separating from you that is hard for your child, not the actual separation after you are gone. Most children stop crying shortly after Mom or Dad leaves. To ease the separation, some parents arrange their schedules carefully to make sure they can spend 15 minutes playing with their child before they leave. Most of these parents discover their child isn't able to relax and enjoy this transition time. Instead they find their child stays very close to them and anxiously asks questions such as, "Are you going now?" or making pleas like, "Don't go yet." In spite of such efforts, the child still cries when the parent leaves. In essence, these parents are only prolonging the sadness their child experiences by drawing out the act of separating. It is better to say good-bye and leave promptly after getting your child situated with his caregiver.

Many children have "cuddlies." A cuddly is an object such as a blanket or stuffed animal that a child sucks on or holds to feel safe and secure. If your child has a favorite blanket or a special "friend", make sure that he has his cuddly when you leave him with his caregiver. If your child doesn't have a cuddly, offer him a familiar object from home to cuddle.

TABLE 1
SUPPORTING YOUR CHILD THROUGH SEPARATION ANXIETY

- Give your child a sense of trust that his needs for food, drink, warmth, and love are always met.
- Provide your child with experiences away from you.
- Always say good-bye before you leave.
- Tell your child when and where you are going.
- Be cheerful and confident when telling your child good-bye.
- Make the act of separating from your child as brief as possible.
- Provide your child with a cuddly.

HANDLING TANTRUMS

The are numerous reasons children between the ages of one and four have tantrums. For example, a young child has a tantrum if he can't get something he wants, doesn't want to do something that you want him to do, or can't get something to work the way he thinks it should work. For instance, your child may scream and begin to cry after you say "no" to his request for a candy bar. If you give him the candy bar after he throws the tantrum, he is more likely to throw another tantrum in the future because he is learning that tantrums get him what he wants. As long as the tantrum is not harmful or destructive, it is best to ignore it. Remember that if you gave in to tantrums in the past and you are now trying to ignore them, the tantrums may get worse before they get better.

To understand why ignored tantrums usually get worse before they get better, think of the following situation: You are watching TV with your spouse, and you ask a question. If your spouse doesn't answer, you are likely to ask the question again, this time in a little louder voice. If your spouse doesn't respond again, you will probably repeat your question a third time, slightly louder and not as politely. After the fourth try, you may finally give up and walk away. The point is that you didn't stop asking the question after your first try. Most children will not stop their tantrums immediately either. When we expect a reaction from our behavior, we persist with the behavior before giving up.

There may be times when you do not want to allow a tantrum to continue where it is occurring. If you are in a store, you may want to take your child to the car until his tantrum is over. Give him a verbal warning, and if the tantrum doesn't stop, take him to the car. Put him in his car seat and ignore the tantrum. *Even though you are ignoring your child, you must stay with him. Never leave him in the car to continue shopping.* While it may be inconvenient to interrupt your shopping, after one or two trips back to the car, most children learn that tantrums don't get them what they want, and their tantrums stop. If you are at home and have company, or if you are a guest in someone else's home, you should change the location of his temper tantrum. For example, if others are around and your child has a loud tantrum in the middle of the living room, give him a warning, and then take him to another room or hallway. Place your child in a *safe spot* and ignore the tantrum. A safe spot is a place where there are no objects on which your child could hurt himself or that he could break. Corners of rooms usually make excellent safe spots.

As mentioned previously, there are two types of tantrums you should not ignore, those that involve your child hurting another person, or your child destroying property. If your child kicks another child or tears pages in a book during a tantrum, give him a time-out. Time-out involves placing your child in a safe and nonstimulat-ing place, such as a corner, for a speci-fied amount of time. The general rule is one minute of time-out for each year of your child's age. So if your child is two-years-old, his time-out is for two minutes. In addition to the passage of time, your child must exhibit appropri-ate behavior to stop or leave a time-out. Your child may leave a time-out when two requirements are met: the passage of a specific amount of time and the presence of appropriate behav-ior. Don't allow your child to leave a time-out when he is screaming or kick-ing, because he may think that the  screaming or kicking behavior was the reason you let him leave. The time-out technique is an effective means of controlling tantrums and other inappropriate behaviors. Chapter 8 "Guiding Your Child's Behavior" describes the time-out technique in detail.

You also should not ignore your child if he is hurting himself during a tantrum or while in time-out. If your child bangs his head, tell him firmly and calmly to stop banging his head. When children are told to stop hurting themselves, most continue scream-ing but stop the harmful behavior. If your child doesn't stop, use your body or a soft object to make sure he doesn't hurt himself. If your child is head-banging, place a pillow or your hand between his head and the surface he is banging on. Even while preventing your child from hurting himself, continue to ignore the rest of the tantrum. Avoid making eye contact with or talking to your child. The more attention the tantrum receives, the more likely he is to have another one.

There may be a point in a tantrum when your child loses control and you sense that he can't regain control on his own. At that point, go to him and comfort him. Try hugging him firmly and rocking him gently from side to side. Continue holding and rocking him until the tantrum subsides.

After the Tantrum

Remember to be calm and consistent when responding to all tantrums. As soon as the tantrum stops or the time-out ends, **praise your child's good behavior verbally.** Say something like, "I like the way you are quiet now. You're doing a good job!" Then **briefly talk about how your child felt and why the tantrum occurred.** For the one- and two-year-old, you will need to do most of the talking. For example, you may say, "It made you angry when Daddy told you to come to the table for dinner. But dinner is ready, and we have to stop playing so we can eat as a family. You

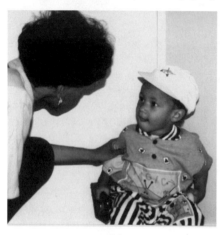

may leave your toys out and finish playing after dinner." You can involve your three-year-old more actively in the discussion by asking him to tell you what happened and adding to it. For instance, he may say, "I no like it when Tommy takes my car so I cried." You may then add, "It made you sad when he took your car." If your child receives a time-out because of harmful or destructive behavior during a tantrum, also **mention why he got the time-out.** "It made you mad when your sister took your toy," you might say. "But you cannot kick her. Mommy gave you a time-out so your sister would be safe and so you would have some time to get it together." After your brief talk, resume your activity—finish shopping, rejoin a party, eat dinner, or continue playing.

Minimizing Tantrums

There are three strategies you can use to minimize the number of tantrums that your child has. First, **set appropriate limits for your child and manage his behavior consistently.** Chapter 8 "Guiding Your Child's Behavior" discusses limit setting and behavior management techniques in detail. Second, **try to determine if there is a pattern to your child's tantrums, and break it.** For example, your child has tantrums only in the late morning when he doesn't get a mid-morning snack. If this is the case, make sure he always gets a mid-morning snack. Third, **provide appropriate opportunities for your child to release his frustrations.** As you decide on an outlet for your child, consider how he acts during a tantrum. Does he kick? hit? scream? Provide him with a similar outlet. If your child kicks when he is angry, give him a special pillow that he can kick or stomp on when he is angry. If your child hits himself or others when he is upset, give him a bop bag to punch. If your child screams during his tantrums, allow him to go to his room and scream. Try to catch your child before he starts a tantrum, and **redirect** him to the pillow or bop bag at that point. If you don't sense his frustration before the tantrum occurs, suggest at the beginning of the tantrum that he go to his outlet. Praise him for doing that if he does it. If he doesn't, ignore the tantrum. During your talk after his tantrum has passed, remind him that he should have gone to his outlet instead.

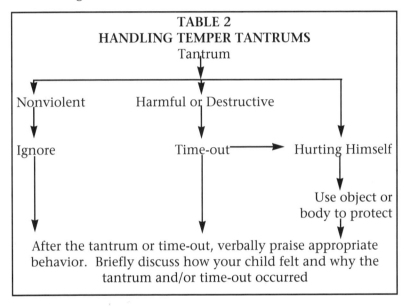

**TABLE 2
HANDLING TEMPER TANTRUMS**

Tantrum

Nonviolent

Harmful or Destructive

Ignore

Time-out ⟶ Hurting Himself

Use object or body to protect

After the tantrum or time-out, verbally praise appropriate behavior. Briefly discuss how your child felt and why the tantrum and/or time-out occurred

A PARENT'S STORY

My son Julio had a lot of difficulty with temper tantrums. This was especially true when we were around other adults. When Julio didn't get my undivided attention just when he wanted it, he would throw a temper tantrum. Before I knew it, we got ourselves into a bad habit. I would be talking to a friend, and Julio would say something to me. I would ignore him so I could finish my conversation, and Julio would scream. I would tell him to stop screaming and would continue with my conversation. Julio would throw himself on the ground, kick his feet, and scream even louder. Embarrassed by the tantrum, I would scoop him up in my arms and hold him. As soon as I picked him up the tantrum always stopped. I would then continue my conversation while I held Julio.

One day Julio had one of his tantrums while I was talking

to Ms. Sanders, his preschool teacher. Ms. Sanders asked me if Julio had tantrums often. I told her that he seemed to have one whenever I tried to talk with another adult. She explained that tantrums were common at Julio's age and suggested that I teach Julio a more appropriate way of getting my attention and that I ignore his tantrums. She told me that a couple months ago a little girl in Julio's class had a similar problem at school— She would hit or throw things to get attention.

Ms. Sanders said they taught her to tap the adult on the knee and say, "Excuse me." The classroom aide, Mr. Drake, spent some time role-playing with the little girl to teach her the new skill. The little girl would pretend to be talking to another person, and Mr. Drake would tap her on the knee and say, "Excuse me." She said they took turns playing this game over the course of a few days. Ms. Sanders suggested that I try this with Julio. She also told me to keep track of how many tantrums Julio has and how long they last. She said this would help me see Julio's progress.

On our way home from school, I thought about what Ms. Sanders had said, and I decided to give her recommendations a try. I also decided that I should praise Julio and give him some immediate attention whenever he tapped my knee or said, "Excuse me." While we were playing that afternoon, I told Julio that I had a new game. We took turns roles-playing as Mr. Drake had done. We even sang a little song we made up: "When you want attention, just tap a knee and say, 'excuse me'." After we played the game for a little while and sang the song a few times, I told Julio that he should tap my knee and say "excuse me" when he needs my attention while I am talking to someone else.

The next time I was talking to someone when Julio wanted my attention, he tapped my knee and said, "Excuse me." I was so surprised and pleased! The second time, he screamed and threw a temper tantrum. I ignored the tantrum. It was the longest nine minutes of my life. After the tantrum was over, I called his name, pointed to my knee, and said, "Remember, when you want attention, just tap a knee and say, 'excuse me.'" He got up off the floor, stomped over to me, tapped my knee and said, "Excuse me." From that time on, I would point to my knee to give him a little hint if I noticed him trying to get my attention in an inappropriate manner. We also did some role-playing from time to time and sang our little song every once in a while. In addition, I tried to avoid having company over at

Julio's nap time. I noticed that he was more likely to have a temper tantrum when he was tired.

Within two weeks, the frequency of Julio's temper tantrums had decreased dramatically, and when he did have a temper tantrum, it only lasted 30 to 45 seconds. It has now been two months since I taught Julio how to get my attention, and he is doing great! Last week he went the whole week without having a single temper tantrum, and he needed only one hint.

HELPING YOUR CHILD GAIN CONTROL OVER HIS FEARS

Most children develop fears at some point in their young life. They are most frequently afraid of large animals, loud noises, and the dark. As they grow older, many children fear getting lost, sleeping alone, and confronting monsters. When a child is afraid, he needs to know that you are not afraid, that you accept his fear, and that you will help him gain some control over his fear.

For example, when a child is afraid of a big bad wolf, searching his bedroom to prove a big bad wolf isn't hiding in the room often does little or no good. When your child is afraid, he needs a way to gain control of his fear. One way is for you to **show your child that he can make the object of his fear go away and stay away**. If your child is afraid of a big bad wolf, try saying, "Let's find the big bad wolf and tell him that he has to go back to the woods. When we find the big bad wolf, we will walk him to the front door, open the door and make him leave. Then we will lock the front door so he can't come back in." The technique of walking the large animal or monster to the door and making him leave is almost always effective.

You can use any other technique as long as it shows your child that you are not afraid, that you accept his fear, and that you will help him achieve some control over the fear. An immediate goal is for your child to believe that the animal or monster has left and won't come back. You want him to say something on this order: "We need to lock the door again, so we make sure the big bad wolf can't get in. The big bad wolf is all gone now. He is in the woods now. He can't get me." A short-term goal is for your child independently to make the animal or monster leave in the future— "There was big bad wolf in my room. But I told him, 'fly out the window, and go back to the woods.' He is back in the woods with his family now." A long-term goal is for your child not to be afraid of the animal or monster and to say in his own words, "Uh oh, there's a big bad wolf behind you. No there's not. I'm just tricking you. Big bad wolves are pretend; they're not real. He is just in my book."

If your child's fears are extreme, **try to desensitize him gently to the object of his fear.** Perhaps he cries and hides behind you every time he sees a cat because he saw two cats fighting in the park

a week earlier. Take the source of the fear, which in this case is cats, and slowly introduce it again in a non-threatening way. In the beginning, show him pictures of cute cats in a book, or watch a movie that portrays a gentle cat. Once he is comfortable looking at pictures of cats, try playing with a

toy cat. Next, go to the pet store to see a cat or arrange to be outside when a friend is walking a small cat on a leash. Finally, when your child is ready, gently encourage him to pet a small, friendly cat. Throughout these new experiences with cats, point out good things about cats.

Minimizing Fears

Although most young children develop fears, there are a few things that you can do to help minimize the number of fears your child has. Before you watch a television show or movie, find out what it is about and whether it contains any scary or violent scenes. Remember to **determine what is scary and violent from your child's perspective.** Seeing a cartoon in which a friendly, purple witch turns a little girl into a ghost may be too scary for your young child. Watching a man throw a dog out a window or viewing one character bopping another over the head with a club may be too violent for him. Also, keep in mind that a G-rated movie may still be too intense for a one-, two-, or three-year-old. Avoid exposing your child to inappropriate material. If your child sees or experiences something that is frightening, explain the situation to him, along with any positive outcomes that may apply—"That man shouldn't have thrown the dog out the window. That was mean. But the dog is okay, and he is playing with the cat now." After the experience, point out any similar, positive occurrences you run across—"Look across the street. That man is letting his dog out the front door. That's a nice way to let a dog outside."

Sometimes you can make a potential fear less intense if you **prepare your child beforehand.** For example, during a bad thunderstorm, hold your child on your lap and speak in ways that will decrease the scariness of the situation. Mention that because it is raining hard, he might hear some loud thunder. Tell him that thunder sounds like drums. Join the thunder by marching around the house while you both drum on pots and pans. If it is nighttime, you could sing a song, like: "Thunder, thunder go away; Come again another day; Little Tommy wants to sleep; Thunder, thunder go away." Often the child will join in the parade or repeat the assuring chant instead of becoming afraid. These types of activities permit him to say or do something that decreases his fear.

FOSTERING THE DEVELOPMENT OF A POSITIVE SELF-ESTEEM

To develop a positive self-esteem, your child needs to feel good about himself. He needs to feel he is competent, lovable, and worthwhile. When you ask your child to do something beyond his means, he may feel badly if he can't do it. By understanding at what ages children learn which skills, you can set appropriate expectations. When you think something might be hard for your child, use phrases like, "**Try** to put your socks on," and "**Try** putting the puzzle together by yourself." Invitations, such as these, encourage your child to try new things without the fear of failing. When you ask your child to do something, give him the time he needs to do it as independently as possible; letting him work at his own pace. This means planning ahead and perhaps allowing an extra ten minutes for everything. This will create a more positive and relaxed atmosphere. Remember to also **praise your child's** <u>attempts</u> **as well as his successes** : "You did a great job trying to put on your socks. You got one on all by yourself! I only had to help you a little bit."

Although your child is growing up and becoming more independent, he still needs time for lots of cuddling. Good times to cuddle with your child include first thing in the morning, before you go to work or begin your household tasks, at story time, and before he goes to bed. While cuddling him at bedtime, talk with your child about his day. Describe two "special" things your child did. Perhaps he went down the slide by himself for the first time, or maybe he helped you set the table. As he gets older, encourage him to describe the good parts of his day. While cuddling him in the morning, talk with your child about the things he can look forward to during the day.

Throughout the day, talk with your child in a **positive and loving manner**. Since gestures and the tone of your voice send messages, **how** you say something is as important as what you say. Your child can feel your love and be very proud when you say, "You're such a turkey," while you smile and rub his head. However, your child feels badly if you say, "You're such a turkey." in a loud, rough voice with a frown on your face.

Spend **one-on-one time** playing and talking with your child every day. It is best if this time is consistent from day to day. It should be a time your child can count on and a time when there are no interruptions. Give him your undivided attention. The best location and amount of time depends on your family's individual schedules and dynamics; for example, playing for half an hour in the morning, an hour after dinner, or 20 minutes at bath time. The

quality of time is as important, if not more important, than the quantity of time. A short, loving, and positive period of time each day is much better than a longer period that has negative comments, anger, and frustration. Play with your child as long as it is enjoyable for both of you. Then take a break or change the play so it is enjoyable again.

Empathize with your child when he is sad, when he misbehaves, or when he is angry. Then discuss the behavior. If your child is crying because he can't have candy before dinner, say something like, "You feel sad that you have to wait until after dinner to eat the candy. If you're really hungry, you may start eating your carrots while I finish making dinner. Let's put the candy on the counter so we don't forget to eat it after dinner." By making such a statement, you acknowledge and empathize with your child's feelings, make accommodations for him in case he really is hungry, and let him know when he may have what he wants. If he responds, "No, I not hungry for salad. I want my candy!", reiterate his feelings and then redirect him. Say, "You're not hungry right now, but you really like candy, and you want to eat it now. But the candy is for after dinner. Let's put the candy on the counter, and the candy can watch you mash the potatoes. Do you want to use a big fork or a little fork?" This response is much better than a speech such as, "You can't have candy until after dinner, and that's that!" The latter response ignores your child's feelings and does not provide him with a positive alternative.

When your child misbehaves, remember **the misbehavior is what is "bad," not your child**. Try not to say things like, "Stop being bad," or "You're so mean!" Both statements convey that you think your child is bad, and neither tells him how to improve his behavior. When your child misbehaves, tell him what he needs to do differently and tell him why. Say something like, "Stop running in the house. Walk so you don't accidentally break something," or "You cannot hit your sister; you might hurt her. If she takes your toy, tell me." By telling your child why he may not do something, you provide him with a rationale that he can use later to direct his own behavior. Similarly, when your child behaves well, praise the specific behavior and let him know why the behavior is desirable: "I like the way you're leaning over your plate to eat. All the crumbs are falling on the plate and not on the floor."

Finally, be a good role model for your child. **Praise yourself when you deserve it**. When you bake a good pie, tell yourself, "I made a good pie." When you finish washing the car, say, "The car is so clean now. I did a good job washing it."

TABLE 3
FOSTERING SELF-ESTEEM

- Set appropriate expectations.
- When you think something might be hard for your child, use words like "try."
- Praise your child's attempts and successes.
- Cuddle with your child.
- Talk with your child in a positive manner.
- Spend one-on-one time playing and talking with your child every day.
- Empathize with your child when he is sad, when he misbehaves, or when he is angry.
- Remember it is the misbehavior that is bad, not your child.
- Give your child a good model, and praise yourself when you deserve it.

SUMMARY

There are five ways to facilitate the emotional development of your child: (1) Understand emotional development so you can better understand your child's behavior, and set appropriate expectations; (2) Support your child through separation anxiety. When you leave your child with another person, always say good-bye and try not to linger. Remember that it is the act of separating that is hard for your child, not the actual separation; (3) Handle tantrums consistently. Ignore the tantrum if it is not violent. Use a time-out if your child is harmful or destructive during a tantrum. As soon as the tantrum stops, praise your child's good behavior and briefly talk about what happened; (4) Help your child gain control over his fears. Let him know that you are not afraid and that you accept his fear. Also, teach him strategies for controlling his fears; (5) Foster the development of a positive self-esteem by praising attempts and successes, cuddling, talking in a positive manner, spending one-on-one time, empathizing, remembering that it is the misbehavior that is bad, not your child, and praising yourself when you deserve it.

REFERENCES AND RECOMMENDED READINGS

Briggs, D. (1975). *Your Child's Self-Esteem.* Garden City, NY: Doubleday & Company, Inc.

Dworkin, P. (1991, Winter). Surefire ways to lessen temper tantrums. *American Baby's Healthy Kids Birth - 3*, pp 40-46.

Dworetzky, J. (1981). *Introduction to Child Development,* pp 225 - 228. New York, NY: West Publishing Co.

Furuno, S., O'Reilly, K., Hosaka, C., Inatsuka, T., Zeisloft -Falbey, B. & Allman, T. (1988). *HELP Checklist.* Palo Alto, CA: VORT Corporation.

Johnson-Martin, N., Attermeier, S. & Hacker, B. (1990). *The Carolina Curriculum for Preschoolers with Special Needs.* Baltimore, MD: Paul H. Brookes Publishing Co.

Chapter 5
Social Skills

Social interactions with peers normally emerges during early childhood. Between the ages of one and four years, children become more and more interested in interacting with other children. Their early social interactions start with watching other children and playing <u>next</u> to other children. But with time, children take part in more sophisticated interactions, which include playing <u>with</u> other children in a similar activity and engaging in organized play with rules.

You can guide your child's social development through four key techniques:

- Set realistic expectations according to your child's personality and age
- Provide your child with opportunities to play with other children
- Teach sharing skills
- Foster appropriate social interactions by understanding and changing aggressive and passive behavior

<u>Parent Perspective</u>
Parents have strong feelings about their child's interactions with other people. Some parents feel personally involved in the way their child treats other people. You may feel that if you are nice to people, then your child will be nice toward others. You may react with disbelief, embarrassment, disappointment, or anger when your child treats another person in a mean or selfish manner. You wonder whether you should intervene or let the children work it out on their own. You may find it exhausting to preserve positive interactions between two or more children. You

may have thought that your child would learn to play with other children as naturally as she learned to walk. It may surprise you to find out that you need to teach social skills.

Child Perspective
Most young children want to interact with other children, but they don't know how. Young children enjoy being around other children because they learn a lot from them. Young children also learn about themselves as they relate with other children. Your child finds ways to keep the toys she wants. She discovers the art of negotiating for what she wants. She learns to handle frustration and disappoint-ment when things don't go her way. Your child also learns from you when you show her ways to solve conflicts with others.

REALISTIC EXPECTATIONS

The most important part of facilitating the social interactions of your child is to set realistic expectations according to your child's personality and age. Realistic expectations help you to understand your child's capabilities and allow you to foster the development of social skills that are within her means.

As a parent, you need to **key into your child's individual temperament and style** when setting expectations. If your child is shy and quiet, you should not expect her to participate with chil-dren in a large group setting the minute she arrives. She will need some time to watch the other children before she is ready to join them. You can help your shy and quiet one-year-old by describing what the other children are doing. Also, suggest ways for her to get involved. If you are the parent of a two- or three-year-old who is slow to warm up, help by asking her to describe what the other children are doing. Also, talk with her about ways she may join in.

Besides thinking about your child's personality, **consider your child's age** when forming social expectations. It is unrealistic, for example, to expect your two- year-old to share her toys indepen-dently and willingly. Such an expectation is out of line with her abilities. It is realistic, however, to expect your three-year-old to share her toys with minimum guidance from you. To know this, you need to familiarize yourself with the developmental progres-sion of social skills for young children.

One-Year-Olds

Most one-year-olds are more interested in toys than in other chil-dren. When one-year-olds play with other children, they almost always engage in solitary play. During solitary play, a child plays alone and independently with toys that are different from the toys children around her are using. The one-year-old shares a toy only at your request, and then she requires a lot of guidance. She uses

---

SOCIAL MILESTONES[1]

One-Year-Olds
• Have more interest in toys than in other children.
• Engage in solitary play.
• Share only when told to do so.
• Need a lot of guidance to share.
• Push and poke as ways of keeping and getting toys.
• Use touch as a way to interact with other children.
• Use words like "mine" and "no" when playing.
• Enjoy playing with parents and familiar adults.
• Like to show toys to parents.
• Have fun playing games such as "Pat-a-Cake," "Ring Around the
    Rosy," and chase.
• May show a preference for one parent over another.

Two-Year-Olds
• Play with other children when adults are around.
• Prefer to interact with adults.
• May be shy with strangers.
• Engage predominantly in solitary play.
• Need supervision while playing.
• Build attachments to their toys.
• Find it difficult to share.
• May pinch, push, kick, and bite to avoid sharing or to get a toy.
• Begin to play with other children without adults.
• Make transition into predominantly parallel play.
• Imitate other children .
• Begin to enjoy dramatic play.
• Can stay in a structured group situation for a short time.
• Start to share voluntarily; sharing remains difficult.

Three-Year-Olds
• Love playing with other children .
• Tend to play equally with boys and girls.
• Continue to engage in parallel play.
• Engage predominantly in associative play.
• Begin to engage in cooperative play.
• May become angry when playing with other children .
• Still exhibit physical aggression when angry.
• Have improved sharing skills .
• Are able to wait for a turn.
• Are willing and able to help a shy or less skilled child.
• Join other children eagerly in play.

[1]Skills are presented in the order that most children learn them.

---

pushing and poking as ways to keep and to get toys. She uses these strategies of touching as her means to interact with other children. She also uses words like "mine" and "no." Although the one-year-old doesn't have any particular interest in playing with other children, she enjoys playing with you and other familiar adults. She likes to show you her toys and to play simple games, such as "Pat-a-Cake," "Little Finger in the Palm," and "Ring

Around the Rosy." As she approaches two years of age, she may show a preference for one parent over another. This is okay. Both parents should continue to play with her and care for her. If she insists that Mommy give her a bath, for instance, have Mom do it. And if Dad wants to be involved in the bath, let him hand the soap and shampoo to Mom. Make it a fun time together. Remind Dad not to feel too rejected; she's a little person and will change her allegiance soon enough.

Two-Year-Olds

Most two-year-olds will play with other children when adults are around, but they still prefer interacting with adults. They like adults because adults seem more predictable and easier to get along with than other children. Although she enjoys interacting with adults, your two-year-old may be shy with strangers. When a two-

year-old plays with other children, solitary play still predominates, and she still needs supervision while she plays. Many two-year-olds build strong attachments to their toys so that they find it difficult to share them. Your child may pinch, push, kick, grab, and bite to avoid sharing or to get a toy.

At around two and a half, children begin to interact more with peers when they are around both adults and other children. Occasionally, the two-and a half-year-old will even play with other children without adults. When she plays with other children at this age, solitary play declines and parallel play predominates. During parallel play, the two-and a half-year-old plays independently with toys like those children around her are using. She tends to play beside other children rather than with them. She is likely to imitate other children, and she adds smiles and laughter to her social interactions. As she nears the age of three, she begins to enjoy dramatic play. She can stay in a structured group situation for a short period. Voluntary sharing emerges at this time, but it remains difficult for her.

Three-Year-Olds

Most three-year-olds love playing with other children. At three, children tend to play equally with boys and girls. While parallel play continues to occur, associative play occurs most of the time. During associative play, children play together in a similar activity. Their conversation centers around the activity, and children voluntarily share toys. For many young children, cooperative play also emerges around this age. In cooperative play,

children engage in organized play that has rules. A three-year-old may become angry while playing with other children, especially when she wants a toy that someone else has, or when someone wants her toy. She may still exhibit physical aggression when she is angry. Her sharing skills are improving, however, and she can wait for a turn—as long as the wait isn't too long. The three-year-old is also willing to help a shy or less skilled child, if she is encouraged. By four years of age most children eagerly join other children in play, with little or no reluctance or hesitation.

PROVIDE OPPORTUNITIES TO PLAY WITH OTHER CHILDREN

The second way to facilitate your child's social development is to provide opportunities for her to play with other children. To develop appropriate social skills, children need experiences with other children. Many children get such experiences with brothers and sisters, neighbors, or in day-care settings. If your child does not interact with children on a weekly basis, you can provide this opportunity by visiting another parent and child. You may also take your child to

an indoor play area or an outdoor playground where other children play. More formal arrangements, such as play groups or nursery schools, can also be considered.

TEACH SHARING SKILLS

Sharing is difficult for young children and is something that must be learned. They do not intrinsically know how to share; generosity can't be forced. When your child takes a toy from another child, let her try to resolve it on her own. If it doesn't bother the other child, mention to your child that she should ask before she takes someone's toy. Intervene if it looks as if the either child will get hurt or upset.

When you intervene, allow the other child—the one who first had the toy—to play with the toy first. Permit him to play with the toy for a set time, or until he is finished with it. Base your decision on the dynamics of the individual children. If the children are young and are beginning to learn how to share, set a specific amount of time. You may even set a timer, so you won't forget. If the children are two and a half years of age or older and are familiar with sharing, allow the other child to play with the toy until he is finished. While he is playing with it, try to interest your child in something else. If your child continues to want the toy, try to distract her in another part of the room or even in another room, until it is her turn. When he—the child who first had the toy—is finished playing with the toy, your child may play with it.

Remember to offer your child the opportunity to play with the toy when the other child is finished with it. It is important to offer your child the toy even if she is happily playing with another toy. In this way you will build credibility—if you promise her a turn, she will get a turn. Otherwise, when you intervene in a dispute later on, to your astonishment, you may be told, "No, I won't get a turn. The other day you said I would, but I didn't get a turn." Follow these same steps if another child takes a toy away from your child:
- Try not to intervene if it doesn't bother your child
- Step in if it looks as if someone will get hurt or upset
  – Allow your child to play with the toy first
  – Let her play with the toy for a set time, or until she is finished with it
  – Offer the other child a chance to play with the toy when it is his turn, even if he has lost interest in the toy

Many two-year-olds build strong attachments to their toys. If your child is possessive about her toys, she probably has difficulty sharing them with other children. However, at another child's house, she may play beautifully with someone else's toys. There are four basic strategies for helping your child share her own toys:

- Share with your child in a realistic manner
- Prepare your child for another child's visit
- Teach your child trading skills
- Implement training sessions about sharing

The amount of guidance your child will need to develop sharing skills will vary according to her individual style and age. For a one-year-old, you should model correct actions, explaining what to do as you do it yourself. For a two- or three-year-old, you can talk her through the steps, having her do the correct actions.

The first strategy is to **share with your child in a realistic manner**. With scarcely a thought, you give your child the toy she wants whenever she wants it while you play with her. You don't care whether you use the white ice cream truck or the blue race car. So if your child wants the blue race car, why not give it to her? Because if you always give her what she wants the minute she wants it, your child may assume that other children should and will do the same. As you know, most children will not share that readily.

You can prepare your child for the rules of sharing by applying them when the two of you play together. This is not to say that you should never give her turns. Instead, explain that it is your

turn with the blue race car and ask her to wait a minute until she may have a turn with it. Redirect her attention to another toy or play with the car together. Occasionally invite her to share a toy with you. Explain to your child that it's nice to share toys.

In addition, let her know that sometimes it's okay to say no when someone else wants her toy. Teach your child how to explain that it's her turn with the toy, to ask others to wait their turn, to offer someone else a different toy, and to give the toy to someone else when she is finished with it.

As a second strategy, **prepare your child for another child's visit**. Tell her a friend is coming over to play. Let her pick out some toys to use <u>with</u> her friend. Toys both children can share equally are best in the beginning. These include blocks, cars, books, and any other toys of which your child has more than one. Explain to your child that her friend will play with the toys, but that he will not take the toys home. While the children play together, you may expect her friend to say, "It's mine," about a toy and for your child to respond, "No! It's my toy!" Your child needs to learn that by saying, "It's mine," her friend is really saying, "It's my turn." Teach your child to say, "It's my toy, but you may play with it." Before the visit, ask your child whether there are any special toys she doesn't want her friend to use—perhaps her new teddy bear from Grandma or her very favorite book. Put these toys away before her friend arrives.

The third strategy involves **teaching your child "trading" skills**. If a situation arises in which your child wants a toy that her friend is playing with, say something like, "Do you want to play with the train that Joel has? What toy may he play with?" Elicit a response from your child, or make a suggestion. Then guide her through the trade—"Go get the car, and ask Joel if he wants to trade toys." In most circumstances, the other child will trade. However, there will be times when the other child will refuse to trade. When this happens, explain to your child that she will have to wait for her turn. Distract her with another toy or some tickles until it is her turn. As soon as her friend is finished with the toy, make sure you offer the toy to your child. Some children are very possessive about their toys and are truly afraid they won't get their toy back.

If these three strategies are not effective enough in helping your child learn how to share, implement training sessions about sharing. During the training sessions, give your child and another child repeated short turns with the same toy. For instance, let your child blow bubbles for 30 seconds, then let the other child blow bubbles for 30 seconds. Continue taking turns in this fashion for about five minutes. Encourage both children to say, "It's your turn now," or "It's my turn now." Communicating during the sharing process can be difficult for young children to learn. However, learning how

to communicate verbally is important, because their ability to verbalize reduces incidents where one child hits another child to get a toy.

FOSTER APPROPRIATE SOCIAL INTERACTIONS

Many young children do not know how to verbalize what they want. Some young children become physically aggressive, hitting or pinching to get a toy or to avoid sharing a toy. Other young children are more passive. They whimper or cry when they want a toy or when someone takes away their toy. To foster appropriate social interactions, you may need to teach your child ways to express her feelings that are effective and socially acceptable.

Understanding and Changing Aggressive Behavior.

Many young children hit, kick, and bite during play to avoid sharing or to get a toy they want. Such behavior, while common, is usually not permanent. Many children go through aggressive phases before they learn to stand up for their rights in a more socially-acceptable manner. If your child is aggressive, show her appropriate ways to express her feelings. When she doesn't want to share, teach her to say, "No, it's my turn." Teach her to explain to someone who wants her toy that it's her turn with the toy, to tell the other child to wait, to offer the other child a different toy, and to give the child the toy when she is finished with it. Make sure that she realizes that using the toy with the other child is another option. Tell her if neither of these ways work, she may get an adult to help her work things out. Encourage her to try to handle the situation by herself first, but provide her with the guidance she needs.

When your child wants a toy that another child has, instruct her to ask for a turn. If the other child doesn't want to share, explain that she can offer to trade toys or ask to use the toy with the child. Teach her to play with a different toy while she waits her turn. Tell her it's best to try to work things out for herself, but that it's okay to tell an adult if she can't handle the situation.

In addition to teaching your child appropriate ways to express her feelings and to stand up for her rights, address the matter of aggressive acts. Tell your child that hitting, kicking, and biting are not nice or permitted. Explain that these actions hurt people. Describe what hands, feet, and teeth were made for— hands are for clapping and hugging, feet are for walking and running, and teeth are for talking and eating.

Teach her to hit or kick a pillow or a bop bag when she feels angry. If it becomes necessary, use the strategies discussed in Chapter 8 "Guiding Your Child's Behavior" to reduce aggressive behavior.

Also consider the amount of aggression your child views on television. Children frequently imitate what they see. If your child watches a lot of aggression or violence on TV, it may be contributing to her aggressive behavior. Talk regularly with your child about what she sees on TV, explaining what is right and what is wrong. Change the shows that include aggression and violence to programs with more positive behavioral messages for your child.

Understanding and Changing Passive Behavior.

Some young children let other children take their toys, then become sad when another child has a toy they want. Parents of passive children often find themselves standing up for their child's rights. They frequently retrieve toys for their child and tell other children to share with their child. A passive child cries when another child takes her fire hat, but does nothing more to get it back. If your child allows another child to take her toy and then appears upset by it, teach her to stand up for her right to play with the toy. A passive child may sadly watch another child play with blocks but does nothing to get a turn. If you notice your child standing off to the side looking longingly at a toy, teach her to offer the other child a trade or to ask the other child to share. Use the techniques presented under aggressive behavior to teach her to keep a toy she has or to get a toy she wants.

A PARENT'S STORY

The interactions between my three-year-old daughter and her three and a half year old cousin amaze me. Here is a ten minute sample of a day with these two children:

Eric goes from the kitchen to the family room.
Amanda runs from the kitchen to the family room.
Eric bounces on two large pillows lying on the floor.
  Amanda: "No!"
Amanda tries to push Eric off the pillows.
Amanda and Eric begin screaming and pushing each other.
I intervene and explain that there are two pillows, one for each of them.
  Eric: "Let's you and me we, lie on it. Make me a sandwich
   in the pillows."
  Amanda: "No."
Eric shrugs his shoulders and lies on his pillow.
Amanda takes her pillow to the couch.

Eric: "You make me a sandwich."

Amanda: "No. I don't want to!"

Eric: "Then I make you a sandwich."

Amanda: "No!"

Eric: "I gonna take one of these (pillows) home."

Amanda: "You can't bring one of these home."

Eric: "You want me to bring them home?"

Amanda: "No."

Eric: "You said I could."

Amanda: "No."

Eric: "Can I bring one of your blocks home?"

Amanda: "No."

Eric: "You have to share. You have to share. It not nice."

Amanda: "No."

Eric: "Let's build a house."

Amanda: "No."

Eric: "Why?"

Amanda: "My tummy hurts."

Eric: "Why?"

Amanda: "I wake up too early. I have go back to sleep and try all over again."

Eric: "You be baby, Amanda."

Amanda: "No. I want be Amanda."

Eric: "You baby girl Amanda."

Amanda: "No, I want be just Amanda. No, I want be just Amanda. No, I want be just Amanda."

Eric: "You baby Amanda."

Amanda: "No!!!"

Eric: "Amanda...Amanda...Amanda...Amanda."

Amanda: "I don't want to talk right now!"

Eric: "Don't yell at me. It not nice. Amanda, you want to play bunnies?"

Amanda: "No. I want to watch a movie."

Eric: "You want to watch scary (Halloween) movie?"

Amanda: "Yes."

Eric: "When that scary part on, can I hold your hand?"

Amanda: "Yes."

Eric: "Let's get the movie. You get scary one."

Amanda: "When there's a scary part, I gonna hold your hand and you gonna hold my hand."

Amanda gets the Halloween movie and begins to bring it to me.

Amanda: "Mom, can you open this for me?"

Eric: "I can! I can!"

Amanda gives Eric the movie and Eric opens it.

Eric: "There."

Amanda: "Let me have the movie 'cause I want to put it in."

Eric gives Amanda the movie and with some guidance from me, Amanda puts the movie into the VCR.

Eric and Amanda go back to the couch to get their pillows.

Eric: "This is my pillow."

Amanda: "No. This is my pillow."

Eric: "No. This was mine."

Amanda: "No. It was mine. I got there first."

Eric: "You got to share with me."

Amanda: "Each us take a pillow."

Eric: "Ooops. I thought that my pillow."

Amanda: "Let's put our pillows together so we can sit next to each other."

Eric: "You can sit here. I sit next to you."

Amanda: "Okay."

Eric and Amanda put their pillows on the floor, one right next to the other. They each sit on a pillow and begin to watch the movie.

Eric: "This scary part. I don't like that purple guy."

Amanda: "I can hold your hand."

Amanda holds Eric's hand.

Eric: "I don't like that purple one."

Amanda: "I like the blue guy."

Eric: "You just like the blue one, not the purple one?"

Amanda: "Yes."

Eric: "Why?"

Amanda: "'Cause I do."

Eric: "Now the scary part over. You can let go my hand."

Eric lets go of Amanda's hand.

Amanda: "No it's not over."

Eric "Are you still scared?"

Eric: "Yes."

Amanda: "I hold your hand some more then."

Amanda holds Eric's hand.

Eric: "You don't like that green guy?"

Amanda: "No."

Eric: "Okay. I don't like this part. I don't like the witch. She bad."

Amanda: "No. She nice."

Eric: "No. She bad."

Amanda: "No. She good."

Eric: "I can say whatever I want to about that witch. She bad."

Amanda: "No. She good."

Eric: "Whatever I want to say to the witch I can. I can say whatever I want to."

Amanda: "No. She nice."

Eric: "No. She bad."

Amanda: "Why she (witch) broke the window?"

Eric: "She bad and crashed."

Amanda: "She should have come in the door, not the window."

Eric: "This is scary."

Amanda: "I holding your hand."

Eric: "I like you holding my hand."

Amanda: "I like you holding my hand also."

Eric: "I got a good idea. I stay the night with you. Does that sound good idea to you?"

Amanda: "That sound good idea to me. You can stay night with me."

Eric: "Scary part over. You can let go my hand."

Amanda: "But I like my holding your hand."

Eric: "Okay. You can hold my hand. I like you holding my hand also."

SUMMARY

Social interactions with peers emerge during early childhood. As a parent, you should consider your child's personality and age when setting social expectations. To facilitate your child's social development, provide opportunities for her to play with other children. Sharing is difficult for most young children. To help your child share: (1) Share with her in a realistic manner; (2) Prepare her for another child's visit; (3) Teach her trading skills; (4) Implement training sessions on sharing. Many young children do not know how to verbalize what they want. Some toddlers are physically aggressive, other young children are more passive. To foster appropriate social interactions, teach your child ways of expressing her feelings that are effective and socially acceptable.

REFERENCES & RECOMMENDED READINGS

For Children:

Dickson, A. (1987). *Don't Be Shy.* New York, NY: Western Publishing Company, Inc.

For Parents:

Bailey, D. & Wolery, M. (1984). *Teaching Infants and Preschoolers with Handicaps.* Chapter 11. Columbus, OH: Charles E. Merrill Publishing Co.

Dworetzky, J. (1981). *Introduction to Child Development.* Chapter 17. St. Paul, MN: West Publishing Co.

Parten, M. (1932). Social participation among preschool children. *Journal of Abnormal and Social Psychology, 27*, pp 243-269.

Rothenberg, B., Hitchcock, S., Harrison, M. & Graham, M. (1983). *Parentmaking.* Menlo Park, CA: Banster Press.

Chapter 6
Self-Help Skills

"I can do it by myself!" is a pet phrase of youngsters from one to four years of age. In these years, young children assert their independence by wanting to do many things for themselves. They also love to watch and copy what they see other people doing.

Your child's eagerness to be independent at this age makes it the ideal time for her to learn basic self-help skills. There are five major types of self-help skills:

- Eating
- Dressing
- Grooming
- Household skills
- Toileting

This chapter discusses the first four types. Toileting, because of its depth, appears in detail in Chapter 10 "Toilet Training."

Parent Perspective
You may wish your child were more independent at skills such as eating, dressing, and grooming. The idea of having your child perform a few simple household tasks may also appeal to you. On the other hand, you may feel that you should let your child spend all her time playing instead of taxing her with lessons on how to pour or dust. Your child's desire to do things that she is not yet ready for may frustrate you. When your child insists on doing something by herself, getting from point A to point B often takes twice as long. If you are as busy as most parents, you may feel upset and even angry, as well as guilty for having such feelings. Try to be patient. Eventually you will be surprised to see how much your child can do if given the opportunity. Imagine

your sense of pride when your child bursts into the room with an ear-to-ear grin to show you how she dressed herself completely for the first time.

Child Perspective
Most young children not only enjoy learning to do new things, but they also strongly desire to do so. Your child truly wants to do most of the things you do for her, and she wants to do these things independently. Since young children learn by seeing and practicing and since they tend to do things slowly when they are first learning, your child needs unhurried time to practice self-help skills. When she does something for herself or when she helps you around the house, she will feel grown-up and proud. When you compliment her for being a big helper, she will beam with joy.

As a parent you can foster the development of self-help skills in four ways. The first way is to **understand the sequence in which young children develop self-help skills.** Understanding when children perform certain self-help tasks allows you to set realistic expectations for your child. This will help you encourage skills that are within your child's capability without thwarting her progress. The second way is to **provide your child with opportunities to develop self-help skills.** For example, to learn how to lace and tie her shoes, your child needs shoes that lace instead of shoes that slip on or close with Velcro. Similarly, for learning how to zip, button, and snap, your child must have pants and shirts with zippers, buttons, and snaps instead of clothing with only elastic or Velcro. Since children, especially those who have disabilities, benefit from systematic and consistent teaching, the third strategy is to **model self-help skills and provide appropriate feedback.** Young children learn by watching and copying others. To teach your child self-help skills such as brushing her teeth, for example, let her watch you brush your teeth. As she tries to brush her teeth, describe aloud what she is doing correctly. Also suggest ways for her to improve her technique. If necessary, physically guide her through the motions. Finally, **allow your child the time she needs to perform the self-help task.** Parents are frequently in a hurry and find it easier, for instance, to wash their child's face or to comb their child's hair than to allow their child to do these tasks herself. In some cases this is okay, but generally, it is better to allow an extra ten minutes so your child can try to do the task herself.

DEVELOPMENT OF SELF-HELP SKILLS[1]

One-Year-Olds

Eating

Feed themselves with a spoon.

Hold a cup by the handles.

Drink from a cup, with little spilling.

Play with their food.

Suck from a straw.

Begin to chew food with their mouth closed.

Give up nursing or drinking from a bottle near the age of two years.

Dressing

Take off their hat.

Take off their socks.

Take off their shoes when the laces are undone.

Unzip large zippers.

Grooming

Enjoy trying to brush their teeth.

Wash and dry their hands with help.

Household

Help with simple household tasks.

Push and pull doors open and shut.

Two-Year-Olds

Eating

Develop food preferences and reject many foods.

Drink from a small cup, using only one hand to hold the cup.

Hold a spoon correctly with their palm tilted upward.

Eat an entire meal using a spoon, with minimal spilling.

Begin to use a fork to spear food.

Spread with a dull butter knife.

Pour liquid from a small container.

Dressing

Put their shoes on with help.

Unbutton large buttons.

Undress with help.

Dress with help.

Grooming

Brush their teeth with help.

Dry their hands independently.

Help bathe themselves.

Blow and wipe their nose with help.

Household

Open and close doors, using the knob.

Understand and stay away from common dangers.

Handle fragile items carefully.

Help put things away.

Three-Year-Olds

Eating

Use a fork to eat meals.

Use the edge of a fork to cut soft foods.

Use a napkin.

Fix a bowl of dry cereal with milk.

Dressing
> Undo fasteners, such as snaps and laces.
> Button large buttons.
> Undress independently.
> Dress with minimal help.
> Distinguish between the front and back of clothes.
> Buckle belts.

Grooming
> Wash their hands independently.
> Brush their teeth independently.
> Blow their nose independently.

Household
> Can set the table with minimal help.
> Know the proper place for their things and can put them there.

[1]Skills are presented in the order that most children learn them.

EATING

Development of Eating Skills

One-Year-Olds

By the time they are twelve months old, most children eat table foods and can finger-feed themselves. Between the ages of one and two years, children learn how to use a spoon. In the beginning a child holds onto the spoon with a closed fist, with the palm tilted downward. When eating with a spoon, a child often turns the spoon over as she brings it to her mouth. At around fifteen months of age, she begins to scoop her food with a spoon and feed herself without turning the spoon over. One-year-olds are messy eaters— they miss their mouth, they drop their food—both accidentally and on purpose, and they enjoy playing with their food. They are, however, learning to chew food with their mouth closed. Most one-year-olds can also drink from a cup. A child between twelve

and eighteen months of age can hold a cup by the handles and drink with some spilling. Between eighteen and twenty-four months of age, most children can hold a cup, without handles, and drink from it with minimal spilling, using two hands. During this time many children learn to drink through a straw. Approaching two years of age, most children give up their bottle.

Two-Year-Olds

Many two-year-olds develop preferences for certain foods and begin to reject all other foods. Between twenty-four and thirty months of age, children learn to drink from a small cup, holding it with one hand. During this time a child also begins to hold a spoon correctly, with the palm tilted upward. A child this age can eat an entire meal using a spoon, with minimal spilling. Between thirty and thirty-six months of age, many children begin using a fork to spear their food, and they learn to spread with a dull butter knife. Near the age of three years, children learn how to pour liquid from a small container.

Three-Year-Olds

By the time they reach the age of three, most children eat independently, needing help only to cut up their food. Between three and four years of age, children refine their eating skills. They begin using a fork more frequently than a spoon, and they learn to cut soft foods with the edge of their fork. At this age children also figure out how and when to use a napkin. Between three and a half and four years of age, a child learns to fix a bowl of dry cereal with milk. By their fourth birthday, most children have outgrown a highchair or booster seat, and they sit on a chair at the table to eat, with only occasional spilling.

Facilitating Eating Skills

Encourage Independence

Let your child be as independent as possible at mealtime. She may make a big mess, but to develop independent eating skills, she needs to practice. Offer her a napkin of her own to use. She will need help to clean her face, but with practice, she will be able to do a decent job of wiping her hands and most of her face. If the mess bothers you, put a body bib or smock on her at mealtime. Or put a plastic tablecloth under the area where she eats. At the end of the meal, simply pick up the tablecloth, shake the contents into the trash can, and if necessary, toss it into the washing machine

While your child is learning to use a spoon and fork, offer her a finger food at each meal. This will give her a chance to feed herself part of the meal with her

fingers, which will increase her feelings of independence and decrease those of frustration. In addition, give her a spoon and a fork of her own to practice using at each meal. You can help with another spoon or fork. To teach your child how to bite corn-on-the-cob, for instance, demonstrate an exaggerated bite from both a face-to-face profile and a side profile. As your child becomes a more independent eater, continue to sit with her while she eats. Mealtime is important for developing social and language skills. It is also a very important family time. Often dinner time is the only time the entire family is together. As your child grows older, dinner time may provide the occasion when you get to hear all about her day. *And it is important for you to stay with your child during mealtime for safety reasons. Left unsupervised, your child could choke, fall out of her chair, or hurt herself by putting a spoon handle down her throat or up her nose.*

Using a Cup

Start with cups that have two handles. At first it is easier for young children to hold on to the handles than onto the cup itself. In the beginning, use a cup with a spill-proof lid, preferably the kind with a slit lower than the lip of the cup. This type of cup is ideal because it allows your child to develop the lip positioning she will need to drink from a cup without a lid. When you give your child a cup with a lid, be sure to tell her not to take the lid off. Explain that it is hard to get the lid off and that the liquid may accidentally spill if she tries to take it off. If not told otherwise, most children will try to take the lid off, spilling the contents of the cup.

When you introduce a cup without a lid, fill the cup only half full. Then, when your child spills—which she will, it's just part of the learning process—you will have less to clean up. Consider taking off her shirt the first time, or let her practice drinking a cup of water in the bathtub. Be sure to introduce a cup without a lid before your child starts preschool. Most preschools use paper cups without lids at snack time. It will be easier for the teachers and your child if she can drink from a cup without a lid before she goes to school.

Drinking from a Straw

Learning to drink from a straw is fun for most children, but it can also be hard work. In their first attempts, many children don't suck on the straw long enough to get the liquid all the way up the straw. Often, once the liquid gets halfway up the straw, the child releases her suck to take a breath, and the liquid falls down back into the cup. This makes the process frustrating for a young child. To help, use a short straw. Cut a regular straw in half. Another challenge is that your child may become so engrossed in getting the liquid up the straw that she may forget to hold the cup steady and straight. To reduce spilling, first insert the straw through the slit in the lid. Once your child can use a straw well, introduce a curvy straw for fun.

Giving up Breast- or Bottle-Feedings

By the time a child is twelve months old, she usually sleeps through the night without needing to nurse or to drink a bottle. If your child nurses or drinks a bottle during the night, wean these feedings first. Wean one feeding every three to four days until your child is not drinking at night. Use the techniques described in Chapter 9 "Sleeping Through The Night" to facilitate sleeping, if needed.

At some time between one and three years of age, most parents think about encouraging their child to give up nursing or drinking from the bottle during the day. Many parents dread this transition because they feel their child will have difficulty without these feedings. You can ease this process for your child by weaning one nursing or one bottle at a time and substituting a special activity for the feeding. Expect it to take about four weeks to wean your child of all daytime breast- or bottle-feedings. To make the transition more slowly and more gradually, extend the number of weeks between each phase.

To begin, wean your child from the breast- or bottle-feedings that she needs least. These often include unplanned nursings or the bottles you give her throughout the day when she wants to drink or gets cranky. Simply substitute these nursings or bottles with a cup of milk, juice, or water along with a hug for reassurance. Weaning these feedings is usually easy; most children give them up without any difficulty. This leaves you with two or three feedings, commonly at morning, nap, and bedtime. Continue these feedings for one week to give your child time to adjust to the fact that she can't nurse or have a bottle anytime she chooses.

Depending on your child's signals, wean the last three feedings so that her favorite feeding is the one saved for last. Wean one nursing or bottle each week. Weaning her slowly gives your child time to adjust. If you are nursing, slow weaning also allows your body the time it needs to slow down milk production enough so that you experience little or no discomfort. Weaning your child from these last three nursings or bottles may be difficult. To make the transition go as smoothly as possible, offer her a special activity during the times when you traditionally nursed her or gave her a bottle. Offer the special activity for three to five days. Having a little tea party with her may work well, since it involves having something to drink and provides your child with the one-on-one attention she used to receive at this time. In their excitement over a tea party or other special activity, many children forget they are supposed to nurse or get a bottle.

Weaning the bedtime feeding is generally the hardest one for young children. Nursing or drinking a bottle at bedtime relaxes most children, helping them move from an active day to quiet time for sleep. If your child cuddles with you on a rocking chair in her room while she nurses or drinks a bottle, begin by offering her "tea" on your lap while you hold her in the rocking chair. Gradually move the tea party from the chair to the bedroom floor to the kitchen before teeth-brushing. Be sure to continue your normal bedtime routine, such as prayers, singing bedtime songs and cuddling your child.

Pouring

Learning to pour various liquids is fun for young children. The first few times you teach your child to pour, use a small pitcher. Young children's little hands make it difficult for them to control a big

heavy container. You can buy miniature pouring pitchers that hold six to eight ounces of liquid at many grocery stores. You can also use a measuring cup as a pitcher. In the beginning, fill the pitcher only one-third to half full. Use water or another liquid that will not stain. The first time your child pours independently, she will probably spill. If she is pouring red grape juice while she is wearing her favorite white shirt, you are likely to have a minor disaster on your hands. Keeping the contents of the pitcher to a minimum will make it easier to clean up. To lessen cleanup chores, consider teaching pouring skills in the bathtub before allowing her to pour in the kitchen. Be sure to show your child how to pour as you describe what you are doing. Caution her to stop pouring before the liquid gets to the top of the cup. Some children, if not warned, will pour until the pitcher is empty without realizing the cup is overflowing. After you show your child how to pour, allow her to practice. If your child hesitates, help her by pouring with her a few times. Once she is fairly good at pouring, allow her to pour her own glass of juice. Also let her pour the milk into her bowl of cereal. Letting her to do these things on a regular basis will make her feel grown-up and will foster her self-esteem.

DRESSING

Development of Dressing Skills

One-Year-Olds

If your child is a year old, you probably already know that the key task is not just to teach your child how to dress or undress. The greater challenge is to get her to stay still long enough for you to dress or undress her. Most one-year-olds are very mobile and don't like to sit still for any length of time. Between twelve and fifteen months of age they want to practice walking; between fifteen and twenty-four months they like to practice running. You can encourage your one-year-old to stay in one place by singing songs, talking about the colors in her clothes, or pointing to her body parts. Between fifteen and twenty-four months of age, a child learns to take off her hat, socks, and shoes—as long as the laces are undone. During this same time, she learns to unzip large zippers.

Two-year-olds

At the age of two, most children are eager and developmentally ready to learn dressing and undressing skills. The dressing skill many two-year-olds learn first is putting their shoes on with help. At about the same time, they learn to push their pants down and to unbutton large buttons. They then learn to take off their shirts and to pull up their pants. They still need help getting pullover shirts over their heads, and pants up over their bottoms. As they approach three years of age, most children can put on  simple clothing items, such as shoes, socks, pants, shirts, and jackets, independently. Even though they can put these items on independently, two-year-olds still need help with tying and fastening.

Three-Year-Olds

Most three-year-olds have mastered several dressing skills. Between the ages of three and four, children refine these skills and move toward independent dressing. They learn to undo fasteners, such as snaps and laces, so that they are able to undress independently. At this age, children also learn to button large buttons, distinguish between the front and back of their clothes, zip front-opening clothes, and buckle belts. These skills allow a three-year-old to get dressed with minimal help. Young children continue to need some help getting dressed until they are close to five years old.

Facilitating Dressing Skills

For a young child, undressing is easier than dressing. Unless your child shows an interest in learning to dress herself, wait until she can undress with some help before you introduce dressing. You don't need to wait until she can unfasten every button and buckle, but make sure she has some of the basic skills. Besides teaching dressing skills when your child dresses in the morning and undressing skills as she undresses in the evening, you might offer a doll or an activity book for her to practice many of these same skills.

When you teach your child to undress and dress herself, incorporate the following four strategies. First, **position yourself behind your child when undressing or dressing her.** By putting her back toward your chest, you will teach her how to undress and dress from her perspective. Second, **describe what you are doing as you undress or dress her.** In the beginning, most fasteners are too difficult for young children. Undo the buttons, zippers, and snaps for your child; describing aloud what you are doing as you do it. While undressing her, say, "Daddy is holding the top of your shirt with his left hand, and he is pulling the zipper tab down with his right hand." When you are dressing her, say, "One arm in, now the other arm...Let's push your arm through the sleeve...terrific!" The third strategy is to **undress and dress your child slowly, using the same sequence of movements she needs to learn.** For example, remove the shirt sleeve from her arm instead of pulling her arm from the sleeve. Finally, **allow your child enough time to practice undressing and dressing.**

As you teach your child to undress and dress, give easy directions and keep the process simple, taking small steps. Some items, such as socks and sweatpants, are easier to take off and put on than others. Teach your child to take off and put on the easier items first, saving items such as turtlenecks for last. Let your child practice and master one step at a time; you do the rest. Letting her do one or more steps independently, even though she can't complete the whole task alone, promotes self-confidence. It also reduces conflicts that arise when she wants to do it herself. Let your child see herself in the mirror when she has finished dressing. Correcting sloppy dressing or mistakes is easier if your child can see them herself. Your child may often spot the

problem and want to correct it without your saying anything. Allowing your child to see herself in the mirror also promotes a sense of pride in her accomplishment.

GROOMING

Development of Grooming Skills

One-Year-Olds

Children usually develop an interest in grooming skills between the ages of one and two. Brushing teeth and washing and drying hands are the two favorites at this age. Children enjoy trying to perform these skills, but they need help.

Two-year-Olds

Between the ages of two and three years, children become more interested in grooming skills and want to do more for themselves. They are better at brushing their teeth, but they still need help to put toothpaste on the brush. They are also better at washing their hands and can even dry their hands independently. In addition, a two-year-old begins to help wash herself at bath time. By the age of three, a child can blow and wipe her nose with some help.

Three-year-Olds

Most three-year-olds want to perform grooming skills indepen-

dently. Children usually learn to wash their hands independently between the ages of three and four. During this same time, they learn to brush their teeth all by themselves. This includes wetting the toothbrush, putting on the toothpaste, spitting out the toothpaste, and rinsing the toothbrush. By four, most children can also blow their nose without help.

Facilitating Grooming Skills

Washing and Drying Hands

For your child to wash and dry her hands independently, she must be able to reach the water, soap, and a towel. If your child is too short to reach these items, furnish her with a sturdy step stool to stand on. The most important part of teaching your child how to wash her hands is instructing her to turn the water on so it is *not* hot. If your sink has two knobs, one for hot and one for cold, *be sure she can identify the cold faucet.* To help her remember which knob to turn, put a sticker on the wall near the cold water knob. If, on the other hand, your sink has only one knob, show your child which way to turn the knob to get cold water. As a reminder, put a sticker on the wall pointing in the direction to turn the knob for cold. As she grows older, teach her how to turn the water on so it is warm. To do this with a two-knob sink, move the cold water sticker to the point where she should turn that knob, and put another sticker on the wall at the point where she should turn the hot knob. With a one-knob sink, simply move the cold water sticker a little to the left where warm water comes out of the faucet. Explain to her that cold water and a *little* bit of hot water make warm water. Show her how this works. Watch her carefully the first few times she washes her hands with warm water to make sure she turns the knobs correctly. Teach her to *test the water* with one finger before putting both her hands into the water.

Brushing Teeth

Even though one-year-olds are old enough to begin brushing their teeth, many children cannot brush their teeth independently and thoroughly until they are four. Until then, a child needs help. When you introduce a toothbrush to your child, let her play with it without toothpaste. Encourage your child to imitate you as you brush your teeth. Buy a soft child's size toothbrush for her. Several cute ones are on the market—some have characters on them; others glow in the dark. If your child complains that your adult toothpaste burns her mouth, use a children's toothpaste with fluoride. Avoid using a lot of toothpaste because when swallowed, it can cause teeth to stain. Teach your child to spit the toothpaste out. This may take time; many children cannot spit purposely and correctly until they are three or four. When you teach your child to spit out the tooth-

paste, emphasize when and where spitting is okay. Otherwise you may suddenly have a child who spits in the living room and wonders why Mom and Dad are angry. (After all, you told her to spit just the night before.) Also teach her to rinse her mouth out with water. Show her how to do it by having her imitate you. Explain that you are not swallowing the water. Tell her you are swishing it in your mouth and spitting it out in the sink.

Most dentists say the goal at this age is for your child to develop good teeth-brushing habits. Try to keep brushing fun. If your child doesn't want to brush, try to motivate her by saying something like, "Let's paint your teeth blue." Many children forget they are brushing their teeth if they can pretend to be painting their teeth with blue toothpaste (paint) using a toothbrush (paintbrush). If your child complains when you check and brush her teeth, approach the task with a sense of humor. Say, "Let's look in the mirror and see what you would look like if you had four arms. Why don't you wave your arms while I pretend that my arms are yours and brush your teeth." To further encourage the development of healthy teeth and gums, avoid sugary or sticky foods that cause tooth decay. Do not let your child sleep with a bottle. When a child drinks a bottle in bed, the liquid sets in her mouth for a prolonged period, coating the teeth. This can cause severe tooth decay. Sleeping with a bottle can also lead to choking and ear infections. If your child needs a bottle at bedtime, give it to her before she goes to bed.

Going to the Dentist

Your child's first trip to the dentist should be around three years of age. Before the first "real" visit, bring her along to the dentist when you go in for a regular checkup. Let her examine the different tools observe what the dentist does to you. If possible, bring along another adult to supervise her during the visit and to explain what is going on. Most two-year-olds will be full of questions and will ask "why?" many, many times. If the dentist is working on your mouth, you will be unable to answer her. Avoid taking your child along for your dental appointment if your gums bleed or if you wince and squirm. You want her observation visit to be a positive one. If your child likes the idea and if your dentist has a spare moment, let your child sit in the chair and "go for a ride." If she is willing, ask your child to open her mouth so the dentist can take a peek. This is enough for the first trip. A few weeks before her first official visit, read a book about going to the dentist or play dentist with your child and her dolls to prepare your child for a positive experience.

Nose Blowing

Since young children learn by watching and imitating, let your child watch you blow and wipe your nose. When she has a runny nose, let her see her nose in the mirror to increase her awareness. Give her a tissue and let her wipe her nose with it while she watches herself in the mirror. Teach your child to do the whole process: Get the tissue, blow and wipe her nose, and throw the tissue in the wastebasket. Do not encourage your child to blow her nose too hard; this could hurt her ears.

Washing in the Tub

When teaching your child to wash herself, it is important that you continue to implement the safety precautions you followed when she was younger. *Always test the water* before you allow your child to get into the water, and teach her to do the same. Always have a *nonskid* surface on the bottom of the tub and *NEVER* leave your child alone in the tub to wash herself. It takes only seconds and a very small amount of water for a child to slip and hurt herself or drown. If you forget something or if the phone rings, take your child out of the tub and bring her with you.

To encourage your child to wash herself, give her an extra washcloth so she can imitate you as you wash her. Help her put the soap on the washcloth, or let her use soapy hands to wash her body. Have your child wash the parts of her body that she can see and reach. You can then do the other parts and touch ups. Name and talk about her body parts as you wash them. Talk about genitals as naturally as you would any other body part. If your child doesn't like taking a bath, try to make it fun by playing more. You can give her an occasional bubble bath to make bath time more enjoyable. *But bubble baths may lead to urinary tract infections, so keep them to a minimum,* and make sure your child rinses off thoroughly after a bubble bath. If she likes taking a bath but doesn't like to wash up, try using a cloth puppet for the washcloth. Try playing games like "Simon Says." For example, say, "Simon says, 'Lift your arm in the air'" before you wash her arm. Most children have so much fun playing the game they forget they are being washed.

HOUSEHOLD

Development of Household Skills

One-Year-Olds

Once young children have mastered walking and running, they usually develop an interest in helping you with simple household tasks. For most children, this occurs between eighteen and twenty-four months of age. In the beginning, their helping makes household chores take a little longer. However, if you allow for the extra time and stay patient, the pride you will see in your child's face as she dusts the table with you will make it all worthwhile.

Two-year-Olds

By two years of age, most children can push and pull doors open and shut. Within another few months, most children can open and close doors, using the knob. If you don't have a deadbolt or chain on the door, *now is the time to install one.* Two-year-olds have been known to walk out the front doors to go outside and play without telling anyone. Between the ages of twenty-four and thirty months, most children learn to stay away from common dangers and they learn to handle fragile items carefully. By the age of three, many children can actually help perform very simple household tasks and can help put things away.

Three-year-Olds

Between three and four years of age, children become real helpers around the house. They can set the table with minimum help and can put their own things away without any help.

Facilitating Household Skills

Helping Around the House

Your child is becoming a little helper. She loves to help perform simple household tasks. Young children have fun helping, and they feel proud when they do adult-type activities. Let your child help you with simple jobs around the house. The jobs should be fun, *safe*, and fail-proof. Table 1 presents examples of excellent jobs for young children. Praise and applaud all the help your child gives. This makes her feel competent and worthwhile. It also does wonders for boosting her self-esteem.

Learning to Stay Away from Dangers

Although your one- or two-year-old may understand the danger associated with many things, her natural curiosity and lack of impulse control require *constant* adult supervision. The exception

---

TABLE 1
HOUSEHOLD TASKS FOR YOUNG CHILDREN

- Wipe the refrigerator or cabinets with a cloth.
- Wash the kitchen table or chairs with a damp sponge.
- Sweep the floor with a child-size broom.
- Vacuum the carpet with a child-size vacuum cleaner.
- Stir and pour at the counter, not at the hot stove, while you cook.
- Hand you clothes as you load them in the washer or dryer.
- Fold washcloths.
- Put clothes into drawers.
- Put groceries away.
- Set the table by putting napkins and silverware on the table. If you store the silverware in a low drawer, your child can get it out independently. Remember to keep all sharp knifes on the top shelf of a high cabinet.
- Water outdoor plants with a small watering can.
- Wash the bumpers of your car while you wash the rest of the car. If your child has a tricycle, let her wash it while you wash the car.
- Open the door to let a dog out or in.
- Fill a pet's bowl with food or water.

---

is when your child is playing in an area that is safety-proofed.

To teach your child to stay away from dangers, explain the consequences of common dangers and how to avoid them. Make these explanations whenever potentially dangerous situations occur during daily activities. For example, when you are cutting food with a sharp knife, say, "Knives are safe for Mommy to use to cut meat, but knives are very sharp. You could cut yourself with a knife, and that would hurt. Never play with or touch a knife." When crossing the street or taking a walk together, say to her, "You must always hold my hand when you cross the street. A car could hit you if the driver cannot see you, and that would hurt. I am bigger, so cars can see me." If your child goes near a dangerous object or situation, ask her to move away or physically move her from the danger. Firmly explain why you do not allow such behavior. If you think she already knows, ask her why she behaved as she did, and then elaborate on her answer as needed.

After one warning, tell her that if she does the behavior again, there will be a consequence. For instance, after you explain why she cannot walk in the street alone, tell her that if she does it again she will have to sit still in a certain spot for three minutes. When choosing your consequence, be sure it is something you are willing to do. If you are looking forward to going to the beach and your child runs into the street while you are loading the car, do not say that she will not go to the beach if she runs into the street again. Try to pair the consequence with the behavior. For example, if she touches a hot stove, she can't help you cook. After two warnings, if your child continues to go to a dangerous situation and if you cannot remove her from the temptation (running into the street, for example), give your child a significant consequence. For example, if your child runs off toward the street after you have given her two warnings, bring her into the house for one hour. Tell her firmly why you are bringing her inside and why running into the street is dangerous and is not allowed. Do not give in!

A PARENT'S STORY

I decided to go back to work when my daughter was three and a half years old. I got a wonderful job working as a bookkeeper for a small company in our town. The pay was good, and the hours were great. I was scheduled to work from seven o'clock to ten o'clock three nights a week. This was terrific because my husband would be able to take care of Jessica in the evenings, and we wouldn't have to pay for child-care. We planned to eat dinner together as a family at five-thirty, and I would leave for work at six-thirty. Dave would clean up the kitchen, play with Jessica for a little while, give her a bath, and put her to bed at eight-thirty. Our plan sounded perfect.

The first night, however, was a disaster for Dave. Jessica threw the biggest tantrum at bath time, screaming, "No! Mommy give me bath!" over and over again. Dave told me that she cried when he tried to wash her hair and that he finally gave up before he washed the rest of her. He asked me what I did with her at bath time—Dave usually went jogging while I bathed Jessica. This was the first time he had ever given her a bath. I told him I didn't do anything special; we played a little, I washed her, we played a little more, and she got out.

The next day Dave came home from work, grinning from ear to ear and carrying a bag full of bath time paraphernalia. He said he had spent the whole morning thinking about what he could do to make bath time more fun. During his lunch break he went to a local toy store and bought soap crayons, a spray bottle, a plastic doll, sponges shaped like the letters of the alphabet, and a cloth puppet. He said proudly that he and Jessica were going to draw on the tub with the soap crayons, rinse the tub with the squirt bottle, give the baby doll a bath, stick wet sponge letters to the tiles while they sang the "ABC Song," and that as a finale, the puppet was going to wash Jessica. I was amazed at how much thought he had put into this. As I drove to work, I crossed my fingers and hoped that Dave's evening would turn out as well as he hoped it would.

When I got home at ten fifteen, Dave was lying on the sofa watching a basketball game. As soon as he saw me, he muted the volume on the television and told me what a great night he and Jessica had spent.

"It was great!" he said. "When I showed her the bag of toys and told her it was bath time, she got so excited that she ran to the bathroom and undressed herself. We started off by drawing on the tub with the crayons. Then Jessica got the idea of drawing on me. She drew circles on my arms, and I made squares and stars on her legs. Then she asked me to draw circles on her arms so our arms would match. We had so much fun drawing with the soap crayons that she got washed without our realizing it. I didn't even need to use the puppet. After we played with the soap crayons, we squirted each other with the water bottle to rinse off. Jessica laughed pretty hard when she got my shirt wet. You know, she's got a good aim. Later, she asked if she might wash the baby doll's hair. So while she washed the doll's hair, I washed her hair. Before I knew it, it was eight forty, and Jessica was still in the tub. When I realized what time it was, I couldn't believe we had been playing for an hour. I told her it was time to get out. She asked if we could play with the ABCs. I let her play with them while the water went down the drain. I was really surprised at how many letters she knows. Then I put her pajamas on, read her a story, and kissed her good night. The best part: As I was leaving her room, she told me that I was a great daddy and asked if I would give her a bath again tomorrow night. You don't mind if I give her a bath tomorrow night, do you?"

SUMMARY

Between one and four years of age, children learn many eating, dressing, grooming, and household self-help skills. As a parent, you can foster the development of self-help skills by: (1) Understanding the order in which young children develop self-help skills; (2) Providing your child with opportunities to develop self-help skills; (3) Modeling self-help skills and providing appropriate feedback; (4) Allowing your child the time she needs to perform the self-help task.

Facilitating the development of eating skills includes: encouraging independence, teaching your child to use a cup and drink from a straw, weaning your child from breast- and bottle-feedings, and showing her how to pour. Facilitating dressing skills involves positioning yourself behind your child and describing what you are doing when you undress and dress her. It also involves undressing and dressing your child using the same sequence of movements that she needs to learn, and providing your child enough time to practice undressing and dressing. Facilitating grooming skills includes teaching your child to wash and dry her hands, brush her teeth, and wash in the tub. Facilitating the development of household self-help skills involves providing your child with simple jobs to do around the house and teaching your child to avoid dangers. When teaching your child self-help skills, always provide encouragement and praise. This will help boost her self-esteem and will foster the development of a positive self-image.

REFERENCES AND RECOMMENDED READINGS

For Children:

Kingsley, E. (1980). *I Can Do It Myself.* New York, NY: Western Publishing Company.

Roffey, M. (1989). *Me & My Friends Downstairs.* Martinez, CA: Discovery Toys.

Roffey, M. (1989). *Me & My Friends Upstairs.* Martinez, CA: Discovery Toys.

For Parents:

Furuno, S., O'Reilly, K., Hosaka, C., Inatsuka, T., Zeisloft- Falbey, B. & Allman, T. (1988). *HELP Checklist.* Palo Alto, CA: VORT Corporation.

Finnie, N. (1975). *Handling the Young Cerebral-Palsied Child at Home.* New York, NY: Dutton.

Johnson-Martin, N., Attermeier, S. & Hacker, B. (1990). *The Carolina Curriculum for Preschoolers with Special Needs.* Baltimore, MD: Paul H. Brookes Publishing Company.

Langone, J. (1988). Self-Help development. In Fallen, N. & Umansky, W. (Eds.) *Young Children with Special Needs.* Columbus, OH: Charles E. Merrill Company.

Leach, P. (1977). *Your Baby and Child.* New York, NY: Knopf.

Parks, S. (1988). *HELP...at Home.* Palo Alto, CA: VORT Corporation.

Wehman, P. & Goodwyn, R. (1978). Self-help skill development. In Fallen, N. & McGovern, J. (Eds.), *Young Children With Special Needs.* Columbus, OH: Charles E. Merrill Company.

Chapter 7
Nutrition and Mealtime Behavior

From week to week, even from meal to meal, the appetites and food preferences of young children change dramatically. At breakfast, for example, a two-year-old may devour a cheese omelet, two slices of toast, and a whole banana. At lunch, the same child may take a bite or two of his sandwich and declare he is "all done." At the next morning's breakfast, he may insist on having a slice of cheese on his toast; but that evening, he may ask you to wash the cheese off his broccoli because he doesn't like cheese. As a parent, you face two major challenges in regard to feeding your child. The first is knowing what and how much to feed him. The second is knowing how to cope with phases of picky eating, decreasing appetite, and misbehavior.

<u>Parent Perspective</u>
Most parents want their child to eat so he can grow and be healthy. Many parents feel that how well their child eats indicates how well they are doing as parents. Some parents don't know what types of food are best for young children, and they don't know how much food to offer. If your child is a picky eater, you may be concerned about his diet. You may wonder, for instance, if it's really okay that he doesn't eat vegetables or like milk. You may become frustrated and upset when your child doesn't eat something you prepare for him; later you may feel guilty that you forced him to eat it. If your child eats less now than he did as a toddler, you may wonder how he can be so active and eat so little. When he doesn't eat much at a meal, you may be tempted to coax him into eating more, even though you aren't sure it's a

good idea. If you are the parent of a child who throws food, kicks the table, screams, or stands on his chair, you probably want to stop the misbehavior, but you may not know the best way to do it. Most parents want mealtimes to be relaxed and pleasant. Many of them want to know how to achieve this while eating with a young child.

Child Perspective
Young children like to eat when they're hungry, and they don't like to eat when they're not. Sometimes young children eat at mealtimes to make Mommy and Daddy happy, as opposed to eating because they are hungry. Your child probably has food preferences and dislikes just as all adults do. But unlike adults, your child may change his preferences from week to week and even from day to day. Because your child doesn't know which foods are nutritious, he needs you to offer him nutritious choices. He also doesn't know which foods are dangerous, so he needs you to make sure that skin, bones, and seeds are removed from his food. Sometimes your child may feel that eating is too time-consuming, because he would rather play. While eating, he may throw his food or dump his drink on the floor because it's fun, or because he's full and doesn't know another way to tell you he is finished eating. He may also do this to get attention. It is important that you include him in conversations when he is behaving so he can learn that appropriate mealtime behavior gets attention.

SAFETY NOTE
Children are at highest risk for choking on food from birth until three years of age and are still at high risk until they are about four years of age. Choking can occur anywhere and anytime there is food. Avoid offering foods that can cause choking, or modify them to make them safer. Always supervise your child when he eats, and encourage him to sit in an upright position and to eat slowly. (See more on choking on page 121.)

NUTRITION
Eating a variety of healthy foods provides your child with the nutrients he needs to build a strong body. It also supplies him with the energy he needs to grow normally, play, learn, and stay healthy. Your child's diet should include foods that contain vitamins, minerals, protein, carbohydrates, fats, and water. Keeping track of your child's nutrient and caloric intake is almost impossible and is not necessary. Offering your child a variety of nutritious foods is the best way to supply the nutrients and calories he needs. As long as your child is growing normally both physically and developmentally, does not have certain medical conditions, and is not on a special diet, he will regulate what he eats to meet his energy needs. If your child is under or overweight, consult with your child's doctor or a registered dietitian for a special diet to meet his needs.

FOOD GUIDE

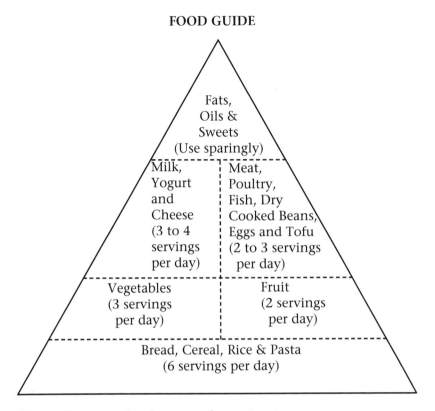

Bread, cereal, rice, and pasta

These foods are a major source of carbohydrates and B vitamins that provide your child with energy for growing and playing. These foods also contain fiber, iron, and zinc. Children need six servings each day. Examples of single servings include one half to three fourths of a slice of bread, half a cup of ready-to-eat cereal, and one-fourth to one-third cup of pasta. Offer your child whole grain choices for some of the servings from this group. Read the labels on whole grain breads, and look for those that list whole-wheat flour as the first ingredient. Wheat flour and unbleached wheat flour are not whole grain choices. Breads with part unbleached flour and part whole-wheat flour are nutritionally preferable to breads made solely with refined white flour. Whole grain choices contain more of some vitamins, minerals, and fiber than other grain products made from refined flour.

Vegetables

These foods are a primary source of vitamins A and C, and they contain other important vitamins and minerals as well. Your child needs vitamin A for normal growth, good vision, healthy skin, and

---

TABLE 1
BREAD, CEREAL, RICE, & PASTA

Whole grain choices:

barley	brown rice	bulgar
corn tortilla	oat bran	oatmeal
pumpernickel	rye bread	Ry-Krisp
wheat germ	whole-grain bread	whole-grain cereal
whole-grain wafers	whole-grain Melba toast	whole-wheat pasta

Enriched/fortified choices:

bagel	breadsticks	cereals
cornbread	English muffin	flour tortilla
rolls	matzo	Melba toast
noodles	pasta	rusks
white bread	white rice	zwieback

Other choices:

biscuits	graham crackers	oatmeal cookies
pretzels	rice cakes	un-enriched breads
un-enriched muffins		

---

tooth development. He also needs vitamin A for proper bone and tissue growth and repair. Vitamin C also helps build and strengthen bones and tissues. In addition, vitamin C builds blood, protects tissues, promotes healing, and increases resistance to infections. Vegetables also provide calcium, B vitamins, carbohydrates,

---

TABLE 2
VEGETABLES

High in Vitamins A & C:

broccoli[1]	Brussels sprouts[1]	cabbage[1]
kale	mustard greens	red and green sweet
spinach[1,2]	sweet potatoes	peppers[1]
Swiss chard	tomato	

High in Vitamin A:

asparagus	carrots[2]	collard greens
mixed vegetables[2]	peas	pumpkin[2]
sugar snap peas	turnip greens[2]	winter squash[2]

High in Vitamin C:

cauliflower[1]	rutabaga	potato (baked)
snow pea pods		

[1]Excellent source of vitamin C.
[2]Excellent source of vitamin A.

TABLE 3
FRUITS

High in Vitamins A & C:

| cantaloupe[1,2] | guava | mango[1,2] |
| nectarine | papaya[2] | |

High in Vitamin A:

apricot[2]	peaches	persimmon
plantain	plums (purple)	prunes
watermelon		

High in Vitamin C:

frozen fortified	gooseberries	grapefruit[1]
fruit juice bars	honeydew melon	lemon
kiwi	mandarin orange	orange[1]
strawberries[1]	tangerine	

[1]Excellent source of vitamin C.
[2]Excellent source of vitamin A.

fiber, iron, and other minerals. Children need three child-sized portions each day, one high in vitamin A and one high in vitamin C. One serving equals one-fourth to one-third cup of cooked vegetables, or one-half cup of vegetable juice. Try to offer your child a wide variety of vegetables, even though he may not want them. Offering the vegetables gives him the opportunity to try them when he wishes. Fresh and frozen vegetables are preferable to canned ones because they often contain less sugar and salt. Many children dislike mushy vegetables; serve your child vegetables that are lightly cooked. To make vegetables fun to eat, serve them with a low-fat dip. For a silly treat, arrange vegetables in the shape of a face. To increase your child's intake of vegetables, you may also add pureed or finely chopped vegetables to soups, eggs, casseroles and pasta sauces.

Fruits

These foods are a primary source of vitamins C and A. They also provide B vitamins, carbohydrates, fiber, iron, and other minerals. Children need two child-sized portions each day, one high in vitamin C and one high in vitamin A. One serving equals half an apple sliced into wedges, half a banana, one-fourth cup sliced fruit, or one-half cup fruit juice. Always peel or thoroughly wash fresh fruits to protect your child from pesticide residues. When buying frozen or canned fruits or juices, always read the label. A label that

reads "100 percent natural," for instance, does not always mean 100 percent fruit juice. Look for juices that contain 100 percent juice rather than water, artificial color and sugar. Choose fruits packed in water rather than in syrup.

Milk, yogurt, and cheese

These dairy products provide calcium, phosphorus, protein, carbohydrates, riboflavin, and vitamins A and D (if fortified). Your child needs calcium for building and maintaining bones, teeth, and muscles. Young children need from three to four servings of dairy products each day. One-serving examples include one-half to three-fourths cup of milk or yogurt, or three-fourths to one ounce cheese. Drinking three to four glasses containing from four to six ounces of milk is all your child needs to meet the recommended dietary allowances for calcium. Drinking more milk may fill your child up, leaving no room for other nutritious foods. Children under the age of two years should drink whole milk. Toddlers need

TABLE 4 DAIRY		
cheddar cheese	cottage cheese	milk
pudding	ricotta cheese	yogurt

the fat and cholesterol for proper brain and nervous system development. For children between two and four years of age, low fat milk is generally the best choice. If your child is underweight, his doctor or nutritionist may recommend for him to continue drinking whole milk. Give your child skim milk only if your child's doctor or nutritionist recommends it. If your child doesn't like milk and refuses to drink it, offer him yogurt, cheese and pudding as substitutes. You can also add powdered milk to casseroles to increase your child's intake of calcium.

Meat, poultry, fish, dry beans, eggs, and tofu

These foods provide protein that your child needs for proper growth. He also needs protein to build, repair, and replace tissues; to fight infection; and to regulate metabolism. These protein-rich foods also contain iron, B vitamins, phosphorus, and zinc. Children need two to three servings of protein-rich foods each day

TABLE 5		
PROTEIN		
Animal-origin:		
beef	chicken	eggs
fish	lamb	liver
pork	poultry-based or reduced-fat cold cuts and franks	turkey
Plant-origin:		
black-eyed peas	garbanzo beans	kidney beans
lentils	lima beans	split peas
tofu		

for a total of three to four ounces per day. A serving is one to two ounces of lean meat, poultry, or fish. One egg or one-fourth to one-half cup cooked, dried beans counts as one serving. Your child will probably like his meats and eggs moist rather than dry and hard. If your child has a hard time chewing meat, prepare meals with ground meat, or dice his meat for him.

Fats, oils, and sweets

Before the age of two, children should not have their dietary fat restricted. Their rapid growth requires a higher percentage of calories from fat, and they need the fat for proper mental and nervous system development. If your child is under two years of age, you can spread some butter or margarine on his pancakes and offer him regular yogurt instead of low fat yogurt. After he reaches two years of age, set the stage for healthy eating by offering your child foods containing fats and oils sparingly. Do this by limiting fried foods, trimming fat from meat, and selecting only lower fat meats. To further reduce your child's intake of fat, teach him to put only small amounts of margarine, salad dressing, and sauce on his food. Offering him fruits, vegetables, or dairy products that are low in fat and cholesterol for snacks instead of chips or sweets will also help. Cookies, cakes, and candy bars tend to be high in fat and sugar, and easily fill a young child's small stomach to capacity, not leaving room for more nutritious foods.

PICKY EATERS

Most toddlers and preschoolers go through phases of picky eating. One day your child may love spaghetti, and the next he may proclaim that he hates spaghetti sauce. It is important to honor your child's food preferences as you would another adult's. If a

TABLE 6
FATS, OILS, & SWEETS

Fats and oils to use in moderation:

margarine	mayonnaise	Neufchatel cheese
salad dressing	vegetable oil	

Fats and oils to use sparingly:

butter	cream cheese	fried foods
gravy	hydrogenated shortening	ice cream
lard	sour cream	whipped cream

Sweets to eat in moderation:

angel food cake	fruit or grain cookies	fruit sorbets
frozen fruit bars	frozen fudge bars	frozen pudding pops
jam	molasses	
sponge cake	sweetened fortified cereals	

Sweets to eat sparingly:

brown sugar	cake	candy
corn syrup	doughnuts	gelatin
honey	maple syrup	pastries
popsickles	rich cookies	sugar

friend told you that she didn't like corn, as you offered her an ear of corn-on-the-cob, you wouldn't tell her how good corn tastes or try to force her to eat some. Instead, you would probably offer her another food item from the table. You should do the same with your child. When preparing meals, always try to include one food that you know your child likes. Put a small amount of each food that you prepare on his plate. If he doesn't want to eat a particular food, don't make an issue of it. Tell him that he can eat the foods he likes. If you give him rice, chicken, peas, and applesauce for dinner, and he eats all the applesauce and asks for more, give him more applesauce without making him eat everything else on his plate. However, don't get into the habit of becoming your child's personal short-order cook. If you keep his preferences in mind when you prepare the meal, as you would for another adult, that's enough.

Some children refuse to eat certain groups of food. If your child will not eat any vegetables, for example, you may need to find nutritious substitutes to make sure he gets all the necessary nutrients. In this case, substitute fruits for the vegetables. However, if your child doesn't like to drink milk and refuses to eat all fruits, substitute cheese and yogurt for the milk, and offer vegetables and fruit juices for the fruits. On the other hand, if your child doesn't like meat, you can offer poultry, fish, eggs, dried beans, and tofu as protein substitutes. Use the information in Tables 1-5 to help find substitutes, according to your child's likes and dislikes. Prepare these substitutes as part of the family meal, not as a separate, special meal for your child.

In addition to finding nutritious substitutes, you can increase the appeal of foods by eating a variety of nutritious foods yourself, letting your child help you prepare the meals, and by making meals fun to eat. The older child can help you by pouring, stirring, and spreading. Simply watching is a lot of fun for many one-year-olds.

DAILY MENU IDEAS FOR PICKY EATERS[1]

Child who loves milk but refuses to eat vegetables:
Breakfast - 1/3 cup cereal with milk and 1/2 cup orange juice.
Snack - One small sausage biscuit cut into bite-size pieces, and six
     ounces milk.
Lunch - 1/2 chicken salad sandwich, two carrot sticks (cooked, then
     cooled), 1/4 cup cantaloupe, and six ounces milk.
Snack - One slice of cornbread and 1/2 cup tomato juice.
Dinner - 1/3 cup spaghetti and meat sauce, 1/2 slice garlic bread, and
     six ounces milk.

Child who dislikes milk and all fruits:
Breakfast - One pancake topped with 1/2 cup yogurt, one sausage link
     cut in half, then sliced, and 1/2 cup orange juice.
Snack - One ounce ricotta cheese, 1/2 oat bran muffin, and 1/2 cup
     vegetable juice.
Lunch - 1/3 cup macaroni and cheese, 1/3 cup spinach, one small
     whole-wheat roll, and 1/2 cup soda juice (1/2 cup salt-free seltzer
     water with two tablespoons cranberry juice).
Snack - Four small cheese strips on four whole wheat low-salt crackers
     and 1/2 cup apple juice.
Dinner - Two ounces of lean beef, 1/3 cup of split peas, 1/4 cup rice,
     and 1/2 cup water with one teaspoon orange or lemon juice.

Child who doesn't like meat:
Breakfast - One slice of whole-wheat toast with one tablespoon tofu on
     top, 1/4 cup strawberries, and six ounces milk.
Snack - One slice of banana bread and 1/2 cup orange juice.
Lunch - 1/2 tuna salad sandwich, one ounce cottage cheese, and 1/2
     cup tomato juice.
Snack - One small corn tortilla with one ounce melted cheddar cheese
     and 1/2 cup apple juice.
Dinner - One slice of quiche, 1/3 cup broccoli, one dinner roll, and six
     ounces of milk

[1]All vegetables listed are cooked. All fruits listed are peeled and pitted.
     A small amount of margarine can be added to breads and vegeta-
     bles.

You can make meals fun by presenting foods in different shapes. For example, you might cut sandwiches into squares, rectangles, and triangles. Or make mouse pancakes with one large and two small circles of batter; for added fun, decorate the face with small pieces of fruit. To liven up fruits and vegetables, present them in the shapes of animals, boats, and characters.

If your child's diet concerns you, reflect over the past three or four days, and think about all the foods that he has eaten. Most children eat a variety of foods over the course of several days. As long as your child is growing normally and eating a variety of nutritious foods, he is getting adequate nutrients. If your child is excluding a whole food group, learn good nutritional substitutes for the foods your child avoids or dislikes. You may also wish to discuss the option of giving your child a vitamin-mineral supplement with your child's doctor. If your doctor thinks your

---

RABBITS, BOATS & CLOWNS[1]

To make a rabbit:
1. Place a canned pear half on a plate as the body.
2. Insert two carrot sticks into the pear half for the ears.
3. Cut a grape into quarters and insert two pieces for the eyes.
4. Add a small mound of cottage or ricotta cheese for the tail.

To make a boat:
1. Peel a cucumber and cut it in half lengthwise.
2. Hollow out the inside by removing the seeds.
3. Fill the "boat" with tuna salad.
4. Place two carrot sticks in the tuna salad as oars.

To make a clown:
1. Put a mound of cottage cheese on a plate.
2. Arrange peas on the cottage cheese to make the face.
3. Place curly carrot strips around the top portion of the cottage cheese for the hair.
4. Add two pieces of broccoli for the bow tie.

[1]Remember to cook all vegetables until soft before serving them. Serve vegetables warm on a cold day or refrigerate them after they are cooked and serve them cool on a hot day. Remember to cut all food items into small pieces or thin slices before your child eats them.

child needs a supplement, ask the doctor to recommend one that is right for your child's age. Because several of the vitamins can reach toxic level if given in large amounts, the supplement should not exceed 100 percent RDA(Recommended Daily Allowance) for your child's age. Stay away from megadoses of single vitamins, such as vitamin C. Giving your child too many vitamins is wasteful at best and harmful at worst.

CHOKING

Children are at highest risk for choking on food from birth until three years of age and are at high risk until they are about four years of age. Choking can occur anywhere and anytime there is food. Avoid offering foods that can cause choking, or modify them to make them safer. Always supervise your child when he eats and encourage him to sit in an upright position and to eat slowly.

Some foods are easier than others to choke on. A food's potential to cause choking is often related to its size, shape, and/or consistency.

Size

Tiny pieces of food, especially those less than half an inch in diameter, most frequently cause choking by getting into the airway when a child tries to swallow food before properly chewing it. Avoid offering your child nuts and seeds, unless you finely grind or chop them. Remove all pits and seeds from fruits that you offer your child. Also, take out all bones from fish, chicken, and meat. Large pieces of food may be harder to chew and are more likely to block the airway if inhaled. Remember to cut your child's food into small pieces or thin slices that he can easily chew.

Shape

Round foods can cause choking, because they are more likely to block the airway completely than other shapes. Cut round foods, such as hot-dogs and carrots, into short strips rather than round pieces. Cut grapes into quarters. Don't offer popcorn and round candies such as gumdrops or sourballs.

Consistency

Foods that are sticky or tough may be hard to remove from the airway. Don't serve your child peanut butter until he is one year old, and then spread it very thinly. Cook tough foods, such as meats and vegetables, until they are soft enough to pierce with a fork. Avoid offering your child raisins or other dried fruit and candy such as caramel. Foods that are firm, smooth, or slick may slip down a child's throat and cause choking. Don't offer your child large pieces of fruit with skin or raw peas. Consistency is another reason for avoiding grapes, peanuts, hard candy, and products like hot-dogs, unless you follow the precautions mentioned above. Foods that are dry or hard may be difficult to chew and easy to choke on. Avoid offering your child popcorn, cookies, nuts, small pieces of raw carrot, seeds, and pieces of pretzels or potato chips for this reason.

Your child may be choking if he coughs, makes high-pitched noises, cannot speak or cry, and/or has trouble breathing. If you think your child is choking, call the rescue squad right away. Knowing what to do when a child chokes could save your child's life. Contact your local chapter of the American Heart Association, American Lung Association, or American Red Cross for pamphlets and classes on preventing and treating choking. The American Red Cross Cardiopulmonary Resuscitation (CPR) course for infants and children includes a lesson on the emergency techniques for choking.

APPETITE

By one year of age, most children have tripled their birth weight and are half again their length. Between one and four years of age, growth slows. Children gain an average of five to six pounds each year during this time. Between one and two years of age, children grow about five inches. They will continue to grow about two inches a year between two and four years of age. As a result of slower growth, you may notice a decrease in your child's appetite. The decrease in appetite may seem contradictory because his activity level increases. Playing, however, requires less calories than growing. If your child's appetite is very small, offer him only the highest quality foods, and watch his liquid intake. If he is drinking too much apple juice or milk, there may not be enough room for food. When you offer food to a child with a small appetite, give him half the amount you think he can eat. When he eats all his food, praise him for eating like a big boy, and offer him some more.

You probably plan your meals to provide your child with a healthy, well-balanced, and tasty diet. You may, however, find that your child's appetite varies from day to day and from meal to meal. Trust your child's judgment about quantity—don't force him to eat food he doesn't want after he indicates that he is finished. Remember that your own appetite varies, depending on your activity level and your desire for the food offered. Your child should determine whether or not to eat and if so, how much to eat—You have no real control over this. You do, however, have control over what foods to offer and when and where your child eats. If you offer him food all day long, even in small amounts, he doesn't have the chance to get hungry, and may find meals uninteresting.

Feed your child primarily at mealtimes with the addition of a small mid-morning and mid-afternoon snack. Such a pattern is likely to produce a better appetite at mealtime. Some children, however, need more than two snacks a day. For instance, a child who eats an early dinner may also need a snack before bedtime. Determine the frequency of snacks based on your child's needs. To assure the best mealtime appetite possible, don't offer him snacks within two hours of mealtime. This includes caloric beverages such as juice and milk. You can, however, offer your child a glass of water to drink while you finish preparing the meal. If your child is consistently hungry before it is time to eat a meal, consider scheduling mealtime a little earlier or offering the snack prior to the meal a little later. For instance, if dinner is at 6:30, and your child almost always gets hungry by 5:30, either change his dinner time to 5:30, or move his 2:30 snack to 3:30.

If your child won't eat, don't force, coax, or make an issue of eating. Doing this usually makes matters worse. A child can sense when mealtime is a battleground, and he may turn eating into a power game. This, in turn, can lead to real feeding problems. As a parent, you need to send the message that mealtime is pleasant. For at least one meal a day, you should try to eat the entire meal with your child instead of bouncing around the kitchen. Dinner is the meal that most families eat together. In some families, however, parents return home from work too late to eat dinner with their child. In such situations, children often eat dinner before their parents eat. If your child eats early but is not in bed when you eat dinner, be sure to acknowledge your child and talk with him while you eat. You might offer him some fruit to eat as dessert while you eat. Doing this will allow him to take part in a family meal. Eating dinner as a family is desirable, but it is not always practical. If you cannot eat dinners together, consider substituting or alternating with breakfast.

HANDLING MISBEHAVIOR AT MEALTIME

At family mealtimes, remember that young children need attention and need to be included in conversations. As long as your child eats his meal and behaves, it is easy for you to engage in a conversation with another adult and forget to pay attention to him.

However, if he throws his food, bangs on the table, or screams, he gets a lot of attention. As a parent, you need to pay attention to good behavior, not just misbehavior. Children are great at learning that certain behaviors bring immediate attention. If negative behaviors attract more attention than eating and behaving well, you are likely to experience more misbehavior then good behavior at mealtime. An easy way to include your child in a conversation with another adult is to prompt your child to ask the adult occasional questions. For instance, prompt your child to ask, "How was work today?" of the other adult. Having your child ask questions allows you to engage in a conversation with another person while, at the same time, involving your child. It also teaches your child how to engage in mealtime conversation.

If your child misbehaves at mealtime, ask yourself the following four questions to help you determine the cause of the problem and possible solutions. First, ask yourself, "What happens before the misbehavior?" When answering this question, you may discover something that happens before the misbehavior is a contributing factor. Pinpointing such a factor often makes finding a solution straightforward. Perhaps your child is just learning to feed himself and overstuffs his mouth when you offer him a plateful of food. If this is the case, try limiting the amount of food that you offer him. Place two or three pieces of food on his plate at a time; when he finishes, add two or three more. Maybe he dumps his plate on the floor when he has finished eating, because he needs to learn a better way to tell you he is full.

The next two questions to ask are "What do I do after the misbehavior?" and "What do I do to encourage appropriate behavior?" Sometimes the attention that children receive after the misbehavior is what encourages the behavior to continue. If you talk to your child more frequently when he kicks the table or screams than

when he eats, you may inadvertently encourage the kicking and screaming. Instead, encourage appropriate behavior by talking with your child when he eats and behaves. Discourage the kicking and screaming by ignoring it. If he says or does things that make you laugh while you are ignoring his behavior, turn away so he cannot see you laugh. As soon as he stops kicking and screaming, provide verbal praise. Say something such as "I like the way your feet are still." Ignoring misbehavior and reinforcing appropriate behaviors is a powerful and effective way of improving mealtime behavior.

However, this technique is not the best choice when the misbehavior involves throwing food. If you ignore food throwing, it will eventually stop, but you will be left with a big mess to clean up. Instead, briefly remove your child's food by putting his plate on the other side of the table. Wait one minute for every year that your child is old, and then return his plate of food. When you remove his plate, explain very briefly that he may not throw food. Tell him to sit quietly and that you will give him his food back in a few minutes. Continue to eat your food during this time; keep talking with him to a minimum. Otherwise, he may continue to throw food to get attention. If your child's behavior becomes worse after you remove his food—for example, he bangs on the table—turn his chair away from the table. Be sure to return the same plate of food to your child. If he throws every piece of food off his plate, refill it with the same or similar foods, not cookies.

If you find yourself repeatedly removing your child's plate or turning his chair around, give him a warning and then end his mealtime. Say, for example, "If you throw your food again, dinner will be all done. You will leave the table and not eat again until snack time." Although it will be difficult, follow through with this. Your child may complain that he is hungry 20 minutes after he leaves the table. If he does, tell him he may eat as much as he wants at snack time. Then keep reminding yourself that he won't starve while he waits another hour for snack time. After you do this two or three times, your child will realize you mean business, and the food throwing or other inappropriate behavior will cease.

Finally, you need to ask yourself, "If my child doesn't eat at mealtime, when and where do I give him food again and what food do I offer?" Mealtime is often the place where toddlers and preschoolers make their first declarations of independence by refusing to eat. When your child doesn't eat at mealtime, avoid allowing him to eat cookies five minutes later while he watches television. If he gets hungry, give him a snack at regularly scheduled snack times, but offer healthy foods, such as fruits and vegetables. Do not save and give him leftover food from his plate. The enzymes from saliva break down food and allow bacteria to set in. These bacteria are

more difficult for young children to handle than for older children or adults. However, you can offer a chicken leg or the other half of a sandwich as a snack as long as your child or another person hadn't started to eat it.

Eating as a family becomes easier as your child grows older. However, some of the misbehaviors that occurred when you first introduced your child to table foods may reemerge from time to time. It is not uncommon for misbehaviors to surface when-

ever your child experiences a change in his life. Big changes include a move to a new home, the birth of a new baby, and the separation of parents. Smaller changes include the transition from a highchair to a booster seat or from a booster seat to a chair. When your child experiences a change, he may misbehave to test the boundaries of the new situation. He may also misbehave to get needed attention.

A PARENT'S STORY

I get off work at five-thirty in the evening, pick my son up from my in-laws at five forty-five, and am home with Mark by six-fifteen. My husband doesn't get home from work until seven o'clock, so I feed Mark his dinner as soon as we get home. I give him his dinner in the neat little plates that are divided into four sections. I like the sections because they help me remember to offer Mark a variety of foods. Mark likes the plates because the sections prohibit one food from touching another food; he has a real thing about his foods getting mixed. The plates are also nice because the sections' sides make it easier for Mark to scoop up his food with a spoon.

While Mark eats his dinner, I put our breakfast dishes into the dishwasher and sort through the mail. Three or four nights of the week, Mark tries to climb out of his high-chair, or he throws his food on the floor. When he stands up in his highchair and tries to climb out, I stop what I'm doing and go to him. I tell him to sit down because he might fall and get hurt. When he throws his food, I stop what I'm doing, go to him, and say something like, "Uh oh, your food is on the floor." Then I give him more food. About a week ago, I got so mad at Mark for standing up in his highchair and throwing his food that I screamed at him. I felt so bad afterward. But when he stood up and threw his spaghetti for the third time, I couldn't take it anymore.

That evening my husband and I talked about Mark's dinner time behavior. The standing and food throwing surprised my husband because Mark is so good when he eats with us in the morning and on the weekends. Suddenly, I realized what was going on. Mark was probably throwing his food to get my attention. He never tried to climb out or threw his food on the days when we didn't get mail. On those days I always sat with him while he ate.

For the next week I sat with Mark while he ate his dinner. I also put the highchair safety belt around him and fastened it. Since then, Mark's behavior has been wonderful—no climbing and no food throwing. I have also enjoyed the time we have spent together. It has been nice to relax and spend uninterrupted time with Mark when I come home. Some evenings I have even eaten my dinner salad with Mark and later eaten the rest of my dinner with my husband.

SUMMARY

A well-balanced diet is important for the growth and development of your child. His diet should include a variety of nutritious foods. If your child is a picky eater, honor his food preferences, and find nutritious substitutes for the foods he doesn't like. You can also increase the appeal of foods by eating a variety of nutritious foods yourself, letting your child help you prepare meals, and by making meals fun to eat. As your child's appetite varies, remember to let him decide whether or not to eat and how much to eat. As a parent, you decide when and where he eats and what foods to offer. If your child is on a special diet, including a vegetarian or diabetic diet, consult with your family doctor or a registered dietitian to make sure his diet is adequate.

At family mealtimes, pay attention to your child and include him in conversations. If your child misbehaves at mealtime, try to determine the cause of the problem and find an appropriate solution. Ignoring misbehavior while verbally praising appropriate behavior often serves as a powerful and effective way of improving mealtime behavior.

Mealtime can be a source of tension or of closeness. Determine what is and what is not acceptable to you. Set firm but flexible rules, and stick to them—take control. Be sure to reinforce appropriate behavior, and periodically include your child in conversation to encourage appropriate behavior.

REFERENCES & RECOMMENDED READINGS

American Red Cross (1984). What should I feed my child? Brochure in *Better Eating for Better Health* packet. Washington, DC: American Red Cross.

Baker, S. and Henry, R. (1987). *Parents' Guide to Nutrition: Healthy Eating From Birth Through Adolescence*. Reading, MA: Addison-Wesley Publishing Co., Inc.

Committee on Nutrition, American Academy of Pediatrics (1985). *Pediatric Nutrition Handbook*. Elk Grove Village, IL: American Academy of Pediatrics.

Food and Nutrition Service, Nutrition and Technical Services Division (1988). *Nutrition Update: Preventing Young Children From Choking on Food*. Beltsville, MD: Food and Nutrition Information Center.

Heslin, J. (1991, Summer). How to feed your picky eater. *American Baby's Healthy Kids, Birth - 3*, pp 18-24.

Hess, M., Hunt, A. and Stone, B. (1991). *A Healthy Head Start: A Worry-Free Guide to Feeding Young Children*. New York, NY: Henry Holt & Co.

Livingston, K. (1990, September). War and peas. *Parenting*, pp 35-36.

Reinisch, N. and Salmen, P. (1990, September). Food for tot. *Parenting*, pp 78-81.

Satter, E. (1987). *How To Get Your Kid To Eat...But Not Too Much*. Palo Alto, CA: Bull Publishing Co.

Satter, E. (1986). *Child of Mine: Feeding with Love and Good Sense*. Palo Alto, CA: Bull Publishing Co.

Sheehan, A. (1989, November/December). Why kids shouldn't always clean their plates. *Child*, pp. 54-56.

Shelov, S. & Hannemann, R. (1991). *The American Academy of Pediatrics Caring For Your Baby and Young Child: Birth to Age Five*. New York, NY: Bantam Books.

Subcommittee on the Tenth Edition of The RDAs (1989). *Recommended Dietary Allowances, 10th Edition*. Washington, DC: National Academy Press.

U.S. Department of Health and Human Services (1991). *Report of the Expert Panel on Blood Cholesterol Levels in Children and Adolescents*. NIH Publication No. 91-2732.

Chapter 8
Guiding Your Child's Behaviors

All parents want their children to behave. However, most young children don't know intrinsically what is safe and what is dangerous, what is socially acceptable and what is not. Helping your child behave involves setting limits that teach your child to avoid danger and to attain socially acceptable behaviors. It also involves guiding your child's behaviors by using "behavior management" techniques to establish and enforce these limits. You can use behavior management to teach, increase, and maintain good behaviors. You can also use behavior management to stop bad behaviors.

Parent Perspective
You want your child to behave. However, you may feel confused about when and how to help your child behave. You wonder if you need more limits or if you have too many. Some days you feel that all you say is "no" or "don't." Other days you feel very proud of your child's behavior. When your child misbehaves, you sometimes become frustrated and angry. At other times you stay in perfect control. You want to do everything possible to help your child learn to avoid danger and to behave in a way that is socially acceptable.

Child Perspective
Young children don't always know what is safe and what is danger-
ous, what is socially acceptable and what is not. Your child runs into
the street to chase her ball without thinking about the car 20 yards

away. She feels confused when you tell her not to go into the street—In her mind she had to go because her ball was there. Your child may take her clothes off and run around the house in the nude, not realizing that she should wear clothes when you have company. When you try to put her clothes back on, she runs away. This is her way of trying to get what she wants. Your child needs you to set consistent and clear limits so she can learn to avoid danger and to act in a socially acceptable way. However, she will test these limits to exert her independence and to see if the rules change. Your child needs you to teach her to follow limits by positively reinforcing appropriate behaviors and by discouraging undesirable behaviors.

SETTING LIMITS

Children need well-defined and consistent limits. Limits help your child learn to avoid danger and to attain socially acceptable behaviors. Limits also put a sense of organization into your child's life, giving her clear boundaries regarding what is and what is not acceptable behavior. Good limits are reasonable and enforceable. When setting limits, consider your child's developmental level, temperament and style. Also, think about what is really important to you. Ask yourself the following questions:

- What limits must I set for my child's safety?
- What limits must I set to teach my child socially appropriate behaviors?
- What limits must I set to facilitate good sleeping, eating, and toileting habits?
- What behaviors can I cope with?
- What behaviors bother me?
- What limits do I need?

Ask your spouse or other adults living in your home to answer the above questions and compare your answers. Then together, **establish a set of limits.** Do this together, so rules regarding limits are consistent. This is important. If the rules between you and your spouse or other adults living in your home are not similar, you will

confuse your child. Once your child has a clear understanding of which rules go with which person, she will learn to go to the person whose rules she likes. Consider, for example, a family in which Mommy doesn't allow snacks right before dinner but

Grandma does. At first this will confuse the child, and she will not know when to ask for snacks. She will probably continue to ask for snacks before dinner because half the time she gets a snack and half the time she doesn't. Within a short period of time, she will learn that Mommy always says "no" and Grandma always says "yes." Knowing what she wants and who to get it from, she will simply go to Grandma.

Minimize the number of limits you set. If there are too many limits, you will have a lot of no's and don'ts. Constant no's and don'ts lead to a negative atmosphere that will frustrate both you and your child. If you find yourself saying "no" or "don't" a lot, check your expectations and the environment. Determine whether you are expecting too much from your child. It is not realistic, for instance, to expect a one-year-old to eat with a spoon instead of her fingers to keep her hands from getting messy. Determine ways to restructure your home so the environment facilitates appropriate behavior. For example, you *should* add child-proof latches to cabinets to prevent your child's access to breakables, poisons, sharp objects such as scissors and knives, and art supplies like glue and paint. If you are the parent of a three-year-old Houdini, rearranging your cabinets to put these items up high may be necessary in addition to having latches. Once limits are developmentally appropriate and the environment doesn't invite misbehavior, the number of no's and don'ts in your home should decrease.

Use substitutions to enforce limits whenever possible. Tell your child what she can do instead of just what she can't do, and briefly explain why. "Couches are not for jumping, but you can jump off your step stool. You may jump off your step stool because it's low. The couch is too high, and you might hurt yourself if you jump off it." When appropriate, add a touch of humor, for example: "Let's go jump off your step stool like a bird. Can you flap your wings like a bird?" Whenever you can, use distraction to reroute your child's behavior. For instance, if your child jumps off a friend's couch, redirect your child's energy by asking her to jump like a bunny in the kitchen and by giving her a book about rabbits to read.

State the rules as positively as possible, but if something is not allowed, say so. While playing outside with his three-year-old daughter, one dad noticed that she was throwing sand out of the sandbox. He said, "Put the sand in the bucket." She obeyed, but then went back to throwing sand out of the sandbox. He suggested, "Make a turtle with the sand mold." She did it, and again went back to throwing sand. He asked her, "Can you make Daddy a cake out of the sand?" She made him a beautiful cake with a stick candle, sang "Happy Birthday" to him, and then dumped the sand cake on the ground. Frustrated, Dad said "Why do you keep throwing the sand out of the sandbox? You never throw sand when you play with Mommy." His daughter looked at him and replied, "Mommy said no throwing sand out of the sandbox. You didn't tell me not to throw sand. You said to make a cake, and I did."

Give your child a five-minute warning before changing from one activity to another. This is very important. Picture yourself at work, typing on a keyboard. Your boss walks in and tells you it's time for a meeting. If she were to say, "Come on! It's time to go. We're going to be late," without allowing you to save what you were working on before you leave, you would be angry. You would prefer for her to give you five minutes to wrap things up; then you

would go willingly. Give your child five minutes to bring her activity to a stopping point. Don't always require her to clean up if she's doing artwork or constructive play. "Five more minutes until lunch time. You may leave your blocks out and finish building your house after we eat." Use a timer to tick off the minutes and to prevent arguments. Many children will come muttering something like, "Stupid timer," but they won't argue with you.

Avoid asking questions if options don't exist. Try not to ask, "Do you want to eat lunch now?" as you put your child's plate of food on the table. She may say no. You will be inviting a small battle. If it is time for lunch, simply say, "It's time for lunch now," after, of course, you have given a five-minute warning. If there are options, give your child a choice. This allows her to exert some independence and gives her some control over the situation. Examples include: "Do you want apple or banana slices with your lunch?" "It's time to cross the street; do you want to walk and hold my hand, or should I carry you?" or "Do you want to wear the red shirt or the blue shirt with these shorts?".

Motivate your child to move to the next activity whenever possible. Young children have difficulty making the transition between activities and places. You can ease these transitions by describing something positive about the next activity or place. You might say, "Let's go home and water your new plant," or "Let's go see what Pooh kitty is up to," instead of "Let's go home." **Have your child verbalize the change as she experiences it.** Encouraging a one-year-old to say something as simple as "'Bye, slides" as she leaves a playground will help her with closure. A two- or three-year-old can elaborate: "'Bye, slides. I going to see Pooh kitty. I coming back another day."

Allow your child the time she needs to go at her own pace. Young children are very inquisitive about the world. Walking from the park to a bus stop can be an adventure with many stops along the way. She may walk a little, stop to pick up a stick, poke a hole or two in the dirt with the stick, walk a few steps with the stick, stop to drum on a fire hydrant with the stick, walk a little, stop to watch an ant, walk a little, stop to watch a plane fly over, walk a little, realize that she has lost her stick and stop to search for another one, walk a little more, and finally get to the bus stop just one block from the park. By yourself, you could walk the 60 feet from the park to the bus stop in a minute; with your child, it probably takes five minutes. As a parent, you can anxiously and impatiently hurry your child along and reach the bus stop in three minutes, or you can go at her pace, enjoy the explorations she makes along the way, and get there in five minutes. Whenever possible, add an extra ten minutes to your time schedule to accommodate your child's pace. This will create a more positive and relaxed atmosphere.

Let your child do as much for herself as possible. Between one and four years of age, children assert their independence by wanting to do things themselves. If you don't allow her to put on her shoes by herself, she may throw her shoes, run away when you try to put her shoes on, or have a temper tantrum. Adding an extra ten minutes to the dressing schedule and letting her put on her own shoes will decrease conflicts and result in more appropriate behaviors. Give verbal or physical guidance to your child if she needs help. To increase her self-confidence, let her do one or more steps independently, even though she can't complete the whole task by herself.

Praise your child when she follows limits. Praise is one of the best ways to encourage your child to follow limits. If your child walks into the living room with a glass of cranberry juice, then immediately turns around and walks back to the kitchen, saying, "Silly me, I forgot 'no drinking' in living room...I gotta drink in here," praise her. Say something like, "Way to go! You remembered to keep your drink in the kitchen."

TABLE 1
GUIDELINES FOR SETTING LIMITS

- Establish a set of well-defined and consistent limits.
- Minimize the number of limits you set.
- Use substitution, humor, and distraction.
- State rules as positively as possible, but if something is not allowed, say so.
- Give a five-minute warning.
- Avoid asking questions if options don't exist.
- Motivate your child to the next activity.
- Have your child verbalize the change as she experiences it.
- Allow your child the time she needs to go at her pace.
- Let your child do as much as possible by herself.
- Praise your child when she follows limits.

Young children forget easily and need many repetitions. Your child may follow a rule one day and the next day not remember the rule exists. Young children also break rules in order to test their limits. Your child may climb on the kitchen table three times before she realizes that you mean business and that climbing on the table is not allowed. Use the behavior management techniques described below to establish and enforce limits.

BEHAVIOR MANAGEMENT

Encouraging Good Behaviors

All parents want their children to behave well. Your role as a parent is to encourage good behaviors. This involves teaching your child new behaviors, increasing some behaviors, and maintaining other behaviors. For example, you may want to teach your child to play outside without running into the street, increase the number of times she comes right away when you call her, and maintain her excellent bath time behavior. You can use positive reinforcement to accomplish all of this.

Positive reinforcement is not a bribe. The dictionary defines a bribe as something given or promised as an inducement to do something bad or illegal. Bribery is a misuse of reinforcement.

Positive Reinforcement

To use positive reinforcement, you provide a desirable consequence following the behavior you wish to develop, increase, or maintain. For instance, if your child puts her toys in the toy box (behavior to increase), clap your hands and smile while telling her that she is a big helper (desirable consequence). Positive reinforcement should always be the first method you use when you are trying to encourage good behaviors.

Positive reinforcers may be social (clapping, for example), tangible (a sticker, for example), loving (a kiss, for example), or edible (candy, for example). It is best to use social or tangible reinforcers when you are trying to encourage good behaviors. Love and food are *inappropriate* reinforcers. Your child should always feel that you love her and that you will feed her. Saying, "I love you when you listen to me," can make a child think you don't love her at other times. A statement like, "It makes me happy when you listen to me," is a better choice. You should not use edibles as reinforcers for two reasons. First, your child should always know you will feed her. Withholding one food until your child performs a behavior may cause her to worry that you will withhold other foods. If you say to your child, "You may have a cookie if you go 'peepee' in the potty," your child may worry that she won't get anything to eat if she can't fulfill your request. Second, providing candy, for instance, when your child does a certain desirable behavior may indeed encourage that behavior, but it may also decrease your child's appetite for her next meal. This may lead to poor mealtime behavior. As a result, using food as a reward can cause eating problems.

TABLE 2
POSITIVE REINFORCERS

SOCIAL
Expressions: smiling, winking, clapping
Proximity: sitting next to your child, standing near your child, holding your child on your lap
Contact: hugging, holding hands, giving a high five
Privileges: getting to go somewhere, watching a video, blowing bubbles
Comments: "I like the way you're sitting." "Thank-you for coming so fast when I called you." "Hip, hip, hooray! Eric's underwear is dry!"

TANGIBLE
Hand stamps, stickers, toys

To keep reinforcers desirable, vary the reinforcers you use. One mom frequently used the phrase, "Good job! You're being such a big girl," when her daughter behaved. After hearing this phrase one too many times, her three-year-old replied, "Good job! Such a big girl! Such a big girl! Is that all you are ever gonna say? I not even a big girl. I still little." An easy method for varying verbal praise is to describe the behavior you are reinforcing: "I like the way you put your toys in the toy box." "Wow! You came as soon as I called you." "You did a great job eating your sandwich."

You can increase or decrease the value of reinforcers through their availability. After receiving ten clown stamps, your child probably won't care if she gets another clown stamp on her hand or not. The value of the reinforcer also varies, according to who is providing the reinforcement. The smiles and giggles of another child may outweigh your stern look of disapproval. The opportunity to play outside at the playground with Mom can be more reinforcing than the opportunity to play with Dad if Dad is the one who usually plays at the playground.

The timing of the reinforcement is also important. Young children often do best when they receive reinforcement immediately after the desired behavior. When you have to delay reinforcement, describe the past good behavior when you provide the reinforcement. If your child is typically uncooperative at bedtime, and a sitter reports an improvement in your child's bedtime behavior, remind your child of the good behavior as you praise her the next morning. "Tisha, remember last night when Olivia was here and you were watching TV? Do you remember when the program ended and she asked you to get ready for bed? She told me that you got up and turned off the TV and went straight to your room to put your pajamas on. Daddy and I are very happy to hear this."

As your child approaches two and a half to three years of age, use sticker paths (see below) and token systems to delay big reinforcers such as a doll or a truck. Sticker paths are more visual and easier for young children to understand than token systems. Begin by using sticker paths, and move on to token systems once your child has mastered the concept of a sticker path.

Sticker paths. To make a sticker path, draw a row of connecting squares (like a sidewalk) on a piece of paper. Make each square large enough for a sticker to fit inside. Make the number of squares equal to the number of stickers that your child needs to collect before she gets her reward. Draw or paste a picture of the reward at the end of the sidewalk. Rewards might include a toy, going to the park, watching a video; the list is endless. In many cases, you and your child can choose the reward together.

To explain a sticker path to your child, tell her three things clearly and simply. First, tell her what behavior earns her a sticker. Second, tell her how many stickers she must earn to get the reward. Third, let her know the reward she is working toward.

To use a sticker path, you and your child place a sticker inside one of the sidewalk squares immediately following the desired behavior. To make the chart as visual as possible, place the stickers in order. Put the first sticker she earns in the first square of the sidewalk, the second sticker in the second square, and so on. In this way, your child can see the stickers getting closer to the reward. After she completes the sticker path, present your child with her reward.

Token systems. The underlying premise of the token system is the same as the sticker path. To use a token system, give your child a small token immediately following a desired behavior. After collecting a predetermined number of tokens, your child turns the tokens in for something special. As you did with sticker paths, always tell your child the behavior required for her to earn a token, how many tokens she must earn to get the reward, and what the reward is.

Almost anything can serve as a token as long as it is *safe*, easy to handle, and durable. Examples of tokens include poker chips, large buttons, and index cards with smile faces. Put a special mark on all tokens to differentiate them from other similar objects in your home. Provide your child with a container and a safe place to keep her tokens. Perhaps she could put her tokens in a shoe box stored on top of her dresser. Maybe she could keep them in a big envelope that you staple to a bulletin board. Selecting a consistent place to put

tokens reduces the chance of your child coming to you with tear-filled eyes, saying she has lost her tokens. In the beginning, it may help to put a picture of the reward on the token container.

TABLE 3
POSITIVE REINFORCEMENT

- Provide a desirable consequence immediately following the behavior you want to develop, increase, or maintain.
- Use social or tangible reinforcers.
- Do not use food as a reinforcer.
- Vary the reinforcers you use.
- Describe the behavior you are reinforcing.
- Increase or decrease the value of reinforcers through their availability.
- The value of reinforcers varies according to who is doing the reinforcing.
- Use sticker paths and token systems as appropriate.

Teaching New Behaviors

To teach your child a new behavior, provide immediate, positive reinforcement every time she performs the behavior. If the new behavior is complex, reward intermediate steps to that behavior. There are three ways to do this. One way is to break a complex skill into several sub-skills and to teach your child one sub-skill at a time. As an example, take teeth-brushing. Table 4 shows the sub-skills your child must learn before she can brush her teeth independently. It is not realistic to expect a toddler or preschooler to learn all these sub-skills at once. When teaching your child to brush her teeth, start by reinforcing her for simply taking out her toothbrush and toothpaste. Another way to teach your child a new behavior is to reinforce increasing accuracy. This is appropriate if for example, you want to improve your toddler's neatness at mealtime. Begin by praising your child for not throwing food, then for not dropping food on the floor, and then for not getting food on her highchair. The last way is to reinforce longer intervals of good behavior. If your goal is for your children to play together for 20 minutes without fighting, begin by reinforcing five minutes of play without fighting, then ten minutes, and so on.

An additional technique for teaching your child a new behavior is allowing her to see a "prestigious" person performing that behavior. The following story is a perfect example. Jennifer's parents were trying to teach their daughter that it was okay for water to get on her face when they wet her hair to wash it. They tried clapping, demonstrating on themselves, and offering an extra bedtime story. But nothing worked. One afternoon when they had guests, Jennifer played in the pool with her cousin Amanda. At two years old, Jennifer looked up to three-year-old Amanda. While playing in

---

TABLE 4
TEETH-BRUSHING SUB-SKILLS

- Taking out the toothpaste and toothbrush.
- Opening the toothpaste, putting toothpaste on the toothbrush, and closing the toothpaste.
- Turning the water on, getting the toothbrush wet, and turning the water off.
- Brushing teeth and spitting the toothpaste out.
- Turning the water on, rinsing off the toothbrush, and putting the toothbrush away.
- Getting a cup, filling the cup with water, and turning the water off.
- Rinsing mouth with the water.
- Emptying any remaining water from cup and putting the cup back.
- Wiping hands and face on a towel.

the pool, Amanda dumped a big bucket of water on her own head and laughed. Jennifer grabbed a matching bucket and dumped water on her own head, as she said, "Me do it, too, Amanda."

To teach your child to act one way under a particular set of circumstances but not another, help her identify the cues that differentiate the circumstances. Keep your explanation brief, emphasizing the most important point. If your explanation is too lengthy, your child may miss the point. In one family, the parents allowed their children to have pillow fights in the family room. However, the parents would not allow pillow fights in the living room. At first this limit was very confusing to their two-year-old, who reasoned that both rooms had a couch, two chairs, and a television. Her parents taught her this limit by talking to her and showing her a difference between the two rooms. They started in the living room and said, "You can't have pillow fights in this room. We have a glass coffee table in this room. It has sharp edges, and it is very hard. If you accidentally crashed into it, you could get hurt and the table might break." As Mom talked, she pointed to the coffee table. Then they led her into the family room, where Dad said, "You and your sister may have pillow fights in here. The family room doesn't have a coffee table that you can get hurt on or that might break."

Increasing Appropriate Behaviors

To increase the occurrence of an appropriate behavior, provide immediate, positive reinforcement after the behavior. There is probably at least one acceptable behavior that your child performs occasionally, but not as often or as consistently as you would like. Sometimes she comes to the table when you say it's time to eat, but at other times she dawdles or runs in the opposite direction. To increase the number of times she comes to the table as soon as you announce mealtime, provide a social or a tangible reinforcer every time she comes right away. For a one-year-old, you might clap your hands and let her wear a special bib with a funny clown on it. For a two- or three-year-old, you might start a sticker path or a token system.

Maintaining Appropriate Behaviors

Once your child has learned a new behavior or is performing a behavior at a satisfactory rate, gradually decrease the frequency of reinforcement. Instead of rewarding your child every time she performs the behavior, provide reinforcement every two, three, or four times. Then continue to provide reinforcement as an occasional, unexpected surprise. You might say, for example, "You put your shoes and coat on so fast! Way to go! Since you got ready so fast, we have a few extra minutes before we have to leave. Let's go outside, and play chase until it's time to go."

STOPPING UNDESIRED BEHAVIORS

You will only need to spend a minimal amount of time stopping undesired behaviors if you set well-defined and consistent limits, use limit-setting strategies, such as substitutions and five-minute warnings, and use positive reinforcement to encourage good behaviors.

When trying to stop undesired behaviors, avoid using harsh words and physical punishment. Avoid harsh words because telling your child that she's bad, sloppy, or mean only lowers her self-esteem. Remember, the behavior is what is bad—It is the room that is sloppy, or the hitting that is mean, not your child. Avoid physical punishment for three reasons. First and most important, you could accidentally hurt your child. Second, physical punishment creates fear. Your child should not be afraid of you; she should trust you so she will go to you whenever she needs you. Third, physical punishment causes confusion. Your child will wonder why she can't hit you or others if you hit her. If you are about to hit your child, scream and hit a table or your own knee instead. Take a deep breath, and then use a more appropriate form of behavior management. Extinction and time-out are described below and are the two best ways to stop an undesired behavior.

Extinction - the art of ignoring your child's behavior

To use extinction, you **ignore** the undesired behavior, allowing the behavior to continue until your child tires of it. Ignoring the behavior works **if** your attention is what your child wants. Extinction works very well for decreasing tantrums. Chapter 4 "Emotional Development" discusses handling tantrums in detail.

Extinction also works well for reducing yelling, talking with a rough or demanding voice, and whining.

Do not use extinction if your child's behavior is harmful or destructive. You don't want to ignore your child if she is hitting her baby brother. While it is true that she is probably hitting her brother for attention, he could get hurt before she tires of hitting him. You also don't want to ignore your child if she is throwing toys or kicking the television. She may throw or kick to get your attention or she may do so because she is angry. Regardless of the reason, you can't ignore the behavior because she could break something and even possibly hurt herself or someone else.

Extinction doesn't work if your child receives additional reinforcement for the behavior. If you smile or laugh while you are trying to ignore your child, you will reinforce the behavior. Although you may sometimes find it difficult to keep a straight face while using extinction, it is very important that your child doesn't see a reaction from you. Turn your face away or turn your back towards your child to hide your reaction—this works nicely as long as you don't laugh aloud. Your child may also receive additional reinforcement from other people in the room. For instance, take a child who is demanding in a rough voice that her mom get her some apple juice. "Get me apple juice now. I said now! You hear me? Do what I say! Get me apple juice. You better listen to me." Her mom can do an excellent job of ignoring her daughter, but if another child laughs, the daughter is likely to continue her demanding behavior.

When you use extinction, remember that the behavior will usually gets worse before it gets better. If your child expects a reaction from her behavior, she will persist with the behavior before she gives up. The fastest way to decrease a behavior is to combine extinction of the undesired behavior with positive reinforcement of an alternative behavior. For example, ignore the demands, but respond to her immediately when she requests politely. Be careful not to do the opposite. Don't ignore an appropriate behavior and reinforce a less desirable one. For instance, don't ignore your child when she asks you politely for another roll at dinner but then hand her a roll when she screams for one.

Time-out

Time-out involves putting your child in a *safe* and boring place, such as a corner, for a specified amount of time. Before giving your child a time-out, give her one warning. "Susie, stop throwing your toys or you will get a time-out." If she continues with the behavior, calmly give her a time-out.

In the beginning, you may need to guide your child to her time-out spot. If she will not go on her own, simply pick her up and carry her to time-out as you would carry her to the car. You may also need to keep her in time-out. It is rare for a young child simply to sit or stand still when you first put her in time-out. Through experience, she will learn that she may not leave time-out until you say that she can. Once she understands this rule, she will probably sit or stand still. Until that point, keep your child sitting in time-out by kneeling behind the chair and wrapping your arms around your child. If your child stands in a corner for time-out, use your body as a third wall to keep her in the corner. While your

child is in time-out, do not talk to her or make eye contact with her.

Allow your child to leave time-out when an appropriate amount of time has passed and your child is behaving as desired. In general, your child should stay in time-out one minute for every year she is old. If your child is two years old, two minutes is an appropriate length for a time-out. Setting a timer is usually helpful. Doing this keeps accurate track of how long your child is in time-out. If your child is screaming and crying, 30 seconds may seem like two minutes, and you may inadvertently let her out too early. Timers are also good to use, because most young children take their anger out on the timer instead of their parents. As a result you are more likely to hear, "Stupid timer. Beep timer! I hate you, Timer." instead of "You're stupid, Daddy. Daddy, may I get out of time-out yet? I hate you, Daddy." Once the two minutes are over and your child is behaving, she may leave time-out. If your child is not behaving when the timer rings, tell her that she may leave time-out once she stops screaming, crying, or kicking. You don't want to allow your child to leave time-out while she is misbehaving because then she may think the screaming, crying, or kicking behavior was the reason you let her leave. This might increase the incidence of misbehavior in future time-outs.

After the time-out, spend a minute or two talking with your child about why she got the time-out and suggesting appropriate behaviors for the future. "You got a time-out because you went in the street. You may not play in the street. Cars drive in the street, and one might hit you if you are playing in the street. You may play in the grass or on the side-  walk."

Whenever possible, return your child to the activity or the place she was before the time-out. This is important for two reasons. First, you should use time-out to stop an undesirable behavior <u>and</u> to teach your child a more appropriate behavior. By returning your child to the activity, you give her the opportunity to practice the new more appropriate behavior. Second, you don't want your child to learn that she can misbehave, get a time-out, and thus avoid an activity or a situation. For example, if your child gets a time-out for pushing another child on the floor and taking away her toy, return your child to the play area and have her ask for the toy in a more appropriate manner.

Avoid threatening to give a time-out at a later time. Delayed time-outs generally don't work. Your child is too young to remember what she did to deserve a time-out and why she did it. If your child deserves a time-out, give her one immediately. There may be times when you will not want to give your child a time-out right where the misbehavior occurred. For example, you may feel uncomfortable giving your child a time-out in a store or in front of others. This is most likely the case if your child screams while she is in time-out. If you are in a store, leave immediately and take your child outside or to the car for a time-out. It may be inconvenient to stop shopping, but most children learn after one or two time-outs that they will not get away with the misbehavior, and their behavior improves quickly. If you are at a party, immediately bring your child to an empty hallway and give her a time-out.

A PARENT'S STORY

My daughter Takera is really a well-behaved three-and-a-half-year-old. She can go weeks at a time without needing a time-out. However, she does need very consistent limits. And she does test us. I would say that every four or five weeks, she breaks every rule to see if limits still exist. On those days, it seems as though we do nothing but give Takera time-outs. My wife and I feel emotionally drained and exhausted by the end of one of those days. And we don't like seeing Takera get upset— She gets very sad when she is put in time-out. One evening after one of those days, I decided that we needed to figure out some way to let Takera know that the limits still exist without her having to break them and spend so much time in time-out. We decided to use a token system.

Every four or five weeks, my wife and I sat down and briefly reviewed our limits with Takera. For instance, we might say, "No throwing balls in the house. If your throw a ball inside, you might break something. If you want to play ball, tell Mommy or Daddy, and one of us will try to take you outside." We don't have that many limits, so the discussions usually went pretty quickly. After reviewing the limits, we told Takera that she could earn one button (our version of a token) at lunch time for following limits in the morning and one button at bedtime for following limits the remainder of the day. We explained to her that once she got six buttons she would get a special treat. Together we decided what the treat would be—One time it was a trip to the park; another time it was a new box of crayons. The system worked great! My wife and I were able to show Takera that our limits still existed without having to give her so many time-outs. But there is a cute little story that I have to share.

One day, while my wife was at the grocery store, Takera came to me, grinning from ear to ear. She proudly held out two buttons that she had obviously taken off the sweater she was wearing and said, "Daddy, I got two more buttons.

See!" She then walked over to her collection of tokens and said, "I'm gonna put these in my button box." When I tried to explain that the buttons from her sweater didn't count as tokens, Takera became very confused and upset. Then in a flash of inspiration, I realized that all the token buttons were red, and the sweater buttons were pink. I quickly explained to Takera that she got red buttons, not pink ones, for following limits. After this brief explanation, Takera looked into her shoe box of red buttons and said, "You're right, Daddy. I get red buttons, not pink buttons. Maybe Mommy can put these pink buttons back on my sweater." As she ran off to play in her room, I sighed with relief and then quietly wondered if Takera had any clothes with red buttons. To be on the safe side, I got out a blue marker and made a star on all the red token buttons.

SUMMARY

Helping your child behave involves setting clear and consistent limits. Limits help your child learn to avoid danger and to attain socially acceptable behaviors. Keep limits to a minimum. If you find yourself saying "no" or "don't" a lot, evaluate and restructure your expectations and the environment. In addition to minimizing limits, you should:
- Use substitutions to enforce limits
- State rules positively, and if something is not allowed, say so
- Give your child five-minute warnings
- Avoid asking questions if options don't exist
- Motivate your child to the next activity
- Allow your child the time she needs to go at her own pace
- Let your child do as much for herself as she wants and as is possible
- Praise your child when she follows limits

Use behavior management techniques to establish and enforce limits.

Behavior management techniques include positive reinforcement, extinction, and time-out. You can use positive reinforcement to teach, increase, and maintain appropriate behaviors. The best positive reinforcers are social or tangible. Do not use love and food as reinforcers. As your child approaches two and a half to three years of age, use sticker paths and token systems to delay big reinforcers. To teach your child a new behavior or to increase the occurrence of an appropriate behavior, provide immediate, positive reinforcement every time she performs the behavior. Once your child has learned a new behavior or is performing a behavior at a satisfactory rate, gradually decrease the frequency of reinforcement and then provide reinforcement as an occasional, unexpected surprise. When trying to stop undesired behaviors, avoid harsh words and physical punishment. Instead, use extinction or time-out. Extinction involves ignoring the misbehavior, and time-out involves putting your child in a *safe* and boring place for a specified amount of time.

Consistency and follow-through are the keys to helping your child behave. If you don't allow something, never allow it. If you tell your child she may have a new toy, buy her one. If you tell your child that she is going to get a time-out, give her one. Throughout the day, provide your child with lots of affection and remember to allow time for cuddling. Cuddles won't spoil your child—she still needs the affection.

REFERENCES AND RECOMMENDED READINGS

Krumboltz, J. & Krumboltz, H. (1972). *Changing Children's Behavior.* Englewood Cliffs, NJ: Prentice-Hall, Inc.

Leach, P. (1992, January/1991, December). Instead of spanking. *Parenting*, pp. 88-93 & 230.

Leach, P. (1989, April). Say what you mean, mean what you say. *Parenting*, pp. 54-59.

Samalin, N. (1991, June/July). Standoff. *Parenting*, pp. 68-73.

Chapter 9
Sleeping through the Night

Sleep problems are a common occurrence in early childhood, affecting about 25 percent of all young children. Difficulty going to sleep at bedtime, nighttime waking, and early morning waking are the three most common sleep problems.

Within the first group of sleep problems is the child who has difficulty going to sleep at bedtime. She may not know how to go from a tired state to a sleep state by herself and therefore, she needs your help. You may need to pat her for twenty minutes or sing her to sleep each night. A child who goes to bed when she isn't tired may also has trouble going to sleep. She may request another story before you leave the room. Ten minutes after you leave the room, she asks for a drink of water. She asks for a second drink just ten minutes after that. Fifteen minutes later she has to go to the bathroom. Ten minutes after going to the bathroom, she needs one more hug or another kiss. Finally, an hour later, she falls asleep.

The second type of sleep problem is nighttime waking. To experience brief periods of arousal each night is normal. We all do this as we go from one sleep state to another. However, some children cannot go back to sleep after these episodes. If the conditions that were present when your child went to sleep are not present when she awakens at night, she may need you to reestablish these conditions for her to go back to sleep. For instance, if she normally falls to sleep at bedtime while you cuddle her and sing to her, she may need you to sing her to sleep after nighttime arousals. The same is true of a child who usually gets a bottle before falling asleep at bedtime. She may have problems falling back to sleep after a period of arousal unless you give her a bottle during the night. This may happen even if she falls asleep by herself at bedtime but if she is used to getting a bottle when she awakens at night.

Early morning waking is the third type of sleep problem. A child who consistently wakes up at five o'clock in the morning and doesn't go back to sleep, no matter what her parents do, may be ready to start her day if she has had enough sleep. She may sleep too much during the day so that she doesn't need to sleep as much at night. Another possibility is that her bedtime hour is too early.

If your child has a sleep problem, perhaps you already have a

strategy for dealing with the problem that works well. Some parents rock their child to sleep at bedtime and night wakings—they enjoy the closeness with their child this affords. Other parents find that having their child sleep with them ends night wakings. But if your child has a sleep problem for which you have not found a satisfactory solution, you should change your child's sleep pattern and/or start sleep training.

Parent Perspective

Deciding to alter your child's sleep schedule is easy. But actually beginning the process of teaching her how to sleep is very difficult. You feel frustrated by your child's sleep problem and exhausted from a lack of sleep. Your head tells you that sleep training is a great idea. At the same time, your heart is torn by the thought of not meeting what your child perceives as a need and of allowing her to cry. Teaching your child how to sleep will probably be one of the most emotionally difficult things you ever do. But once she and you are sleeping through the night, you will feel that teaching her this skill was one of the best things you did.

Child Perspective

If you adjust her sleep schedule gradually, she will probably change with little or no difficulty. Sleep training, however, frequently results in some crying by young children. Initially, sleep training will be a confusing process for your child. She will not understand why things are not happening the way they used to, and she will cry in an attempt to get back what she had. When your child doesn't get what she wants, she will protest louder and longer. She will finally fall asleep exhausted from her efforts. Gradually, as she begins to *understand that the rules have changed and that crying doesn't help, she will learn to sleep independently.*

Other less common sleep problems such as nightmares, night terrors, sleepwalking, and night fears may also occur. These problems are very different from those previously mentioned, and they require different interventions. Therefore, they are in a separate section at the end of this chapter.

CHANGING SLEEP PATTERNS

A child who takes too many naps, naps late in the day, or goes to bed too early can have difficulty sleeping through the night because of a poor sleep pattern. The amount of sleep each child needs varies. Nevertheless, knowing the average amount of day and night sleep young children need helps you understand how much sleep your child needs. With this knowledge, you can look at her sleep schedule and determine if adjustments are necessary.

The average night and day sleep patterns for children vary slightly according to age. Between one and four years of age, most children need about ten hours of night sleep. At four years of age, most preschoolers sleep about eleven and a half hours each night. The night sleep hours increase as daytime naps decrease. Between one and two years of age, toddlers typically sleep three and a half hours during the day. These hours are usually divided in a morning and an afternoon nap. Around two years, most children give up their morning nap. The afternoon nap can last from one to three hours. At three years, the afternoon nap generally decreases to one or two hours. By four, most preschoolers no longer take naps.

TABLE 1
AVERAGE NIGHT AND DAY SLEEP PATTERNS[2]

Age	Night Hours	Day Hours
12 months	10 1/2	3 1/2
18 months	10 1/2	3
2 years	10	1-3
3 years	10	1-2
4 years	11 1/2	0

[2]Adapted from Barnard & Erickson (1976), Coley (1978), Ferber (1985).

Too Many Naps

A three-year-old who takes a two-hour nap in the morning and a two- hour nap in the afternoon may have trouble sleeping at night. She may resist going to sleep at bedtime because she is not tired, or  she may wake up early because she has had enough sleep for that day. If your child is more than two years old, takes two naps a day, and has difficulty sleeping at night, drop the morning nap. To do this, delay her morning nap by ten minutes each day. At the same time, shorten the length of the nap by ten minutes each day. Continue delaying and shortening the morning nap until it no longer exists, keeping one afternoon nap.

Late Afternoon Naps

A child who takes a two-hour nap at 5:00 p.m. has trouble falling asleep at 8:30 p.m. because she isn't sleepy yet. Late afternoon naps become a common problem between two and four years of age. If your child naps in the late afternoon and has difficulty sleeping at night, gradually change the time of the nap by making it ten to fifteen minutes earlier each day. It is best if afternoon naps begin before 3:00 p.m. Continue changing the nap time until your child sleeps in the early or mid-afternoon. If she refuses to sleep in the afternoon but consistently falls asleep at dinner time, she may be ready to give up her naps. As she is making this transition, allow her to take a brief nap before dinner. The nap must be short, or it will interfere with nighttime sleep. Thirty minutes should be long enough to keep the grouchies away but short enough to allow her to sleep well at night.

Early Bedtime

A child who goes to bed at 7:00 p.m. may have difficulty going to sleep because it's too early. If your child goes to bed at one time but consistently falls asleep two to three hours later, her bedtime may be too early for her. A simple solution is to delay her bedtime until the time she usually falls asleep. However, this is not an appropriate long-term solution if your child goes to bed at 10:30 p.m. and falls asleep at 12:30 a.m. If your child goes to bed late and consistently falls asleep even later, temporarily delay her bedtime. After a few nights, advance her bedtime and the time of her morning waking by

HELPFUL STRATEGIES FOR NAPS

- Use an abbreviated version of the bedtime routine at nap time.
- Put your child to sleep for naps in a similar fashion as at night. In other words, if you use the Gentle Technique at night, use it at nap time.
- Implement the 2-In & 15-Out or Gradual Method (as discussed in Sleep Training Step 3) during naps to facilitate day sleep. Use the same method that you are using at night.
- If your child is in her room for an hour and does not take her nap, let her get up.
- As your child makes the transition from one nap to not napping, provide an hour of quiet rest if she won't nap in the afternoon. Play calm music on a radio alarm clock for an hour. Explain that she may get up when the music stops playing.

HELPFUL STRATEGIES FOR NIGHTTIME

- Wean your child of any night nursing before you begin sleep training. Wean one feeding every three to four days until your child is not nursing during the night. Keep the bedtime nursing as long as you like.
- The first time you discuss new sleep rules with your child, do so before the bedtime routine. This will prepare your child for the changes you plan to make.
- If you have another child who does not have a sleep problem, tell that child what is going on and explain why there will be some crying. If possible, arrange for that child (the one without the sleep problem) to spend a night or two (not necessary to include the days) at Grandma's or a friend's.
- Put bells on your child's door if she gets out of her bed and leaves her room during the night. They will let you know when your child gets up so you can immediately put her back to bed. Bells are helpful if your child likes to crawl into bed with you in the middle of the night. Many parents don't realize when their child crawls into bed. The bells will wake you so you can prevent your child from making it to your room.

HELPFUL STRATEGIES FOR NAPS AND NIGHTTIME

- Provide your child with a small stuffed animal or a special blanket. A bed companion will give her something to hug and hold onto. It will also make separating from you a bit easier.
- If potty training, put a potty chair in the bedroom to avoid an excuse to get out of the bedroom.
- Consider using a gate at the doorway to impede escapes. This is not recommended if your child will climb over it and get hurt.
- Provide rewards for following sleep rules. Tell your child, for example, that if she goes to sleep at night without crying, you will read her favorite story in the morning. At nap time, tell her that if she stays in her bed, she may blow bubbles when nap time is over.
- Remind your child of the sleep rules and rewards as you tuck her in bed.
- Promptly return your child to her bed if she leaves her room. Stay with her for two minutes the first time she leaves her room. Explain that it is time to sleep and that she must stay in her bed. Tell her good night, give her a kiss, and leave the room. If she gets up again, promptly return her to bed and leave the room immediately.

10 to 15 minutes each day. Continue advancing bedtime and wake time until the timing of her night sleep is acceptable.

Remember that young children only need to sleep ten to eleven and a half hours each night and three and a half or less hours each day. It is unrealistic to expect any child to go to bed at 7:00 p.m., sleep until 9:00 a.m., nap from 10:00 a.m. to noon, and to nap again from 3:00 p.m. to 5:00 p.m. However, it is realistic to expect a two-year-old to go to bed at 9:00 p.m., sleep until 7:00 a.m., and nap from 2:00 p.m. to 4:00 p.m. If your toddler has trouble sleeping through the night and her sleep pattern needs improvement, adjust her schedule before initiating sleep training. Once a child is on a good schedule, night sleep often improves.

SLEEP TRAINING

Sleep training involves teaching your child to go to sleep by herself and to sleep through the night. This does not mean that your child will not wake up during the night. It means that she will have the skills needed to put herself back to sleep without your help. Most children are capable of sleeping through the night, and can learn how to do so if they are not.

Sleep training is not appropriate for some children, including those who have central nervous system (CNS) disorders, who are on medications, or who are ill. Children with CNS disorders, such as epilepsy and cerebral palsy, often experience sleep problems, but these problems are medical in nature and are not appropriate for sleep training. If your child has a CNS disorder, you should discuss sleep prognosis and treatment with your child's pediatrician/physician.

Some medications, such as antibiotics, antihistamines, and stimulants, affect sleep patterns. If your child is taking medication, check with the pediatrician before beginning sleep training to be sure the medication is not causing the problem. If it is, request a different drug or a change in dosage or timing. If the medication must remain exactly the same, sleep training is not appropriate because the reasons for her difficulties are beyond her control and yours.

Finally, some common childhood illnesses, such as an ear infection, a strep throat, or a urinary tract infection may alter your child's sleep. When your child recovers and no longer needs your comfort, she may still request it out of habit. Once your child's pediatrician has assured you that she is better, you may start training.

There are four basic steps to teaching your child how to sleep. To teach her to sleep through the night as quickly as possible, be consistent with each step. The time it takes to teach a young child to sleep through the night varies. Most parents see improvement

SAFETY PRECAUTIONS

If your child is in a crib:
- Make sure all toys in the crib are safe.
- Toys should not have buttons or other small pieces that your child might choke on.
- Toys should not have sharp edges that your child might get cut on.
- Toys should not have long ribbons or strings that your child might get caught in.
- Remove large stuffed animals or toys that your child might use to climb out of the crib.
- Use a night light so your child can see clearly in the room. (This is essential for children with hearing impairments.)

If your child is in a bed:
- The entire room must be safety-proofed.
- Make sure all toys in the room are safe.
- Put dangerous toys and items out of reach or in another room.
- Put safety covers on all outlets.
- Use bed rails, if needed, to keep your child from falling out of bed.
- Use a night light so your child can see clearly in the room. (This is essential for children with hearing impairments.)

by the third night. By the end of one week, most children are sleeping through the night.

Step 1. Implement a Bedtime Routine.

Take from ten to thirty minutes each night to set up a consistent routine that your child will associate with getting ready for bed. The activities that make up this routine are not as important as that they are calm in nature, consistent, and replicable by others. Examples of appropriate activities include brushing teeth, taking a bath, putting on pajamas, reading a story, and singing a song. If you don't like your child's current bedtime routine, this is an excellent time to introduce a new one.

Step 2. Put your child into bed using the gentle or the Regular Technique.

Gentle Technique
Put your child to bed when she is already asleep. In your child's dimly lit and quiet bedroom, put her to sleep any way that you like. After your bedtime routine, you may wish to rock her or nurse her to sleep. When she is asleep, put her gently into bed. If she wakes up once she is in bed, your child must return to sleep independently. Implement the 2-In & 15-Out or the Gradual Method (described in Step 3) if your child wakes up and has difficulty going back to sleep. The Gentle Technique works well for many families. Most young children can learn to go to sleep one way and to go back to sleep another way. The important distinguishing factor is the bed. If your child is in bed, she must go to sleep by herself.

Regular Technique
Put your child into bed sleepy but awake. Put her to bed awake so she will put herself to sleep independently. This way, when she experiences brief arousals during the night, she will know how to put herself back to sleep without your help.

After completing her bedtime routine and receiving her final good night kiss, your child may ask for a drink of water or another song. Although you don't like to ignore her requests, you must stay consistent with bedtime rules. Explain that it is time for her to go to sleep and for you to leave. Give her one more kiss and leave the room. Implement the 2-In & 15-Out or the Gradual Method if she has trouble falling asleep. Use the same method if she wakes up during the night and has difficulty returning to sleep.

When unique circumstances exist, you can bend the bedtime rules. If your child is sick, an extra song or additional cuddling is appropriate. If she hasn't had anything to drink since dinner and she asks for a drink, offer one glass of water as a special treat. If you recently started toilet training and she asks to go potty, take her to the bathroom. Avoid such requests in the future by offering a drink of water and having her go potty as part of the bedtime routine. If she continues to ask to go potty after she is in bed, despite going during the routine, put a potty chair in her room. If a child is asking to go potty as a bedtime-delaying tactic, her requests will probably stop when the potty is in the room. After all, what fun is it if you don't get to walk down the hallway and check things out on your way to the bathroom? When you do deviate from the rules, explain why you are doing so, for example, "I'm going to bring you a drink of water as a special treat. You may have a drink tonight because you haven't had anything to drink since dinner. Tomorrow night you will get a drink before you go to bed." This will help your child learn that you are consistent but flexible under certain conditions.

Choosing a Technique

The technique you choose to use in Step 2 is a matter of parental preference. However, under a few circumstances the Regular Technique is a preferable choice.

Use the Regular Technique before changing your child from the crib to a bed. It is easier to teach a child to go to sleep independently at bedtime when she is in a crib. A crib restricts a child to the crib. A child in a bed has access to the entire bedroom and, if she can open the door, she has access to the whole house. Children usually change from a crib to a bed between the ages of eighteen months and three years. As long as your child fits in her crib and cannot climb out, you can keep her in it. Six weeks before making the change to a bed, take your child to a store that sells beds for children. Allow her to look at, touch, and sit on the beds. Tell her that one day she will sleep in a "big girl" bed like one of these. A few days later, look at bedding in a catalogue with her. Ask her which sheets she likes. A couple days later, explain that when she can go to sleep by herself at bedtime, she will get a "big girl" bed with "big girl" sheets. On the same evening, remind her about the bed and implement the Regular Technique. Within three to seven days your child should go to sleep independently at bedtime. Take three to four weeks to establish this new pattern, and then change her to a bed. Do not make the new bed a surprise. The change to a bed will go smoother if you take her along to buy it at the store or allow her to help assemble it at home. Giving her a lot of verbal praise during her first week in the bed will further facilitate the change.

Also use **the Regular Technique if, while using the Gentle Technique, your child resists going to sleep or wakes up as you put her into bed.** Your child may fight going to sleep because she doesn't want you to leave. Her eyes may pop open every time they close. She may wake up and cry when you put her into bed. Since she is in bed, you must implement one of the methods to get her back to sleep. If you spend more than thirty minutes trying to get your child to sleep while using the Gentle Technique or implement the 2-In & 15-Out or Gradual Method because she has difficulty transitioning into bed, the Regular Technique will be easier in the long run.

> ## BOTTLES IN BED
> It is best if you don't allow your child to drink bottles while lying in bed. Drinking a bottle while lying in bed can lead to ear infections. The Eustachian tubes in the ears of young children are short, wide, and almost horizontal. When a child drinks from a bottle lying down, the fluid can drain from the mouth into the Eustachian tubes. The fluid can then get trapped in the tubes, resulting in middle ear infections. Drinking a bottle in bed can also damage the enamel of the teeth and lead to cavities. The sugar from the milk or juice sets in the mouth, coating the teeth and causing the damage.

Step 3. Facilitate sleeping through the night using the 2-in & 15-out or the gradual method.

2-in & 15-out Method

The 2-In & 15-Out Method is the fastest way to teach your child to sleep through the night. Using this method, most children can learn to sleep through the night in less than one week. Use the 2-In & 15-Out Method whenever your child is in her bed and has trouble falling asleep. This may be at bedtime, after a nighttime waking, or after an early morning waking. When your child fusses after you leave the room at bedtime or when she awakens during the night, wait a few minutes to see if she will calm down and go to sleep independently *[If she is crying and may be hurt, go into her room right away. Be sure to know when your child is crying to complain versus crying because of pain.]* If she continues to cry, go into her room for two minutes **to reassure her that you are there and that she is okay.** During this time rub her back, explain that nighttime is for sleeping, and tell her that you love her. However, do not take her

out of bed. After spending **two minutes** with your child, leave the room for **fifteen minutes.**

Continue going in for two minutes and leaving for fifteen minutes **until your child falls asleep by herself.** Expect your child to cry when you leave the room. Crying is a normal reaction. You are not doing things her way, and crying is her way of protesting the change. Staying out of her room for fifteen minutes before returning may be very difficult for you. This will probably be the first time you have allowed her to cry. You may even cry yourself because she is crying. If it is too difficult to stay out for fifteen minutes, stay out for five minutes the first time. The second time, stay out for ten minutes. Starting with the third time, stay out for fifteen minutes. While you are out of the room, do things to occupy yourself—fold a load of clothes or clean out the refrigerator. Sitting in the hallway, with a baby monitor in one hand and a watch in the other, will only make this a more agonizing task for you.

Your child may cry for an hour or more before she finally goes to sleep. Continue going in for two minutes and leaving for fifteen minutes until she falls asleep. You may want to take your child out of her bed and rock her to sleep after an hour of crying, but don't unless she is crying because of pain. Doing this will teach her to cry for a very long time to get what she wants. As a result, she may cry longer the next night. If you are consistent with the 2-In & 15-Out Method, you both should be sleeping soundly through the night in less than one week.

Gradual Method

Teaching your child to sleep through the night will take longer if you use the Gradual Method. This method generally takes from ten to fifteen nights. However, the Gradual Method feels better to some parents. It allows you to do the 2-In & 15-Out gradually. The Gradual Method **involves slowly moving farther away from your child in three-night intervals.** As with the 2-In & 15-Out Method, use the Gradual Method whenever your child is in her bed and has trouble falling asleep. This can be at bedtime, after a nighttime waking, or after an early morning waking.

On the first night, instead of leaving the room after her good night kiss, sit nearby, but not on, your child's bed until she falls asleep. After three nights, sit near the doorway until she goes to sleep. On night seven, sit outside the doorway with the door open until she is asleep. While you are sitting near your child, keep interactions to a minimum. Every fifteen minutes, spend two minutes reassuring her that you are there and that she is okay. Explain that you will sit with her until she falls asleep, but that you will not sing, read stories, or lie down with her. Tell her that you love her,

but nighttime is for sleeping. You should not take her out of bed during this time. After two minutes, return to the spot where you were sitting. Continue to reassure her every two minutes and to sit for fifteen minutes until she falls asleep. Starting on the tenth night, close her bedroom door and use the 2-In &15-Out Method if needed.

Step 4. Provide a Morning Signal.

A morning signal lets your child know that it is time to wake up and get out of bed. It helps her understand when you will and will not let her get up. Examples of morning signals include turning on the light, opening blinds, and singing a good morning song. For a three-year-old, the time on the clock may be a morning signal. Tell her what time she may get out of bed and show her that time on the clock. If she has a digital clock in her room, write the number on an index card and tape it to the top of the clock in the correct position. Explain to her that she may get up when the number in that spot matches the number on the card. If she has a clock with hands, put a sticker by the number where the little hand needs to be. Explain that she must wait until the little hand touches the number with the sticker before she may get up.

Provide your child with the same signal each morning. If your signal is to sing a song, sing it every morning before she gets out of bed. If the time on the clock is your signal, point out the time before she gets up. Most children learn their morning signal quickly. After initial sleep training, many young children go back to sleep with little protest if they do not get the signal when Mommy or Daddy enters the room. For instance, if your signal is to open the blinds, your child may stop crying and lie back down with a groan if you do not go to the window when you walk in.

NIGHTMARES, NIGHT TERRORS, & SLEEPWALKING

Nightmares, night terrors, and sleepwalking are less common sleep problems that may also occur in early childhood. They are very different from the problems previously mentioned and require different interventions.

Nightmares

Nightmares occur during the REM sleep stage, usually near morning. REM stands for the Rapid Eye Movements that occur under the closed eyelid during the sleep stage associated with dreaming. Many children wake up from a nightmare recalling scary visions and feeling frightened. Most young children cannot separate the dream from reality. When your child awakens upset from a bad dream, quickly reassure her that she is okay. Comfort her as you talk about pleasant things to turn her scary thoughts into happy ones. Point out her favorite toys and mention the fun things that you will do together the next day. Do not take your child out of her bed during this time, but encourage her to go back to sleep as quickly as possible. As your child approaches school age, she will talk about her dreams and make a separation between dreams and reality.

Night Terrors

Night terrors, even less common then nightmares, happen during non-REM sleep, usually within the first few hours of sleep. Non-REM sleep occurs during sleep stages not associated with dreaming. During non-REM sleep, there is no evidence of rapid eye movements under the closed eyelid. Night terrors last about 15 minutes and may include loud screaming, fierce thrashing, or wild running. It is difficult to wake a child during a night terror, and doing so generally makes getting her back to sleep even more difficult. If your child has a night terror, stay with her until it is over to make sure she is safe. If she thrashes, put pillows by the wall, headboard, or other hard surfaces, so she doesn't hurt herself. If she runs, close the door to keep her from leaving the room, and use your body to block her from running into dressers or walls. When the night terror is over, tuck her into bed, give her a kiss, and leave the room. Night terrors generally fade by school age.

Sleepwalking.

Sleepwalking occurs during a partial waking from non-REM sleep. As with night terrors, it is hard to wake a sleepwalking child and doing so will make getting her back to sleep difficult. If your child sleepwalks, make her surroundings safe. Keep her bedroom door closed, or put a gate in the doorway. Also, put gates at the top and bottom of all stairs. Keep floors clear of toys and other objects that she could trip on. When she sleepwalks, guide her back to bed, wait until she returns to a full sleep, give her a kiss, and leave the room. Sleepwalking can begin as soon as a child can crawl or walk, but is more common in mid-childhood and adolescence.

A PARENT'S STORY

Teaching Tanya to sleep through the night was the hardest thing that I ever had to do. She was 12 months old and waking up two or three times every night. I would get up every time she did and rock her back to sleep. Everything was fine for her—she was getting what she wanted. Everything was fine for my husband—I got up most of the time. Things were not okay for me though. Getting up in the middle of the night exhausted me. The fact that it took me 30 to 45 minutes to go back to sleep after getting up to help her frustrated me. I didn't like being sleepy and grouchy during the day. I wanted Tanya to sleep through the night so I could sleep through the night.

I did some reading, talked to our pediatrician, and discussed our options with my husband. We decided to use the Gentle Technique and the 2-In & 15-Out Method to teach Tanya how to sleep through the night. On the first night we did our bedtime routine, and I nursed Tanya to sleep. She was in her crib by 9:00 p.m. When she woke up at 1:00 a.m., my heart began to beat fast, and I became nervous. I knew that I had to stick to my plan, but I also knew that it was going to be hard on her. I waited a few minutes to see if she could handle things on her own and then went into her room. Tanya was standing up, holding onto the crib rail, and crying. I went to her crib, kissed her on the head, and laid her down. I rubbed her back and explained that nighttime was for sleeping. I told her that I loved her, but that she had to go back to sleep by herself. After two minutes, I gave her one more kiss and left the room. Before I got to the door, she was standing up again and crying louder than ever. I left the room, shut the door, and returned to my room. I turned on the monitor, watched the clock, and cried with her.

This was the first time that I had let Tanya cry, and I felt terrible. I tried to wait 15 minutes before I went back into her room, but I couldn't. After ten minutes, I went to her room and spent another two minutes with her. This time when I returned to my room, my husband was awake. He asked me if I knew what I was doing and told me that it didn't feel right to him. He said that he thought this was going to traumatize Tanya for life. I explained that the doctor said we should do this and told him that the doctor had reassured me it would not harm her.

The first time she woke up, she cried for two hours and ten minutes before falling asleep. She slept for an hour, and then woke up again. The second time she cried for 50 minutes before going to sleep. She woke up once more at 6:15 but went back to sleep in 20 minutes. On the second night she woke up twice. The first time she cried for a little over an hour, and the second time she cried for 25 minutes. That night I didn't listen to the monitor, and I didn't watch the clock constantly. Instead, I set a timer for 15 minutes and washed the kitchen floor. When the timer rang, I went to her room for two minutes. Although Tanya was as upset the second night, it was easier for me. On the third night, she only woke up once and went back to sleep in less than 15 minutes. On the fourth night, Tanya only woke up once, but this time she cried for an hour before returning to sleep. On the fifth night, and from then on, she slept through the night and so did I!

SUMMARY

One out of every four young children has trouble sleeping through the night at some point. The three most common sleep problems are: (1) difficulty going to sleep at bedtime; (2) night waking; and (3) early morning waking. Adjusting sleep patterns and sleep training are two strategies for getting a child to sleep through the night.

A child who takes too many naps, naps late in the day, or goes to bed too early may have difficulty sleeping through the night because of a poor sleep pattern. Adjusting the sleep pattern of such a child can be helpful. To drop a nap, delay it by ten minutes, and shorten its length by ten minutes each day until the nap no longer exists. To change the time of a late nap, make it 10-15 minutes earlier each day until the nap is in the early or mid- afternoon. To change an early bedtime, delay it by an hour or two. Sometimes, adjusting a child's sleep pattern is all that is necessary to promote sleeping through the night. At other times, sleep training is needed.

Sleep training is a process for teaching children to sleep through the night. The four basic steps are: (1) Establish a bedtime routine; (2) Put your child into bed using the Gentle or Regular Technique; (3) Facilitate sleeping through the night using the 2-In & 15-Out or the Gradual Method; and (4) Establish a morning signal. Most children are capable of sleeping through the night and can learn how to do so if they are not. Depending on the specific method used in Step 3, a child can learn to sleep through the night in less than one week.

Teaching a child to sleep through the night is one of the most difficult things a parent has to do. But once it is done, most parents see it as one of the best things they have ever done.

REFERENCES & RECOMMENDED READINGS

Barnard, K. & Erikson, M. (1976). *Teaching Children With Developmental Problems: A Family Care Approach.* St. Louis, MO: Mosby Co.

Coley, I. (1978). *Pediatric Assessment of Self Care Activities.* St. Louis, MO: Mosby Co.

Douglas, J. (1987). Coping with sleep problems. *Health Visitor, 60,* p. 52-53.

Ferber, R. (1985). *Solve Your Child's Sleep Problems.* New York: Simon & Schuster.

Ferber, R. (1985). Sleep, sleeplessness, and sleep disruptions in infants and young children. *Annals of Clinical Research, 17,* p. 227-234.

Gilman, L. (1989, February). KIDFILE: Sleep. *Parenting,* p. 87- 100.

Schmitt, B. (1985). The prevention of sleep problems. *Clinics in Perinatology,* 12 (2), p. 453-457.

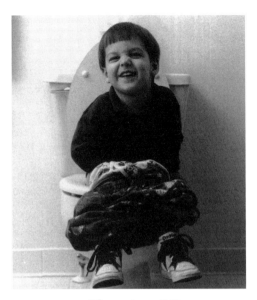

Chapter 10
Toilet Training

Toilet training involves teaching your child to go to, and use the toilet. It includes recognizing the need to go to the bathroom, walking to the bathroom, pushing pants and underwear down, getting on the toilet, and urinating or having a bowel movement. It also includes getting the right amount of toilet paper, wiping clean from front to back, putting toilet paper into the toilet, getting off the toilet, pulling up underwear and pants, flushing the toilet, and washing and drying hands. Most toilet training occurs during the first six weeks once you begin. The whole process, however, may take a long time. It is not unusual for a child to need help until the age of four or five. He may need help wiping after a bowel movement or a reminder to wash his hands. The length of time it takes a child to go all day and night without having an accident varies. The key to making this a short and stress-free experience is to make sure that your child is ready for toilet training when you begin.

Parent Perspective
Deciding when to begin toilet training may be difficult. You may be eager to start before your child is ready. Waiting is hard if you are experiencing social pressure from relatives or friends. Nursery school toileting requirements may add pressure. Frustration from the never-ending task of changing diapers may also motivate you to begin training early, especially if you are expecting another baby.

On the other hand, you may be hesitant to begin training when your child is ready. You may fear that toilet training will be a new ground for battles. You might not begin training because you don't know how to proceed.

Child Perspective
Many young children are comfortable "peeing and pooping" in their diapers. Some don't understand why they have to recognize the need to "peepee or poopoo," to hold it until they reach a potty, then to let it go down a hole. Your child also may feel that the only reason for going "peepee or poopoo" in the potty is to please you.

When he does "poopoo" in the potty, he may wonder why you are flushing the "poopoo" away when it made you so happy. To some children, their "poopoo" is a prized possession and they want to save it to show everyone. Your child may not realize that it is the act of going "poopoo" in the potty that you are proud of rather than the "poopoo" itself. Instead of disappointing your child, the flush may frighten him. He may think the toilet flush sounds like a big lion's roar. Depending on your child's readiness, temperament, and desire to please, he can range from being compliant to being resistant to this request.

READINESS

Most children have the muscle control to regulate themselves between eighteen months and three years of age. Children with disabilities such as mental retardation may not have this ability until they are four or five years old. Medical problems, such as urological disorders and paralysis, may delay or prohibit your child from developing the muscle control needed for self-regulation.

More important than chronological age is each child's level of readiness. There are 14 signals of readiness (see Table 1). Your child does not need to exhibit all of these before you begin training. However, the more signals your child exhibits, the easier and faster training will be. Thus, training will be easier if he has ten readiness signals as opposed to only six of them.

There are four groups of readiness signals. The first group of signals deal with your child's motor and cognitive development. The first signal of readiness is that your child is **over the excitement of learning to walk and run.** Children who have recently learned to walk or run have difficulty sitting for any length of time. If your child is still thrilled with his new ability to walk and run, it is not the time to begin toilet training. This leads directly to the second signal—being **able to sit down and play quietly for about five minutes.** If your child can do this, then you know he has the ability to sit still. If he will not sit for five minutes during training, it is probably due to a lack of desire rather than a lack of skill. The **ability to help dress and undress himself** is another signal of

TABLE 1 READINESS SIGNALS

- Over the excitement of learning to walk and run.
- Able to sit down and play quietly for about five minutes.
- Able to help dress and undress self.
- Shows imitative behavior.
- Wants to put toys and other possessions where they belong.
- Able to understand and follow simple directions.
- Takes pride in accomplishments.
- Not in a period of negativism.
- Has bowel movements at regular times every day.
- Bowel movements are well formed.
- Able to remain dry for about two hours at a time.
- Able to urinate a good amount at one time.
- Aware of the process of elimination.
- Has a name for urine and bowel movement.

readiness. This includes skills such as pushing down his pants after you unsnap them and pulling them back up. The more he can help dress and undress himself, the more independent he will be in the bathroom. **Showing imitative behavior** is also a readiness signal. Ask yourself if he copies activities that you do—dusting furniture, cutting the grass, or shaving. Your child will learn a lot about toileting by watching you. If he can imitate, teaching him toilet skills should be easier for you. The **ability to follow a simple direction** is another signal. During the toilet training process, you will be asking him to follow many directions. An example of one such direction would be, "Tear off a small piece of toilet paper."

The second group of readiness signals has to do with your child's state of mind. **Showing evidence of wanting to put toys and other possessions where they belong** is the sixth readiness signal. Your child's desire to put toys in the toy box or his shoes in the closet, for instance, tells you he is interested in learning where things go. It also shows a desire to be neat. He should then be able to make a smooth transition to a desire to have a clean bottom and an interest in learning to use the toilet. **Taking pride in accomplishments** is also a readiness signal. If your child is happy about learning a new skill, chances are good that he will take pride in learning to use the toilet. If he is **not in a period of negativism,** he has the eighth signal. However, if your child is saying no to everything, this is probably not the time to begin training. Starting now would just give him something else to say no to.

The third group of readiness signals relates to your child's <u>ability to control bladder and bowel functioning.</u> **Having bowel movements at regular times every day** is the ninth readiness signal. You may need to note his bowel habits over the course of three days to determine if he has a regular pattern. It is common for young children to have a bowel movement after one of their meals. In addition to noting when he has his bowel movements, consider the consistency of his stools. It is better that your child has **well formed bowel movements** as opposed to stools that are loose. Being **able to remain dry for about two hours at a time** is another readiness signal. If your child cannot stay dry for two hours, he may not yet have the muscle control to hold urine that long. Or he may be wetting frequently because he drinks a lot. Consider the amount of urine. Is your child **able to urinate a good amount at one time** rather than dribbling throughout the day?

The fourth and final group of readiness signals deals with your child's <u>understanding of bladder and bowel functioning.</u> Showing an **awareness of the process of elimination** is a signal of readiness. Signs of awareness range from tugging at a wet diaper to saying "I do poopoo." It includes behaviors like grimacing or straining, hiding behind a couch, and pointing to puddles on the floor. Once your child exhibits signs of awareness, determine if he exhibits these signs after the fact, during the act, or beforehand—the latter being optimal. If your child **has words for urine and bowel movement,** he has the last readiness signal. He must be able to communicate with you throughout the toilet training process. Words like "peepee" and "poopoo" will allow him to do this. If your child is not yet speaking or is unable to speak, you may teach him the sign for toilet. To sign toilet, make a fist and place your thumb between your index and middle finger, then move your hand and wrist in a back and forth motion.

In addition to considering readiness signals, make sure your child is not experiencing a stressful situation when you start toilet training. Stressful situations for young children include weaning from the breast or bottle, the birth of a new baby in the family, and changes in child care arrangements. A separation from parents (due to, for example, a business trip or vacation), hospitalization of the child or another family member, or moving to a new home also cause extra stress. Wait four to six weeks after the stressful situation is over before beginning toilet training.

PRE-TOILET TRAINING

Pre-toilet training activities lay a solid base for toilet training. Engaging in these activities with your child make the training process an easier one for both of you. You can begin pre-toilet training for your child as young as fifteen months of age. This process should continue until your child has enough readiness signals to begin toilet training. If your child is ready to begin toilet training immediately, you should spend one week in this phase first. This will allow him to enter the toilet training process with the skills and knowledge that this phase provides.

There are four aspects to pre-toilet training. **Naming urine and bowel movements** is the first. When you notice that your child has a wet or dirty diaper, mention what has happened, using the words that your family has chosen—"You have 'poopoo' in your diaper..." or "You went 'peepee. . . .'" The words you choose to use should be simple. Consistency in using these words is more important than which words you choose. Using the same words consistently will help your child learn their meanings. If your child is in a day-care setting, you may want to use the same words as his caregiver.

The second aspect of pre-toilet training involves **allowing your child to watch you or other family members use the toilet.** This provides your child with opportunities to see, ask questions, and learn. You can facilitate this learning process by occasionally describing what you are doing, saying, "I'm going 'peepee' in the potty. . . .I'm getting a small piece of toilet paper. . . .I'm wiping myself from front to back so I can feel dry and clean...." When showing your child how to have a bowel movement, do not strain or grunt. Your child may interpret this as a sign of pain

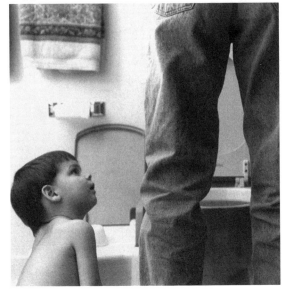

and may reason, "When my Mommy goes 'poopoo' in the potty, she makes faces and funny noises. It must hurt to go 'poopoo' in the potty. When I go 'poopoo' in my diaper it doesn't hurt. I'm not going 'poopoo' in the potty."

The third aspect of pre-toilet training revolves around issues of **changing your child's diaper**. Change his diaper as soon as possible after it becomes wet or dirty to prevent his becoming comfortable with, or even liking, wet and dirty diapers. When you change his diaper, never make him feel he is bad for wetting or soiling it. Also avoid making faces or negative comments, no matter how foul it smells. Instead, simply label what he has done. Then comment on how good it will feel to be clean and dry again. If possible, change your child's diaper in the bathroom. This will accomplish a few important toilet training tasks before initiating training. Dropping the discards from the diaper into the toilet will help him learn that the toilet is where "poopoos" go. If you encourage him to help flush the toilet, he may learn how to flush. By flushing, your child may understand later that it is the act of "going poopoo" in the potty that you are proud of. If your child is afraid of the flushing sound, do not force his participation. Simply flush the toilet once he is out of the bathroom, easing him into it.

Finally, **praise** your child when he tells you verbally or with a gesture that he has gone "peepee or poopoo." Let him know that by telling you this, he is being a big helper. You may say, "Yea! You told me you have 'poopoo' in your diaper. So now I know it's time to change your diaper." Later during the training phase, change your statements to include both praise and encouragement: "Yea! You told me you have 'poopoo' in your diaper. Now I know it's time to change your diaper. But next time, if you tell me before you go 'poopoo,' we can try to go 'poopoo' in the potty." Once he develops voluntary control, he can tell you before the fact. Be sure to provide praise then, too, remarking, "Yea! You told me you have to go 'poopoo.' Let's go potty now."

TOILET TRAINING

Once your child has enough readiness signals, and once he has spent at least one week in the pre-toilet training phase, you can begin toilet training. There are seven basic steps to toilet training. Your child should master and feel comfortable with each step before moving onto the next. The time frame presented is meant as a guideline. Some children take a little longer to progress through the steps, and others move a little faster. While implementing steps one through five, you should continue with pre-toilet training activities.

Placing your child on an adult toilet may make him feel insecure—the hole is bigger than he is, his feet dangle in the air, and he is dependent on you to hold him in place. A potty chair or a child's seat that attaches to the toilet makes him feel more secure. Many parents find a potty chair more convenient for them as well as more comfortable for their child. Several good potty chairs are on the market. Some of them convert to step stools or to child-size seats for the toilet. Some parents begin with a child's seat attached to the toilet so they don't have to make a transition to the adult toilet later. Whichever type you choose is not

important, as long as your child feels comfortable and secure when sitting on it.

Throughout the training process, it is helpful to keep your child in loose clothes that can be taken off and put back on easily. This will allow him to feel more independent, and it may prevent failures due to fumbling with buttons and zippers. Although not necessary, you may find it helpful to provide your child with tangible reinforcers from time to time. Stickers, although a favorite among young children, often lose their appeal quickly. If you feel your child needs the extra encouragement of tangible rewards, use a sticker or smile path (see Figure 1). Finally, you should expect your child exhibit curiosity about his genitals and yours. Toilet

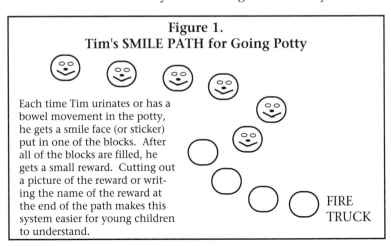

Figure 1.
Tim's SMILE PATH for Going Potty

Each time Tim urinates or has a bowel movement in the potty, he gets a smile face (or sticker) put in one of the blocks. After all of the blocks are filled, he gets a small reward. Cutting out a picture of the reward or writing the name of the reward at the end of the path makes this system easier for young children to understand.

FIRE
TRUCK

TABLE 2
TOILET TRAINING STEPS

WEEK ONE
Step 1: Keep a running list of when your child urinates or
has a bowel movement.
Step 2: Casually introduce your child to his potty.
Step 3: Have him sit on the potty several times a day with
his clothes on.

WEEK TWO
Step 4: Encourage him to sit on the potty several times a
day with his pants and diaper off.

WEEK THREE
Step 5: For a period of time each day, leave your child's
diaper and pants off.

WEEK FOUR (OR FIVE, OR SIX. . .)
Step 6: Transfer your child into training pants and then
underwear.

WEEK EIGHT (OR NINE, OR TEN. . .)
Step 7: Transfer the toileting functions that you are
performing over to your child.

---

training is a natural time for this curiosity to emerge. It provides
you with an opportunity to label the genitals with correct terminol-
ogy, as you do any other body part to which your child refers.

Week One

Step 1. Keep a running list of when your child urinates or has a bowel movement.

This will help you identify his elimination pattern. He may urinate
once every two hours and have a bowel movement within 15
minutes after a meal. Knowing his pattern will help you in Step 4.
If you have difficulty telling when you child urinates because he
wears disposable diapers, consider using cloth diapers for a little
while. Implement Steps 2 and 3 while you collect this information.

Step 2. Casually intro-duce your child to his potty.

Put the potty in the bathroom and wait for your
child to inquire about it.
This gives him not only the
role of initiator but also a
sense of control. It also
avoids a negative response

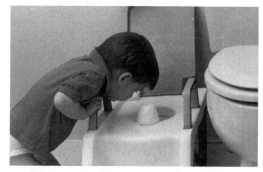

to your initiating the process—"No, I no wanna see potty." Respond to his inquiries with simple answers, and try to avoid overloading him with all the facts of toileting at once. If he asks "What's this?", you might respond by saying, "This is a 'big boy' potty. Do you want to touch it?" Allow your child to explore the potty at his own pace and in his own style.

This may include looking at the potty, touching it, and turning it over. If necessary, draw his attention to the new potty by bumping into it.

Step 3. Have him sit on the potty several times a day with his clothes on.

This will get him into the habit of sitting on the potty in a non-stressful manner. Keep the potty-sitting period brief—one or two minutes is enough. Encourage your child to sit on the potty by providing him with a special activity to do. To keep the activity desirable to him, only allow it when he sits on the potty. Make sure the activity is new. Taking away something that he routinely enjoys and allowing it only at toilet-ing times may make him resent toilet training. Activities such as playing with stickers or stamps and examining a bowl of shells or marbles are favorites among young children. Reading magazines or books and drawing with chalk or markers are also good activities. Engaging in an activity will also keep your child from becoming tense and bored while he sits on the potty. Over the course of his toilet training experience, you may need to alternate activities to keep his interest.

Week Two

Step 4. Encourage him to sit on the potty several times a day with his pants and diaper off.

The goal for your child at this point is to become comfortable sitting on the potty, his skin against plastic. Don't expect him to urinate or have a bowel movement in the potty. Just praise him for sitting on the potty like a big person. If he urinates or has a bowel

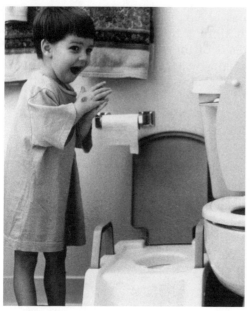

movement while he is on the potty, make a big deal out of it and give him lavish praise. You might clap together while saying, "Yea!", give each other a high five, or sing a little song like "Tim went peepee in the potty, Tim went peepee in the potty! Yea, Tim!!!" If you are putting your child on the potty at the right time and are involving him in an activity, you are likely to experience a couple of successes.

A good time to put your child on the potty is close to the time he usually urinates or has a bowel movement (from information gathered in Step 1). A natural time for putting him on the potty is at bath time, when his clothes are already off. Also try putting him on the potty if he wakes up dry. As in Step 3, keep potty-sitting periods brief. Start with a minute or two, but never leave him sitting more than five minutes, unless he wants to sit longer. Remain with him the entire time unless he requests privacy. If your child wants privacy, wait outside the doorway, and *be certain that his potty arrangements are safe.*

When you take your child to the potty, use a matter-of-fact approach. Approaches like "Let's go sit on the potty and play with your shells" often meet less resistance than "Do you have to go potty?". Do not ask your child if he has to go to the bathroom unless you are willing to respect the answer "no." Instead, simply say it is time to try, and then reinforce his efforts and successes. If you see signs that tell you he is about to urinate or have a bowel movement, take him to the bathroom. You might want to comment on the signal you noticed and explain that you are taking him to the bathroom. For instance, you might say, "You're holding your penis, and when you do that, you usually have to go 'peepee.' Let's try going 'peepee' in the potty." Avoid rushing him to the bathroom as you notice these signs, since doing so may cause him to become anxious and tense. If walking at your normal pace doesn't get you there in time, simply say something like, "Oh oh, we didn't make it, maybe next time. Thank you for trying. I like the way you're trying to put your 'peepee' in the potty."

TRAINING LITTLE BOYS

When training a little boy, teach him to urinate sitting down rather than standing up. Toilet training requires your child to be in the right position so when he urinates, it goes into the potty and not on the floor. Standing up requires him to stand still and to control the direction of his urine, both of which are difficult tasks for most young children. Also, standing makes it difficult for him to engage in an activity while waiting and makes it easy for him to wander away.

If you are using a splash guard with a little boy, you should help him get on and off the potty, so he doesn't hurt his penis on it. If you do not use the splash guard, your child may get on and off by himself. However, make sure that one of you keeps his penis pointing down into the potty, so you and the rest of the bathroom stay dry. As he grows more comfortable with toileting and gains some confidence, he may ask to sit on the adult toilet without a child's seat. This is fine as long as he can support himself on the toilet or you can hold him in place. Be sure that his penis in pointed low enough so the urine goes into the toilet and not out through the crack between the lid and the bowl. You may also have him sit on the toilet backwards (facing the tank). This position avoids any chance of your getting wet.

Week Three

Step 5. For a block of time each day, leave your child's diaper and pants off.

This will help your child learn that "peepee and poopoo" come from him. The longer the time the better, but a minimum of 30 minutes is best. Accidents will occur, so you should think carefully about where you will and will not allow your child to wander. The more restricted the space, the shorter you should make the time. If your child's diaper will only be off for a short period, try to pick the times when he is most likely to urinate or have a bowel movement. If you wish to leave the diaper off for an extended period and if your child will be playing in carpeted areas, cover your carpet with a couple of old blankets. The blankets will catch the accident instead of your carpet and will make cleaning up a lot easier. You might also consider letting him play outside in the backyard if the weather is warm.

When you take his diaper and pants off, explain that big boys go "peepee and poopoo" in the potty. Show him where his potty is, and tell him to sit on the potty when he has to go "peepee or poopoo." If you are using a potty chair you may find it helpful to move it into the room where he is. That way the potty chair is always visible and near.

Reassure him that you will be there to help him, and then allow him to play. While he is playing, avoid asking, "Do you have to go potty now?" every five minutes. Instead, bring toileting back to his attention by asking him a related question every twenty or thirty minutes. You could ask, "Where do big boys go potty?" or "I can't find your potty, where is it?" If two or more hours have passed since your child last urinated and you know that he usually goes every two hours, now would be a good time to encourage him to sit on the potty. As before, allow him to do an activity while he is on the potty. If he is successful, praise him and positively reinforce him. If he sits on the potty and tries to go, but doesn't, still praise him for trying. This allows him to feel successful about his attempts as well as his successes and avoids his feeling any sense of failure.

When your child has an accident, simply say: "Oh, oh. You had an accident. Let's clean it up. Maybe next time you'll get your

'poopoo' in the potty." Try to react very calmly. It will be hard to respond calmly when your child has his fourth or fifth accident in a row. Remind yourself that accidents are inevitable and are an important part of the learning process. Typically, a young child will have many accidents in the beginning. He will then start to have some partial successes with his accidents. A partial success is when he starts to urinate or have a bowel movement, notices it coming out, stops, goes to the potty, and gets the rest in the potty. Gradually, the accidents will decrease, partial successes will increase, and complete successes will emerge. Remain in Step 5 until your child has had ten complete successes.

Week Four (or five, or six...)

Step 6. Transition your child into training pants and then underwear.

First, have your child wear training pants all the time instead of a diaper. There are three types of training pants: thick cotton, thick cotton with a plastic outer lining, and disposable. Some training pants are plain while others have designs on them. When you are at home, put him in the thick cotton pants. This type, while more absorbent than underwear, allows leaks to occur and makes it easier for him to feel wet or dirty. You may want to use the cotton and plastic or disposable ones when you are out because they are less likely to allow his clothes to become wet or soiled. This will reduce the number of times that you will need to change all his clothes after an accident.

Complete nighttime control usually occurs later than daytime control. If your child urinates during the night, use the cotton and plastic or disposable training pants at bedtime. Some parents keep their children in diapers at bedtime and training

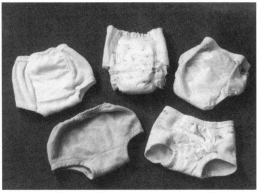

pants during the day. This is an option. However, some children do not want to wear diapers once they have worn training pants because it makes them feel like a baby. Another point to remember is that some children, though capable of staying dry, will continue to wet at night because they are wearing diapers and in their mind diapers are for "peepee and poopoo."

Emptying his bladder and moving his bowels in the potty is a new habit for your child. Continue to expect some accidents and partial successes, with an increasing number of complete successes. As you did before, reinforce all attempts and successes, and treat accidents as calmly as possible: "Oh well, your pants are wet. Let's put on some dry ones." It may take a couple months of training before he can go a few days without having an accident. When he can do this, let him wear underwear instead of training pants. Once he goes a few nights without wetting, let him wear underwear at bedtime. The reason to make this change is financial—underwear is less expensive.

Week Eight (or nine, or ten...)

Step 7. Transfer the toileting functions that you are now performing over to your child.

This includes pushing pants and underwear down, getting on the toilet, getting the right amount of toilet paper, wiping clean from front to back, putting toilet paper into the toilet, getting off the toilet, pulling up underwear and pants, flushing the toilet, and washing and drying hands. Once your child is wearing underwear, he is ready to assume more toileting responsibilities. At this point, he will probably be doing much of this himself. If he is not, use modeling and physical guidance to teach him one function a week until he has mastered independent toileting. He will still need you to provide reminders and help from time to time—especially in the area of wiping. To avoid rashes and infections, make sure that he is wiping properly and not just grazing the surface of his skin with the paper.

HELPFUL STRATEGIES

- Make sure your child exhibits enough readiness signals before you initiate toilet training.
- Spend at least one week in the pre-toilet training phase.
- Avoid grunting and straining when demonstrating how to have a bowel movement.
- Avoid rushing your child to the bathroom.
- Do not ask "Do you want to go potty?" unless you will respect a no answer.
- Teach boys to urinate sitting rather than standing.
- Provide a special activity for your child to do only while on the potty.
- Have your child wear loose clothes.
- Reinforce all attempts and successes.
- Use tangible reinforcers and sticker paths if needed.
- Treat accidents matter-of-factly.
- Handle curiosity about genitals with honesty and sensitivity.
- Relax training for a week if you run into a problem.
- Use the pictures in this book to tell your child a story about toilet training.

WORKING OUT PROBLEMS

If you run into a problem during the toilet training process, stay on the step you are on and address the following questions. First, ask yourself, "Was my child ready for training when I began?" If he only had half of the readiness signals, it may be a good idea to relax the training until he develops a few more signals. Consider whether or not he has lost some of the signals he had earlier. Perhaps he is now in a stage of negativism he wasn't in before.

The second question to ask is "How far did I get before we ran into the problem?" and "Did something happen before that point that may have been a contributing factor?". If you can pinpoint such a factor, the solution is often straightforward. In one situation, a toddler who was making great progress with six total successes in Step 5, suddenly began to cry whenever his diaper was taken off. After stopping to think about the problem, Dad remembered that a couple of days before the new behavior emerged, the family had gone to visit a relative for the day. The relative was training her puppy at the time of the visit. Whenever the puppy had an accident, the relative spanked the puppy and rubbed his nose in it. Once the parents realized their toddler was probably afraid of receiving the same treatment if he had an accident, they relaxed training for a few days. They reassured their son that training puppies was very different from teaching little boys to use the potty. They also shared several books with him that depicted parents responding to accidents in a calm manner.

Finally, you need to ask, "Are there any other issues that might be interfering with the toilet training process?" One such issue is your child's diet intake. If your child is having problems with loose or hard bowel movements, try to determine whether or not he is eating or drinking something that can cause diarrhea or constipation. Another issue is the consistency and regularity of training. If you are busy and unable to provide your child with toilet training opportunities daily, the process is going to take longer.

Besides addressing the questions above, discuss the problem with your child's pediatrician or your family practitioner. Your child's doctor should know him well and may be able to provide some very useful advice.

A PARENT'S STORY

My wife and I began toilet training our son once he had all the readiness signals, and we had done pre-toilet training for about three weeks. I think he was about thirty months old at the time. We did all the things we heard we should do. First, we had Justin sit on a potty chair with his clothes on. Next, we had him sit on the potty chair a couple times each day with his pants and diaper off. Justin usually needed to pee when he woke up in the morning and after his afternoon nap. He also needed to go to the bathroom a couple of hours after breakfast and again after lunch. So we put him on the potty at these times. I also put him on the potty before his bath when he was undressed.

I remember the first time he peed in the potty. I think it surprised him as much as it surprised me. He was sitting on the potty chair playing with a boat while I was filling the tub with water. He peed without either of us knowing; with the sound of the water running neither of us heard him pee. After the tub was full, I asked him if he was ready to get off the potty. He said yes. As I helped him off the potty chair, I saw that he had peed. I was so thrilled that I said, "You did it! You did it!" He looked at me rather confused, not really knowing what he had done. I had him come over and look in the potty. When he did, he was so excited—he clapped his hands and said ,"Yea for me! Yea for me!"

The next week, we covered our living room carpet with old blankets and let him run around in just a T-shirt. Justin's first accident was an eye-opening experience for him. It was as though a light bulb went off in his head, as he realized that pee came from him. He stood there looking at the puddle, his wet leg, and his penis for couple minutes, and then said, "My peepee." After two more accidents, he peed on the potty chair every time. My wife and I were ecstatic!

He had gone three days in a row without an accident, when my wife and I realized that Justin had not pooped in four days. That afternoon we were playing in the living room when Justin stood up, began screaming, and running in circles. I looked at him and didn't know what was going on. I sat him down on my lap, and he said, "I need a diaper. I need a diaper." I asked him if he had to go potty, and he told me he had to go poopoo. I tried taking him to his potty chair, but he insisted on a diaper. My wife went to our son's room and brought us a diaper. We put the diaper on Justin. As soon as we did, he ran to the bathroom, stood by the sink, and pooped in the diaper.

For one month, he peed in the potty but insisted on wearing a diaper to poop. My wife and I were so confused we didn't know what to do. We knew that children who potty-trained for pee before poop were usually harder to train for poop, but we didn't expect this. We talked to a friend who worked with kids, and she recommended a system for helping Justin poop in the potty. The system involved giving Justin some control, using a sticker path, and gradually weaning Justin off the diaper.

The plan involved making a sticker path with 18 squares on it. The squares were color-coded into groups of three. For instance, the first three squares were red, the second three squares were blue, and the third three squares were purple. Each section of colored squares represented a new task. For the first section, Justin needed to sit on the potty with his diaper on to get a sticker in one of the red squares. He didn't need to poop; all he had to do was sit there for ten seconds. For the second section, Justin needed to poop while sitting on the potty with his diaper on to get the sticker. To get a sticker in the third section, Justin needed to poop while sitting on the potty wearing a diaper taped on only one side. In the fourth section he got a sticker if he pooped while sitting on the potty wearing a diaper not taped at all. He earned a sticker in the fifth section if he pooped on the potty wearing half of a diaper. In the sixth and last section he had to poop in the potty without a diaper to get a sticker. In all sections, Justin could earn two stickers if he pooped in the potty without wearing a diaper. Since there was a picture of a big truck at the end of the sticker path, Justin was motivated to get through the squares as fast as possible.

We told Justin that we had a plan for helping him poop in the potty. We explained that he could get stickers to earn a toy. We looked through a catalogue, and he picked out a big truck. We told him that to earn the first three stickers all he had to do was sit on the potty with a diaper on. He got the first three stickers within ten minutes of our putting up the chart. Next, we told him that he had to poop on the potty to get a sticker. We explained that he would get one sticker if he pooped wearing a diaper and two stickers if he pooped on the potty without a diaper. We didn't go into the details of each section of the path.

Throughout the sticker path period, Justin wore training pants and had the option of wearing a diaper when he told us that he needed to poop. The hardest part of the path was getting Justin to sit on the potty the first time that he had to poop. After that we were surprised at how fast things went. He pooped on the potty wearing a diaper twice and then pooped on it without asking for a diaper. The fourth time he asked for a diaper. We were in the purple section, the third section, of the path. That meant Justin could sit on the potty wearing a diaper taped on only one side. Before this section, I removed the tape from one side of all our diapers. We made a joke about the diapers being made wrong, and Justin thought it was funny. He went poop on the potty wearing the diaper taped on one side twice. He asked for a diaper once more, and we gave it to him. From that point on, he never asked for a diaper. Within one week, Justin was pooping in the potty without a diaper all the time!

SUMMARY

Toilet training is the process by which you teach your child to go to the bathroom at his own signal and to use the toilet with little or no help. Although most toilet training occurs during the first six weeks after you begin, the whole process can take a long time. The key to making this a short and stress-free experience is to make sure that he is ready for toilet training before you start.

There are 14 signals of readiness. Your child does not need to exhibit all of these before training begins. However, the more signals your child exhibits, the easier and faster the training will be. Most children are ready for toilet training between the ages of eighteen months and three years. Pre-toilet training can begin as early as fifteen months of age and can continue until your child has enough readiness signals to begin toilet training.

Once your child has mastered enough readiness signals, and once he has spent at least one week in the pre-toilet training phase, you may begin toilet training. There are seven steps to toilet training. Your child should master and be comfortable with each step before moving onto the next. If you run into a problem during the toilet training process, relax the training and try to find a solution.

REFERENCES & RECOMMENDED READINGS

For Children:
Cole, J. (1989). *Your New Potty*. New York, NY: Morrow Junior
    Books.
Frankel, A. (1980). *Once Upon A Potty*. Happauge, NY: Barron's.
Rogers, F. (1986). *Going To The Potty*. New York, NY: Putnam.

For Parents:
Brazelton, T. (1976). *Doctor & Child*. New York, NY: Delacorte Press.
Leach, P. (1978). *Your Baby & Child*. New York, NY: A. A. Knopf.
Mack, A. (1978). *The Picture Book Techniques for Children and
    Parents*. Boston, MA: Little, Brown.

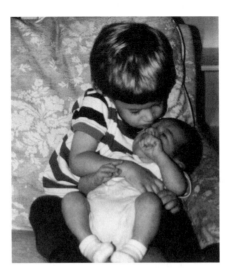

Chapter 11
Preparing for and Adjusting to a New Baby

Helping your child prepare for and adjust to a new baby involves teaching, including listening and loving. The process evolves over time in three phases. The first phase occurs during pregnancy and involves **preparing a child for the addition of a new baby** to the family. The second phase takes place while Mom is in the hospital. Its focus is on **easing the separation that occurs at that time and assuring the child that Mommy and Daddy still love him.** The third and final phase begins when the baby comes home from the hospital and continues through early childhood. It is during this last phase that a young child begins **adjusting to a new sibling**, as he realizes that things are different and the new baby can't go back where she came from.

<u>Parent Perspective</u>
Most parents anticipate the birth of a new baby with great joy. However, many of them admit they also feel apprehensive. As an expectant parent, you may feel uneasy about the coming separation your child will experience while you are in the hospital. You worry about your child's reaction to the new baby—will he be mean or will he be sweet? You may be concerned that the relationship between you and your child will change for the worse— will he suddenly become clingy and fussy? You may dream that your child will have as loving and caring a relationship as you had with a younger sibling. Sometimes you wonder if you'll love your new baby as much as you love your child. You want to do everything possible to prepare your child for the birth of his sibling, to

minimize any separation problems during your hospital stay, and to support him as he adjusts to the new baby at home.

Child Perspective
Most young children experience mixed feelings about the idea of having a new baby brother or sister. Your child may be excited about the prospect of having a playmate who can go outside and play with him. But he may be very disappointed when he learns that new babies can't crawl or play. He may get angry at seeing the nursery set up with his old crib and toys. He will feel important when you ask his opinion on names for the baby. He may feel sad and abandoned when you leave him with a sitter while you keep a doctor's appointment. He feels jealous when you receive gifts for the new baby at a shower. As your due date approaches, he nurses fears that you may never come back when you go to the hospital to have the baby. He worries that you won't love him anymore once you have a baby to love. Many toddlers and preschoolers have difficulty expressing these feelings in words, so they act them out through their behavior.

PREPARING FOR A NEW BABY

Without adequate preparation, it is almost impossible for a young child to grasp the idea of a new baby. Most toddlers and preschoolers envision an older baby who crawls, eats mushy food, and plays with toys. Many young children are excited about the prospect of having a new playmate. Such inaccurate expectations often make adjusting to a new baby more difficult for a young child. Teaching your child about the appearance, abilities, and needs of a newborn will foster the development of realistic expectations. Talking about things he may do to help once the baby arrives and including him in activities, such as doctor appointments and shopping for the baby, can develop feelings of involvement and may facilitate adjustment.

Preparing your child for a new brother or sister is extremely helpful. Preparing him for the hospitalization that will occur when the baby is born is also important. The best time for these preparations is while you are pregnant. In preparing your child, it is important to consider his developmental level. While the same activities are appropriate for the one- to four-year-old, the depth of explanations should vary. If your child is between one and two and a half years, keep your explanations simple and concrete. Simplicity is also best for the two- and a half- to four-year-old, but your explanations should include some details and specifics.

The first step in preparing your child for a new baby is to **prepare him for hearing that Mommy is pregnant.** Before telling your child that you are pregnant, spend some time talking about babies in general. Read him a book about babies, and visit a friend

---

TABLE 1
PREPARING FOR A NEW BABY

• Prepare your child for the news that Mommy is pregnant.
• Tell him that Mommy is going to have a baby.
• Ask your child if he would like to see what the baby looks like inside of Mommy.
• Briefly explain how a baby is born.
• Discuss what a newborn looks like and does.
• Talk about the things a new baby needs.
• Describe ways that your child may help when the baby is born.
• Explain safety rules.
• Prepare him for the hospitalization that will occur when the baby is born.
• Involve your child as much as possible.

---

or a relative who has a baby. You can also read a book on baby animals and visit the zoo, pet store, or petting farm. All are excellent ways of introducing babies in a non-threatening manner.

After you introduce your child to the concept of babies, **tell him that Mommy is going to have a baby.** When you tell your child that the family is expecting a new baby, do not ask him whether he wants a new brother or sister. By asking him this question, you are implying that he has a decision to make. If you are pregnant, the decision has been made, and it is too late for such a question. Instead, remind him of the book that you read or the baby that you visited,

and tell him that soon there will be a baby in his family.

Carefully watch and listen to his reaction to the news. He may say that he doesn't want a stupid baby; he may say "okay" and run off to play; or he may clap his hands and say "Yea!" Regardless of his reaction, respond with understanding. If he appears distressed by the news, react in a non-judgmental and sympathetic manner. Let him know that it's all right to express how he feels. Reassure him that Mommy and Daddy love him and always will. If he is noncommittal, take his lead; drop the subject for now, and play with him. If he appears to be excited, tell him that you are glad he is happy. Let him know that he may help the family get ready for the new baby. Answer, as honestly as possible, any questions your child asks.

A few days later, **ask your child if he wants to see what the baby looks like inside of Mommy.** Show him the picture of the pelvic bones, the uterus, and the baby (see below). Tell him the picture shows what it would look like if he could see inside Mommy's tummy. Explain that everyone has pelvic bones, and that the hip bones and tail bone are part of the pelvic bones. Help him find his hip bones and tail bone. Have him point to your hip bones and tail bone. Mention that the baby is in Mommy's uterus, and that the uterus rests in her pelvic bones. Explain that the umbilical cord is a food tube that brings food right to the baby's stomach. Describe how he had an umbilical cord when he was a baby. Tell him that his belly button is where his umbilical cord used to be. Have him point to the picture of the baby. Explain that the baby will grow inside of Mommy, and that Mommy's tummy will get bigger as the baby gets bigger. Mention that once the baby is big enough, it will be born.

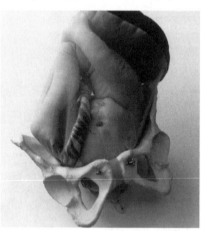

When your child asks you how the baby will get out, **briefly explain how a baby is born.** Tell him that the uterus will open at the bottom and the baby will come out of Mommy's pelvic bones through the vagina. If your child asks "Does the baby comes out where peepee comes out?", explain that there are two parts to a vagina—a place for "peepee" to come out and a place for babies to come out. If you know that the baby will be born by Cesarean section, you may describe that birth process. Tell your child the doctor will get the baby out through Mommy's tummy. Explain that the doctor will cut Mommy's tummy and uterus open to get to the baby. Tell him that the doctor will give Mommy medicine so it will not hurt.

At another time, **discuss what a newborn baby looks like and does.** An excellent way of doing this is to show your child pictures of himself as a newborn. Talk about how small he was and how much or how little hair he had. Mention the things that he is doing in the pictures—sucking a pacifier, sleeping, taking a bath, nursing, looking at a toy, getting a kiss. Ask him to tell you some things that babies can and cannot do. Point out similarities and differences between what he can do and what the baby can do. Reinforce how great it is that he is big and can do some things that babies can't. If you have any, show your child pictures of yourself as a baby. In addition to looking at these pictures, read books about babies, color in a coloring book on babies, draw pictures of your family with the new baby, or do some role playing and pretend to be babies.

TABLE 2
THINGS THAT BABIES CAN AND CANNOT DO

Babies can:	Babies cannot (but your child can):
Hold a rattle.	Play in a sandbox.
Drink from breast or bottle.	Drink from a cup.
Cry.	Talk.
Listen to voices and music.	Sing songs.
Look at faces and toys.	Throw balls .
Wet and dirty diapers.	Use a toilet (maybe).
Burp and spit up.	Eat foods.

Before shopping for items for the baby, **talk about the things that a new baby needs.** Ask your child what he thinks the new baby will need. Look at books and catalogues to get ideas. Together, make a list of six or seven items that the baby needs. Look around the house to see if you already have some of these things. If you find an item that your child used as a baby—his crib, for instance—prompt him to say that it's okay for the baby to use it. Take him shopping to buy the remaining items. When appropriate, let your child choose the color or style of the item. Make the shopping trip a special outing; eat lunch together at the park or a restaurant before you come home. After you get home, thank your child for being such a big helper.

When appropriate situations arise, **discuss ways your child can help once the baby is born.** For example, when you buy diapers, mention to your child that he may bring you a clean diaper when the baby needs her diaper changed. Let him know that in addition to bringing you things such as diapers and pacifiers, he may help put things away. Point out the fun things that he may do with the baby. Explain to him that he may play with her by making silly faces, singing songs, and showing her rattles or other *safe* toys. Tell him that when you feed the baby, he may help burp her. Mention that he may rub lotion on the baby after she has her bath. Also tell him that he may hold the baby *as long as an adult is there to help*

him. If your child appears interested, let him practice some of the things on a doll that he will be allowed to do with the baby.

As you discuss and practice ways that your child may help, **explain safety rules.** There are six basic safety rules that young children should follow. The first is: *always wash your hands before playing with the baby.* Most toddlers and preschoolers play on the floor and learn by touching everything. Some young children are notorious for putting their fingers in their noses. Explain to your child that although his hands may look clean, they may have invisible germs on them. Tell him that he should wash the germs away before he plays with the baby. The second rule is: *hold the baby only when an adult is there to help.* Explain that he should always ask permission from an adult before he holds the baby. Tell your child that he is too little to pick up the baby, so that the adult will give him the baby. Mention that he will need to sit while he holds the baby. Using a floppy doll, teach him how to support the baby's head with his arm or a pillow. Let him know that when he tires of holding the baby, he should ask an adult to take the baby. This is an important part of the holding rule because some young children will simply stand up when they are tired of holding the baby, allowing the baby to roll off their lap. The third rule is: *always ask before giving the baby a toy.* In his eagerness to interact with the baby, a toddler may share a toy that is too heavy (his overloaded box of blocks) or too small (his favorite miniature car). The fourth rule also relates to sharing. Tell your child that he should *never put anything on the baby's face.* Explain that if he wants to play Peek-A-Boo with the baby, he should hide his face, *not* the baby's. Needless to say, you don't want him putting a pillow on the baby's face during a game or at any other time. The fifth rule is *never give the baby food.* Your child probably likes taking bites of your food and may think that he is being nice by sharing his food with the baby. Explain that babies can only drink breast milk or formula. The last rule is that your child *should always be gentle with the baby.* Talk about how little the baby will be and how easily she could get hurt. These six rules are the basic safety rules. Depending on individual circumstances, you may need to add more rules. When discussing safety issues with your child, do so a little at a time; so that your child can remember as much as possible.

TABLE 3
SAFETY RULES FOR YOUNG CHILDREN

- Always wash your hands before playing with the baby.
- Hold the baby only when an adult is there to help.
- Always ask before giving the baby a toy.
- Never put anything on the baby's face.
- Never give the baby food.
- Always be gentle with the baby.

In addition to preparing your child for a new brother or sister, **prepare him for the hospitalization that will occur when the baby is born.** Unless your child brings up the issue first, save discussions about the hospitalization until close to the due date. A few weeks before your due date, discuss the fact that Mommy will be going to the hospital to have the baby. Tell him that Mommy will only be gone for a day or two. Mention that Daddy will be at the hospital for part of the time too. Point out that he can visit you at the hospital. Take your child on a tour of the hospital so he can envision where you will be. Many hospitals have tours specifically designed for toddlers and preschoolers. If the hospital where you are delivering does not have tours for children, ask to bring him along on the adult tour. Unfortunately, some hospitals do not allow children on the maternity unit at all. If this is the case, take your child to the hospital to see the building, lobby, and cafeteria. When discussing the hospitalization, be sure to tell your child who will take care of him while Mommy and Daddy are at the hospital. Try to develop some extra closeness between your child and that person before the birth.

Throughout the pregnancy, **involve your child as much as possible.** Such involvement will make him feel that he is a part of this change, and it may facilitate his adjustment. Take him along to a couple prenatal doctor appointments. At one of the appointments, let him listen to the baby's heartbeat. Prior to his listening to the baby's heartbeat, let him hear his own. Arrange his other visit so he may be present during an ultrasound. Seeing the baby on TV fascinates most toddlers and preschoolers. In addition to attending appointments, involve your child in activities such as shopping for the baby and setting up the nursery. If

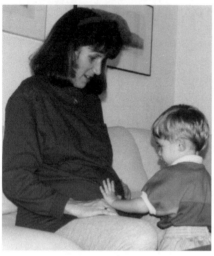

the new baby will be using some of your child's baby items or your child's nursery, it is important to let him participate in arranging the nursery. When you include children in simple decisions, they are better able to accept those decisions. Having your child help with pushing furniture in place and arranging the room transfers some of the power to him. He may not be enthusiastic about sharing his baby items, but your allowing him to participate teaches him that he has some power that affects family decisions. Finally, involve your child by encouraging him to kiss and hug the baby through Mommy's tummy.

EASING SEPARATION DURING MOM'S HOSPITAL STAY

When it is time for you to go to the hospital, tell your child that Mommy is going to the hospital to have the baby. Remind him of the arrangements you've made for his care. Let him know when you will call and when he may visit. Give him a big hug and kiss before you leave.

During your hospital stay, your child will do best if he stays with someone who is familiar, warm, and loving. Although this is the most important factor, there are a few additional things you or his caregiver may do to ease this separation. One idea is to mark a calendar to show your child how long it will be before Mommy comes home. Draw a smiling face on the day Mommy will come home. Each evening, draw an X through the day and count how many days are left until Mommy comes home. Second, give your child an audio tape of Mommy reading a bedtime story or singing a bedtime song. Prepare the tape several weeks before the due date so your child will have it to listen to at bedtime or whenever he misses

Mommy. Provide him with a picture of Mommy to hold and look at while he listens to the tape. Finally, arrange daily visits and phone calls with Mom.

When your child visits the hospital, he will probably want to see and hug Mom before he takes a look at the new baby. If possible, have the new baby in a bassinet when your child arrives for his visit, keeping Mommy's arms free to hug her older child. Be sure to have a picture of your older child in the hospital room. Show your child the picture and explain that Mom looks at the picture whenever she misses him. This will assure your child that Mommy has not forgotten him. After a few minutes of cuddling him and catching up, introduce him to his new sibling. A good idea is to have a small present for your older child to give to the new baby and another for the new baby to give in return. A big brother button or T-shirt makes an excellent gift for a toddler or preschooler to receive. Either makes a great gift because your son may wear either one proudly, and it will attract attention— attention he may now have to seek since the new baby naturally attracts so much.

Most hospitals have unlimited visiting hours for siblings. Bring your child to visit as often as you like. If the hospital doesn't permit siblings to visit, allow your child to call Mommy at the hospital. If possible, have Daddy bring him a picture of Mommy and the baby. If the picture of the older child is in the background of the picture of Mommy and baby, it will let him know that Mommy is thinking of him.

Some children become upset with short visits or talks with Mommy—what they really want is to have Mommy all to themselves for a long time. Prepare for this reaction by planning a fun activity for the older child after the visit or phone call. Going out for an ice cream cone is usually an excellent distraction. Unless your child responds in an extremely negative way to visits or phone calls, it is important to continue daily contacts.

When it is time for Mom and baby to leave the hospital, your child may go along to get them or await their arrival at home. The latter is generally the better choice because the discharge process is often long and boring for a toddler or preschooler. It usually involves physical exams of Mom and baby, discussions with nurses or doctors, paperwork, packing, and loading the car. It is also difficult to predict the exact time that you will leave the hospital. As a result, your child may have to wait an hour or more before it is actually time to bring Mommy and baby home. Unless you have some toys or another adult to entertain your child, he may have more fun waiting at home with a friend or a relative. Encourage them to make a welcome home card or banner for Mom and baby. Or suggest they make a birthday cake to celebrate the birth of the new baby. If your child waits at home, arrange to have Dad or another adult carry the baby in from the car so Mom's arms are free to greet and hug the older child.

ADJUSTING TO A NEW BABY

The addition of a new baby to the family creates many dramatic changes for your child. He needs to learn what a baby can and cannot do, and what he may and may not do to the baby. He has to share his old baby items and possibly his bedroom. Even more, he has to share his mom's and dad's attention with the baby. He is not able to get what he wants as quickly as he used to. He wonders why you want this baby. He feels afraid that you love this baby more than you love him. He fears that you don't need him now that you have another child. He is likely to feel jealousy towards the new baby.

Jealousy is a normal reaction to a new sibling. Young children, however, often cannot express this emotion verbally. Instead, your child may express his jealousy through anger, stubbornness, hostility, withdrawal, or regression. As a parent, you must recognize the jealousy, empathize with your child's feelings, and limit his jealousy to safe expression. If your child is abusive towards the baby, give him a doll or a bop bag to take his aggressions out on. Both will provide him with an excellent outlet for dealing with his negative feelings.

At the same time you are helping your child handle several strong emotions, you may also struggle with an emotional balancing act of your own. Chances are, you feel overwhelmed by the task of raising another child. You may feel incompetent, because you don't have enough time or energy for the children, your spouse, and other household tasks. You might resent the intrusiveness of your older child, as you try to form a close bond with your new baby. You are likely to feel badly because you aren't able to give your new baby as much attention as you gave your older child. And you may feel guilty for not spending the amount of time with your child that you did before the baby was born. Your feelings of guilt may tempt you to let your child get away with breaking rules to make things easier for him. But ignoring the usual limits will only cause your child to feel unsure and may result in his testing his limits to reestablish his boundaries. To facilitate your child's adjustment to the new baby, implement the appropriate strategies from Table 4.

TABLE 4
STRATEGIES FOR FACILITATING ADJUSTMENT

- Keep limits stable.
- Involve your child in the care of the baby.
- Stress the positives of being the older child.
- Spend special time with your child each day.
- Provide your child with a "big boy box."
- Have some inexpensive gifts to offer your child.
- Delay undertaking major developmental tasks.
- Assure your child that you love him.

Maintain consistent limits

If your child was not allowed to jump on the couch before the arrival of the baby, do not permit this after the baby is born. By maintaining rules to the greatest extent possible, you will not push your child to test all his limits. Instead, he will only need to test boundaries with regards to the baby. The fewer the incidents of testing, the easier things will be for all of you.

Involve your child

Involve your child in the care of the baby *to the extent that it is safe*. While you are feeding the baby, your child may help burp the baby by gently patting her back. During a diaper change, he may get you a clean diaper and take Babywipes out of the container. While you dress the baby, he may hand you items of clothing. At bath time, he may entertain the baby by singing songs and showing her small bath toys. After the bath, your child may help rub lotion onto her arms, legs, and stomach. Make sure his helping with the baby is an option, not a duty. Otherwise, he may resent his sibling

for the extra work he has to do. *You will need to provide a lot of supervision and reminders while your child is helping.* You may also need to teach him how to be gentle with the baby.

Compliment your child when he does something for himself. Tell him how great it is that he can drink his milk from a cup without spilling and how strong he is that he can carry a small bag of groceries inside. Comment on what a grand structure he is building with his blocks. Mention that he can do these things, but the baby cannot. From time to time, you may notice your child regressing into babyish behaviors. Regressions, such as bedwetting or baby talk are normal and indicate a need for reassurance. Engaging in babyish behaviors is one of your child's ways of seeking the attention that the baby receives. Try not to punish him for this. Punishment will only increase his feelings of insecurity. As you reassure your child that you love him, the behavior will fade rather quickly.

> **ASKING TO NURSE OR DRINK FROM A BOTTLE**
> Having your toddler or preschooler ask to nurse or drink from a bottle is a tough regression for many parents to handle. The request may represent curiosity on the child's part. It may also be his attempt to get the attention and love the baby receives during feedings. One strategy is to offer the breast or bottle to your child. Most toddlers and preschoolers find the confinement to Mom during a feeding boring. After a few minutes most children will say they are "all done" and will decide they prefer to play. However, if you make this offer, you need to realize that your child may like nursing or drinking from a bottle. An alternative is to remind the older child that he is too old to nurse or take the bottle. If you opt to do this, do it in a loving manner and offer another way to spend some special time together. Perhaps the two of you may plan a trip to the park without the baby.

Spend special time with your child each day

Your older child may be accustomed to getting a lot of your attention. You will find it impossible to provide him with the same attention once the baby is born. Your child will miss this attention, and he will feel that the new baby is threatening his place in the family. He may tell you that he wants the baby to go back where she came from. Responding that babies can't go back may end the conversation, but it will not deal with the feelings that he is expressing. Instead, respond in a way that shows your child that you understand his position. Tell him that you know it is hard for him to share Mommy and Daddy with the new baby. Make plans for Mommy and Daddy to spend fifteen minutes each alone with him every day. Then, when your child demands attention that you cannot provide, you may remind him of the special time that you spent together earlier that day or that is coming up later that day.

Provide your child with a "big boy" box

There are going to be times when you will be busy with the baby, and your child will want you to play with him. For those times, a "big boy" box may be a helpful solution. This can be, for example, a shoe box filled with a few fun, safe, and independent activities. The types of activities will vary according to the age of your child. Suggestions include little books, paper, washable crayons or mark-

ers, cars, bubbles, blocks, and stickers. Use the box only when you are too busy to interact with your child. If you allow him to play with it whenever he wishes, the box will quickly lose its appeal. Even with limited usage, you should change the contents of the box every few weeks. Each time you refer your child to the box be sure to go to him as soon as you finish with the baby. Thank him for playing independently, put the box away, and give him a few minutes of special attention.

Have some inexpensive gifts for your child

During the first months after the birth of the baby, friends and relative often bring gifts for the new baby. Watching a younger sibling get attention and gifts is hard on a toddler or a preschooler. He may feel left out. He may think that people don't love him enough to give him gifts. He may also resent the baby for getting so many gifts. Occasionally provide your child with a small, inexpensive gift during this time. This will make him feel valued and loved.

Delay undertaking major developmental tasks

Adjusting to the arrival of a new baby is a major effort for your child. So that you don't overload him with new expectations, it is best to undertake one developmental task at a time. Wait a couple of months until your new routines are established before you initiate another developmental task—such as toilet training—with your older child.

Assure your child that you love him

Seeing his mommy and daddy care for and play with the new baby may concern your child. He fears that he will lose your love. Assure your child many times every day that you love, care for, and need him. Remember that words and actions are both important. Tell him that you love him, and give him kisses and hugs to show him.

A PARENT'S STORY

I became pregnant with my second child when David was 26 months old. I had really mixed emotions about being pregnant— Part of me was happy and excited, but part of me was a little sad and anxious. I was sad for David because he wasn't going to be the baby anymore, and he wouldn't be the only one getting my attention. I was anxious about how David would react to the new baby.

When I was six months pregnant, I told David that I was going to have a baby. I did all of the things that you should do to prepare a child for the birth of a new baby. I think the best thing I did to prepare David was to attend a sibling preparation class with him. The class was great! The teacher showed the children what the baby looked like when it was inside of Mommy. She taught them about how babies are born. She talked with them about the things that a baby can and can't do. She taught them how to hold a baby. She showed them a movie about babies. She took the children and parents on a tour of the hospital. She pointed out where Mommy would be when she had the baby and where Mommy would be afterward, stressing that there was a phone in each room. David was glad to know that he could talk to me whenever he wanted to. She also showed them the nursery. After the tour came David's favorite part, a birthday party for the new babies. The children ate cupcakes, drank juice, and listened to stories about having a new baby in the family. At the end of the class, the teacher gave the girls a button that read, "I'm ready to be a big sister!", and the boys one that read, "I'm ready to be a big brother!" David talked about the class for the next three weeks.

We were all playing in the living room when I went into labor. I told David that it was time for Daddy and I to go to the hospital to have the baby. He looked a little apprehensive. I gave him a kiss and told him not to worry. I reminded him that Grandma and Grandpa would take care of him and that they would bring him to the hospital as soon as the baby was born. My parents were at our house within twenty minutes. Grandpa was great. He came with a new car and a new puzzle. Distracted by the new toys, David waved bye, barely taking the time to glance up as he did so.

The labor and delivery went extremely well, and Christina was born five hours after we got to the hospital. As promised, my mom and dad brought David to the hospital right away. We were still in the recovery room when David arrived. The nurse was bathing Christina. That was great because my arms were free to give him a big hug. When the nurse was done with Christina, he brought her to me. David was sitting on my left, so I put Christina on my right. A minute or two later, David popped off the bed, ran around to the other side, and climbed back into bed next to Christina. He snuggled under the covers, leaned over, gave her a kiss, and said, "I like her." My husband and I looked at each other and smiled, as a wave of relief and joy swept over us.

The first two weeks at home were wonderful! My husband took the time off from work to be with us, and his help was immeasurable. Everything fell apart during the third week—my husband had to go out of town on business, and I had to deal with things on my own.

The morning after my husband left, David cried and said that he was hungry when we were in the bathroom trying to bathe Christina. We had just finished breakfast thirty minutes before, but he was so insistent that I stopped bathing Christina, and we all went to the kitchen to have a snack. An hour later, David hit me when I started to nurse Christina. I asked him why he was hitting me. He hit me again and ran to his bedroom. Christina was screaming and needed to eat, so I nursed her. I felt bad about not running after David, but I could hear him playing with his cars in his room and knew that he was okay. Later that afternoon, when I began to nurse Christina, David hit me again. After hitting me, he ran behind the couch and began to cry. This time before nursing Christina, I calmed David down and set him up with his favorite video to watch. He hit me again when I went to nurse Christina that evening. And when I got the infant tub filled with water to try to finish Christina's bath, David cried and said that he wanted something to eat. This happened although I had purposely offered him a snack before going into the bathroom to bathe Christina. For the next two days, David continued to hit me when I nursed Christina, and he continued to insist on eating when I bathed her.

On the third night, after David and Christina were in bed, I sat on the couch and cried. I knew that I couldn't handle another day like the three we just had. After crying for twenty minutes, I called my sister. She is the mother of four children, but lives 800 miles away. Our talk helped a lot. She helped me see that David was jealous of the attention that I was giving Christina, and that he probably missed his Daddy. She helped me come up with a few ideas for helping David out.

The next day when I nursed Christina, David and I read a story together. I had him sit on the side opposite the one that Christina was nursing on. I told him that Christina was keeping one side of me warm, but the other side of me was cold. I asked him if he could help keep that side of me warm. With a smile on his face, he gladly cuddled next to me. Each time that I nursed Christina, David and I sat close to one another and read a story, sang songs, or watched a video. Much to my relief, there was no hitting. Bath time also went a lot better. I decided to bathe Christina in the kitchen. I put her infant tub on a big towel on the kitchen floor. Right next to her tub, I put a snack and drink on a placemat for David. During her bath, he ate his banana and drank his juice.

Two mornings later, when David and I were reading his favorite story (while I was nursing Christina), he closed his book and said, "I tired of sitting here. You feed Christina, I gonna play with my trucks. Okay?" Five minutes later he suddenly stopped playing with his trucks and ran to his room. My heart stopped for a moment. Before I could get up to see if everything was all right, David was back in the living room handing me his blanket saying, "Here, Mommy. You can use this if you get cold." From that point on, I continued to ask David if he wanted to cuddle and read or sing when I nursed Christina. About half of the time David would cuddle, and about half of the time he would happily entertain himself. I continued bathing Christina in the kitchen for the next few months. I think David looked forward to bath/snack time and that it actually became an important part of his routine.

SUMMARY

Helping your child prepare for and adjust to the birth of a new baby is a process that evolves over time in three phases. The first phase occurs while you are pregnant and focuses on preparing your child for the new baby. It involves telling him that you are pregnant, teaching him about the baby and what he can do to help, and explaining safety rules. It also includes preparing your child for the separation that will occur when the baby is born. Easing this separation is the second phase. It encompasses providing your child with a loving person to care for him while you are in the hospital, allowing him to call and visit, and making Mom's arrival home with the baby a positive experience. The final phase is facilitating your child's adjustment to the new baby. It involves eight key strategies.

When preparing your child for a new baby and helping him adjust to the birth of a baby, listen to his comments and questions carefully. Respond with sensitivity and honesty. Throughout the process, reassure him daily that you love him and that you always will.

REFERENCES & RECOMMENDED READINGS

For Children:
Catano, J. (1988). *A Coloring Book for Kids: Helping Mommy Breastfeed.* Minneapolis, MN: International Childbirth Education Association.
Fujikawa, G. (1963). *Babies.* New York, NY: Grosset & Gunlap Publishers.
Hendrickson, K. (1985). *Getting Along Together: Baby and I Can Play.* Seattle, WA: Parenting Press, Inc.
Hoban, R. (1964). *A Baby Sister for Frances.* New York, NY: Harper and Row Publishers.
Szekeres, C. (1989). *The New Baby.* New York, NY: A Golden Book.
Tillema, S. (1983). *The Children's Activity Book.* Madison, WI: Program Development and Management Associates, Inc.
Watson, J., Switzer, R., & Hirschberg, J. (1986). *Sometimes I'm Jealous.* New York, NY: Crown Publishers, Inc.
Weissman, J. (1988). *Games to Play with Babies.* Overland Park, KS: Miss Jackie Music Company.

Young, R. (1987). *The New Baby.* New York, NY: Viking Kestrel.

For Parents:

Brazelton, T. (1976). *Doctor and Child.* New York, NY: Delacorte Press/Seymour Lawrence, Chapter 9.

Weiss, J. (1981). *Your Second Child.* New York, NY: Summit Books.

Chapter 12
Preparing for and Supporting Your Child through Preschool

Preschool has replaced kindergarten as the first school experience for most children, for some, their first experience away from home. In preschool, many children acquire the skills they need for kindergarten and learn to socialize with other children. Like all parents, you want your child's preschool experience to be a good one, but you may not be sure how to find your way through the maze of preschool options you hear other parents talking about.

Ensuring that your child's preschool experience is successful involves three phases. **Choosing the right school** is the first phase. Most preschools conduct registration for the fall during the prior winter. To meet possible deadlines, be prepared to decide on a preschool six to eight months before your child begins. **Preparing your child for school** is the second phase. This process usually occurs during the summer before your child starts preschool. The third phase, **supporting your child throughout the preschool years**, begins on the first day of school and continues until she graduates to kindergarten.

<u>Parent Perspective</u>
While you may be interested in preschool for your child, you may not know when she should start. Deciding on the best preschool for your child may seem confusing. If you do not know how to evaluate a preschool, you may be concerned about your ability to choose a good one. Looking at preschools may be frustrating as you realize that some are too expensive, some are too far from home, and some just aren't right for your child. Once you find

the right school and register your child, you may wonder if you did the right thing. As the school year approaches, you may worry about how your child will handle separating from you. It makes you nervous to realize that you will no longer know everything that happens in your child's life. At the same time you may look forward to the extra time you'll have, once your child is in school. You will feel good thinking about the new experiences your child will have in preschool. On the first day of school, your heart will break if your child cries when you leave, or you will feel relief if she kisses you good-bye and runs into the room. One day a few weeks later, when she walks out of the classroom proudly waving an art project and sputtering tales of what she did in school, you will smile to yourself, knowing that you chose the right school for your child.

Child Perspective
Before going to preschool, most children have no idea what it is. They don't know what a preschool looks like physically. They don't know who is in a preschool. They don't know what goes on at preschool. Your child may have some basic notions about preschool if she has friends in preschool or if she has visited one. But for the most part, she will rely on you to teach her about preschool. Once she knows more about preschool, she will probably not be anxious about starting school until the first day. On the first day of school, she may feel apprehensive about separating from you. She may be afraid that you won't come back to get him. She may worry that she won't like preschool or that the teacher won't like her. She may cry when you leave, but chances are she will stop crying within a few minutes. The act of separating from you will probably be harder for her than the actual separation. At the end of the day, she may cry when you pick her up. She does this because she is afraid you will leave again. In a couple weeks she will learn that Mommy or Daddy always picks her up and that preschool is an okay place. Instead of crying and saying that she doesn't want to go to school, she will probably tell you to hurry up so she isn't late.

CHOOSING THE RIGHT SCHOOL

There are five steps to choosing the right school for your child and family. The first step is to determine your philosophy on preschool and decide which of the four types of preschools meets your needs best. The next step is to locate the preschools in your area that are the right type. The third step is to narrow your list of preschools. In the fourth step, you evaluate the preschool programs on your list through observations and interviews. The final step is to pick the best preschool for your child.

Determine your philosophy on preschool

Many parents begin to think about preschool when their child is

---

TABLE 1
CHOOSING THE RIGHT PRESCHOOL FOR YOUR CHILD

- Determine your philosophy on preschool.
- Locate the preschools in your area.
- Narrow your list of preschools.
- Evaluate the preschool programs on your list.
- Pick the preschool you want for your child.

---

between eighteen months and three and a half years of age. Preschool frequently means different things to different parents. Some parents think of preschool as a place for their child to develop basic academic skills. Other parents view preschool as an opportunity for their child to develop good peer relationships. You need to decide what you want a preschool experience to do for your individual child. You may want your child to become comfortable in group situations, or you may want her to develop intellectual readiness for kindergarten. Some parents feel strongly about their level of involvement in their child's preschool program. Some want daily involvement while others wish to have little direct involvement. Once you decide what you want a preschool to be, you are ready to match your goals with one of the types of preschools.

There are four types of preschools—traditional, co-op, university, and structured. Traditional preschools emphasize the social-emotional and motor development of young children. Co-op preschools usually have a traditional emphasis with regular parent involvement. At most co-ops parent participation ranges from assisting the teacher during sessions to cleaning the school. In this type of preschool, parents often make decisions about the curriculum and the actual running of the school. University preschools also have a traditional emphasis. In addition, these schools serve as sites for conducting research and training future teachers. Structured preschools emphasize pre-academic learning, preparing children for the structured learning they will receive in kindergarten. Montessori programs fall into this group. Many structured preschools also integrate play, socialization, and motor skill development into their programs.

Locate the preschools in your area

Once you know your philosophy on preschool and once you have a good feeling for the type of preschool that you are looking for, the next step is to find the preschools in your area that are the right type. Most county and state Education Departments have on file a list of approved preschool programs for your geographic area.

Calling the Department of Education in your area is generally all it takes to get a copy of the list. Your local phone book is another way to locate preschool programs. The phone numbers are often in

sections such as Early Childhood Services or Schools. The phone book usually presents the listing according to type. For example, a list of co-op preschools will be under the heading, Co-op Preschools. Some communities hold annual fairs to introduce parents to the preschool programs in the area. In addition to helping parents locate preschools, fairs provide parents with an opportunity to get literature on various programs and to speak with area directors.

Streamline your list of preschools

Before conducting observations and interviews, you may need to streamline your list of preschools. Knowing the type of preschool that you want reduces the number of schools that you need to contact. Your first contact with the preschools will probably be over the phone or in person at a fair. When you talk with preschool personnel, verify the type of preschool and ask about the school program's philosophy. Also inquire about the school's location. Consider the location of the school as you narrow your list. If the school is far from your home, think how much traveling you and your child will do. For some families, this is not a big issue; for others, it is. In addition, find out what the fees are. The cost of sending a child to preschool varies according to the type of preschool, number of days per week the child attends, and the geographic location of the school. Tuition may be as low as $250 a year for one morning a week at a rural co-op preschool or as high as $3,600 a year for five full days a week at an urban structured preschool. Based on all this information, narrow your list of preschools. Schedule appointments to observe the remaining programs on your list. Request some time with the director or a teacher after the observation so you may ask questions. Evaluate the preschool programs on your list.

There are seven aspects of a preschool program that you should consider during the observation and interview. As you observe, evaluate the physical environment, classroom schedule, activities offered, and teacher-child interactions. During the interview, consider the school's discipline policy, level of parent involvement, and qualifications of the school and it's staff. Use the Preschool Evaluation Checklist provided in Table 2 on pages 204-206 as a guide during your assessment.

Pick the best preschool for your child

The Preschool Evaluation Checklist can help you make an informed choice about the best preschool program for your child. Use the information that you gather on the Preschool

Evaluation Checklist, with your gut reaction to the schools, to pick the preschool where you will send your child. Call the director of the program you choose to find out about registration procedures. Take the necessary steps to register your child.

If your child has special needs, determine whether services such as physical therapy or speech therapy are available at the school. Do this before you register. Many preschool programs do not offer such services. This does not, however, mean that your child cannot attend the school of your choice. You may be able to devise a plan with your county intervention program where: (1) Specialists go to your child's school to provide services; (2) Specialists teach your child's preschool teacher how to provide needed intervention; (3) Your child sees specialists after preschool. **Remember that your child has a legal right to education in the least restrictive environment possible.** Most school systems will do all that they can to ensure this occurs.

PREPARING YOUR CHILD FOR PRESCHOOL

Many children experience some anxiety about starting preschool. The fear of the unknown—not knowing what the preschool looks like, not knowing what happens at preschool, not knowing what a teacher does, not knowing what they will do, and not knowing if they will like it—creates much of this anxiety. To relieve it, introduce the concept of preschool to your child and show her the school.

TABLE 2
PRESCHOOL EVALUATION CHECKLIST

The checklist is for use during your observation and review of the program. To use the checklist: read the statement, observe or ask about the item, and check off those items that reflect the preschool you are observing. It is desirable for a preschool to have most, if not all of the following attributes:

PHYSICAL ENVIRONMENT
Activity Centers
     Designed to accommodate different activities
     Visual barriers created by shelves are high enough for children to feel
        privacy but low enough for adults to see over
     Child-size furniture is available
Supplies And Equipment
     Adequate number of supplies, toys, chairs
     Condition of supplies, toys, chairs is good
     Safe supplies and toys are stored on shelves or in bins accessible to children
     Dangerous supplies are stored out of reach or in locked cabinets
Displays
     Pictures And Posters
       reflect ethnic variety
       portray men and women in nonsexist roles
     Children's work is displayed attractively at child's eye level
Personal Space For Hanging Coats And Storing Backpacks
Room Is Clean And Safe
Bathroom/Diaper Changing Area Is Clean And Safe
Playground
     Space for running, throwing, etc.
     Equipment for climbing, sliding, etc.
     Area for playing outside is safe
     Outside play occurs on a regular basis

SCHEDULE
Predictable With Some Flexibility
Balanced
     Quiet and active times provided
     Sitting activities followed by active ones
     Opportunities for independent, small group, and large group play/work
Arranged So Children Are Greeted By Teacher Or Aide And Receive Support
     Needed If Separating From Parent Is Difficult
Structured/Teaching Activities Conducted Early When Attention Span And
     Concentration Is Best
Allows Children To Do Real Things Like Cooking And Taking Care Of Plants Or
     Animals
Incorporates Field Trips

ACTIVITIES
Thinking Skills
     Small group times are provided for developing readiness skills such as letter
       and number recognition
Understanding And Using Language
     Books are read
     Flannel boards are used to tell stories

Songs and fingerplays are taught
Self-expression is encouraged in children
Using Large Muscle Movements
    Time and place for:
        running
        jumping
        riding tricycles and other ride-on toys
        throwing and catching
        climbing
        sliding
        dancing
Manipulating Small Objects
    Time and place for:
        water and sand play
        puzzles
        stringing beads
        block building with figures and vehicles
        playing musical instruments
        art
          drawing with crayons
          painting with brushes, fingers, sponges
          simple block printing
          making collages
          stitchery
          using glue
          using scissors
          using clay
Socializing
    Time and place for free play
    Social toys such as games, dramatic play props, and blocks are
        provided
    Toys are developmentally appropriate
    Snack time occurs in groups of two or more
    Interactions between children are encouraged
Self-Help
    Opportunities to learn how to:
        put on and take off coats
        wash and dry hands
        set and clear table at snack time
        feed self different foods
        drink without sippee lids
        pour, scoop, and spread

TEACHER-CHILD INTERACTIONS
Style Of Interactions
    Warm interpersonal atmosphere
    Teachers have respect for children
    Teachers make eye contact when talking with children
    Teachers listen attentively to what children have to say
    Teachers speak naturally
    Frequency of interactions is sufficient but not interfering
    Appropriate teacher-child ratio (laws vary from state to state but
    ratios like 1:4 for 2-year-olds, 1:6 for 3-year-olds, 1:8 for 4-year-olds
    are good)

DISCIPLINE
Appropriate Limits Are Set
Limits Are Enforced With Reasoning And Consistency
Teachers Disapprove The Misbehavior, Not The Child
Discipline Is Handled In A Manner That You Like
Hitting Is <u>Never</u> Permitted

PARENT INVOLVEMENT
Policy Matches What You Want

STAFF AND SCHOOL QUALIFICATIONS
Licensed By State Department Of Health And Safety, Department Of
     Education, etc.
Program Director Has, At Minimum, A Bachelor's Degree Or A Teaching
     Credential In Early Childhood Education
Some, Preferably All, Teachers Have A Bachelor's Degree Or A Teaching
     Credential In Early Childhood Education
Staff Turnover Is Minimal

Introduce the concept of preschool

Talking with your child about a friend who goes to preschool is an excellent way of introducing the topic of school to your child. Talk about the things this friend does at school and how much her friend likes school. Reading books about preschool is another way to familiarize your child with preschool. Playing preschool is an excellent way to prepare your child for the routine of her preschool. For example, take turns with your child playing the roles of the teacher and the student. Playing the roles, act out circle time, free-play, art time, and snack. Find out what the school rules are, and include them in your role play. For example, if the program does not allow children to bring pacifiers or toys to school, act this out in play—whoever portrays the pretend student resolves the issue in a positive manner. If your child will ride a bus to school, pretend

to ride a bus or sing the song, "The Children On The Bus." Play school with your child, using figures and objects representing the school. Many stores sell toy school buses and play schools equipped with tables, chairs, and/or figures. You can make a bus or school out of a box by cutting out doors and windows and using smaller boxes for seats and tables.

Show your child the preschool

Although playing school with you helps prepare your child for the routine and rules of her school, she may still have trouble picturing what school will be like for her. Actually showing your child her preschool provides her with a visual image of her school and helps her more accurately imagine what school will be like. If possible, arrange for your child to see one of the classrooms in her school. Since many schools close for the summer, schedule the tour during the spring before she starts school or during staff orientation and preparation, usually a few weeks before school starts in the fall.

While visiting the school with your child, point out the toys, books, art supplies, and games. Show her where she will hang her coat and put her backpack. Take her to see the bathroom and playground. If her teacher is available, introduce her to her teacher. During the summer, wave "Hi!" to the school when you drive past it. A few weeks before school starts, purposefully drive past the school so your child can wave to it. Stop at the school once or twice so she can play at the playground.

The process of preparing your child for preschool should occur during the summer before she starts school. When you talk about preschool, always be honest with your child. If you won't be able to stay with her, let her know so she can prepare herself. But do not make school too much of a big deal before she starts. Talking about school a few times, playing school occasionally, visiting the school a couple times, and waving to the school periodically is enough. Too much will just make your child more nervous and anxious.

SUPPORTING YOUR CHILD THROUGHOUT THE PRESCHOOL YEARS

Supporting your child through her preschool experience begins with her first day of school and continues until she graduates to kindergarten. During the first few days of preschool, most of your support revolves around easing separation. Communicating with your child's teacher and talking with your child about preschool become the focus of support throughout the preschool years.

Supporting your child's preschool experience during the first few days of preschool

During the first few days, avoid arriving at the school too early. It only prolongs the act of separating for your child. For most children, the act of separating from their parent is more difficult than the separation itself. If you do not plan to stay at school, let your child know this ahead of time. When you get to school, motivate her to start her first activity, give her a kiss and a hug, say good-bye, and leave. If you can't resist peeking in a window to see how she is doing, make sure she doesn't see you. As difficult as it may be, do not remove your child from the classroom if she cries. Bringing her home because she cries may reinforce the crying and may even increase the crying throughout the adjustment period. As long as she is in a loving environment, the teacher, aide, or director will give her the support and gentle encouragement she needs to make this transition. Do something special together after her first day or week at school to celebrate—serve her favorite meal for lunch or dinner, go on a picnic, or have a special ice cream treat for a snack.

Supporting your child throughout the preschool years

Communicating with your child's teacher is an important part of supporting your child's preschool experience. Speak with your child's teacher weekly. After school is typically a better time than before school. Find out how your child is doing, and ask what the class will be working on the next week. Ask about show-and-tell-days or parties. Your child wants to participate in these activities, but she may not communicate this information to you. Prepare her for school by telling her what she will be doing—"Today you're going to bake cookies at school" or "This week Mrs. Smith is going to teach you about Indians." Arrange to have a more in-depth parent-teacher conference twice a year. This is the time to find out what your child has learned and how she interacts with other children.

Ask if the teacher has any concerns about your child. Find out what global concepts the teacher plans to work on in the next few months, so you may reinforce them at home by incorporating them in everyday life. For instance, if the teacher plans to work on counting, ask your child to give you five grapes for the fruit salad or two slices of bread for a sandwich.

Besides communicating with the teacher, talk with your child about preschool. Each morning before school, talk briefly about what she will do at school that day. On the days you do not plan to pick her up after school, tell her so and tell her who will pick her up instead. Remember that nobody is as good as Mommy or Daddy. If she is expecting to see you, she will be disappointed if her favorite uncle picks her up.

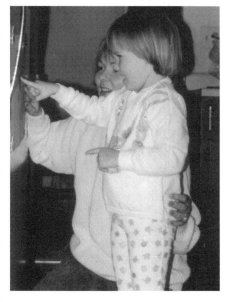

Each day after school, take a few minutes to talk about her day at school. For the two-year-old, ask prompting questions like, "What did you have for snack?", " Did you play outside today?", or "Did you paint?". For three-year-olds, open-ended questions usually work well. When your child brings home art work, ask her to tell you about it, and display it proudly in the house. Many children feel sad when school closes for a holiday. Prepare her for this ahead of time, by mentioning that it will be the last week of school before winter break. In the same way, prepare her for the summer break. Tell her, for example, that she will go to school two more times, and then school will close for the summer. If she will return to the school in the fall, let her know that she can go back after summer ends. If she will go to kindergarten in the fall, tell her so.

A PARENT'S STORY

When Donna was eighteen months old, a friend asked me which preschool I was planning to send her to. I thought to myself, "Preschool...she's only eighteen months old; she's still a baby; she's not ready for academics." I said, "I'm not sure yet. Are you sending Sarah to preschool next year?" She replied rather animatedly that, of course, she was sending Sarah to preschool. She proceeded to tell me about all the preschool programs in the area. How this one emphasized socialization, that one had an academic focus, a third was primarily a play group, and a fourth worked on readiness skills and socialization. Her knowledge of preschool programs was impressive, so I asked her how she knew so much. She told me about a preschool fair that took place in our community the previous week. It was a relief to hear that the fair was going to be held again the following weekend.

That weekend my husband and I, with Donna in tow, went to the fair. We learned so much and got the opportunity to meet with program directors and teachers. I was so glad that I went because most programs were conducting registration the next week. That astounded me. It was January, and the schools were accepting registration for the fall already. We narrowed our choices to three schools and made appointments to observe them.

During our third observation we knew we had found the perfect school for Donna. This school was, in our opinion, so much better than all the rest, and we really wanted Donna to go there. My husband asked the director about the registration process. She told us that in-house registration had occurred the week before and that open registration would be the following Saturday morning at 9:00. I asked how many two-year-old slots there were, and she told us there were 11. I thought to myself, "I really want Donna at this school. Tim (my husband) will have to get to the school by 8:00 a.m. to make sure that Donna gets a spot." The director thanked us for visiting, and as we were leaving, she mentioned that last year parents started lining up at 6:00 a.m.

On Saturday morning Tim went to the school at 5:30 a.m.. To make a long story a little shorter, he was the twenty-second person in line; the first person was at the school at 1:00 a.m. Fortunately, being twenty-second in line was good enough, and Donna got a spot. Tim registered Donna for one morning a week.

The first day of preschool was great! Moms and Dads attended, with their children along, to orient everyone to the program. Throughout the next week, Donna talked about how wonderful school was and how excited she was about going back the following week. We reinforced her comments and gently mentioned that only children and teachers would be in the school the following week. On the morning of her second day, it was a different story. She told me that she didn't want to go to school because she loved me so much and wanted to stay home to play with me. I told her that school was a fun and happy place and proceeded to take her to school. At the door to her classroom, she broke into tears. I gave her a kiss and hug, told her that I would pick her up before lunch, and said goodbye. She was crying, and I felt terrible. As I left the school, I walked around to the back of the classroom to peek in a window. It had only been a minute or two since I left her, and I was sure that she would be crying hysterically. I just wanted to see if the teacher was giving her the support she needed to make this transition. To my surprise, there were no tears; she was sitting at a table doing a puzzle. I let out a sigh of relief and went home. The following week she cried again, but only for a minute. On the fourth week, her lip quivered as I said good-bye. On the fifth week she saw her teacher, smiled, and ran into the room without saying good-bye.

Donna has been in preschool for nine months now, and I am so glad that we decided to send her. It was hard to think of her being ready for school when she was eighteen months old, but by the time fall came, she was twenty-six months and ready. Donna loves school and has learned a lot. She now has some nice pre-academic skills like color and shape recognition. She has also learned how to make new friends. Most importantly, she has developed a love and an eagerness for learning.

SUMMARY

Preschool is the first school experience for most children. All parents want their child's preschool experience to be a good one. Making your child's preschool experience successful occurs in three phases. Choosing the right school is the first phase. This involves determining your philosophy on preschool, locating the preschools in your area, streamlining your list of preschools, evaluating the preschool programs on your list, and picking the best preschool for your child. Preparing your child for school is the second phase. It involves introducing the concept of preschool to your child and showing her the school. The third and final phase is supporting your child throughout the preschool years. It involves easing separation, communicating with your child's teacher, and talking with your child about preschool.

REFERENCES AND RECOMMENDED READINGS

For Children:
Elliott, D. (1983). *Grover Goes to School.* New York, NY: Western Publishing Co.

For Parents:
Bailey, D. & Wolery, M. (1984). *Teaching Infants and Preschoolers with Handicaps.* Columbus, OH: Charles E. Merrill Publishing Co., Chapters 5 & 6.
Bradley, B. (1991, March). How to choose the best preschool. *Parenting.*
National Association for the Education of Young Children. *Some Ways of Distinguishing a Good Early Childhood Program.* To order, send 25 cents to: NAEYC, 1834 Connecticut Avenue, N.W., Washington, D.C. 20009.